A Short History of U.S. Interventions in Latin America and the Caribbean

Viewpoints/Puntos de Vista
Themes and Interpretations in Latin American History

Series Editor: Jürgen Buchenau

The books in this series will introduce students to the most significant themes and topics in Latin American history. They represent a novel approach to designing supplementary texts for this growing market. Intended as supplementary textbooks, the books will also discuss the ways in which historians have interpreted these themes and topics, thus demonstrating to students that our understanding of our past is constantly changing, through the emergence of new sources, methodologies, and historical theories. Unlike monographs, the books in this series will be broad in scope and written in a style accessible to undergraduates.

Published

A History of the Cuban Revolution, Second Edition
Aviva Chomsky

Bartolomé de las Casas and the Conquest of the Americas
Lawrence A. Clayton

Beyond Borders: A History of Mexican Migration to the United States
Timothy J. Henderson

The Last Caudillo: Alvaro Obregón and the Mexican Revolution
Jürgen Buchenau

A Concise History of the Haitian Revolution
Jeremy D. Popkin

Spaniards in the Colonial Empire: Creoles vs. Peninsulars?
Mark A. Burkholder

Dictatorship in South America
Jerry Dávila

Mothers Making Latin America: Gender, Households, and Politics Since 1825
Erin E. O'Connor

A Short History of U.S. Interventions in Latin America and the Caribbean
Alan McPherson

A Short History of U.S. Interventions in Latin America and the Caribbean

Alan McPherson

WILEY Blackwell

This edition first published 2016
© 2016 John Wiley & Sons, Inc.

Registered Office
John Wiley & Sons, Ltd, The Atrium, Southern Gate, Chichester, West Sussex, PO19 8SQ, UK

Editorial Offices
350 Main Street, Malden, MA 02148-5020, USA
9600 Garsington Road, Oxford, OX4 2DQ, UK
The Atrium, Southern Gate, Chichester, West Sussex, PO19 8SQ, UK

For details of our global editorial offices, for customer services, and for information about how to apply for permission to reuse the copyright material in this book please see our website at www.wiley.com/wiley-blackwell.

Library of Congress Cataloging-in-Publication data applied for

9781118953990 (hardback)
9781118954003 (paperback)

A catalogue record for this book is available from the British Library.

Cover image: President Theodore Roosevelt collecting debts and patrolling Central America and the Caribbean with his "big stick", cartoon by William Allen Rogers, 1904. The Granger Collection / TopFoto.

Set in 10.5/13.5pt Minion by SPi Global, Pondicherry, India

1   2016

To Luc and Nico, with all Papa's love

Contents

Series Editor's Preface

Each book in the "Viewpoints/Puntos de Vista" series introduces students to a significant theme or topic in Latin American history. In an age in which student and faculty interest in the Global South increasingly challenges the old focus on the history of Europe and North America, Latin American history has assumed an increasingly prominent position in undergraduate curricula.

Some of these books discuss the ways in which historians have interpreted these themes and topics, thus demonstrating that our understanding of our past is constantly changing, through the emergence of new sources, methodologies, and historical theories. Others offer an introduction to a particular theme by means of a case study or biography in a manner easily understood by the contemporary, non-specialist reader. Yet others give an overview of a major theme that might serve as the foundation of an upper-level course.

What is common to all of these books is their goal of historical synthesis. They draw on the insights of generations of scholarship on the most enduring and fascinating issues in Latin American history, and through the use of primary sources as appropriate. Each book is written by a specialist in Latin American history who is concerned with undergraduate teaching, yet has also made his or her mark as a first-rate scholar.

The books in this series can be used in a variety of ways, recognizing the differences in teaching conditions at small liberal arts colleges, large public universities, and research-oriented institutions with doctoral programs. Faculty have particular needs depending on whether they teach large lectures with discussion sections, small lecture or discussion-oriented classes, or large lectures with no discussion sections, and whether they teach on a semester or trimester system. The format adopted for this series fits all of these different parameters.

In this ninth volume in the "Viewpoints/Puntos de Vista" series, Professor Alan McPherson provides an interpretation of history of United States occupations in Latin America, with a focus on the twentieth century. Somewhat provocatively, Professor McPherson places political motivations – not economic or cultural ones – at the causative center of the repeated decision of United States policymakers to send troops to occupy Latin American territory and thus violate the sovereignty of Latin American nations. To make his case, Professor McPherson aptly distinguishes these government-sponsored military occupations from the more broadly defined concept of interventions, and even from the privately sponsored filibuster expeditions that figured significantly in United States imperialism in Latin America during the nineteenth century.

This volume's publication is timely, coinciding with a fascinating period in inter-American relations. As the United States is finally taking historic steps to mend relations with socialist Cuba – a nation that was a repeated victim of United States occupations at the turn of the twentieth century – this volume helps us understand why and how the United States government once came to view Latin America as its own backyard and sent military expeditions to the region with astonishing regularity.

Jürgen Buchenau
University of North Carolina, Charlotte

Acknowledgments

I wish to thank Viewpoints/Puntos de Vista Series Editor Jürgen Buchenau and Peter Coveney at Wiley for believing in this project. The three anonymous reviewers were very helpful. Thanks also to Dominic Granello for bringing me heaps of books, articles, and documents, and for cobbling together the bibliography. As always, Heather Dubnick did a wonderful job with the index. Finally, I owe a debt to all the collaborators of my *Encyclopedia of U.S. Military Interventions in Latin America and the Caribbean*, on whose shoulders I stood to draft this book.

List of Illustrations

Maps

Figures

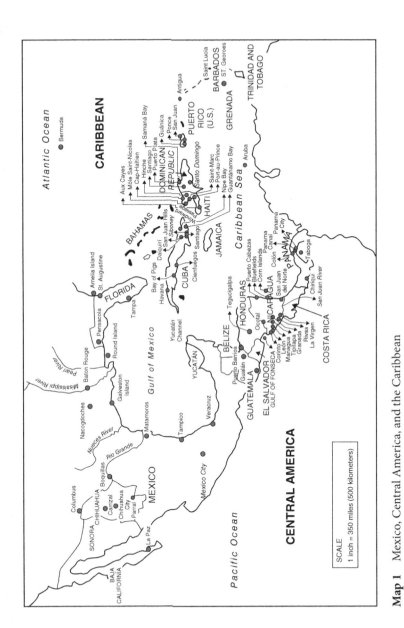

Map 1 Mexico, Central America, and the Caribbean

Map 2 South America

Introduction

Topic and Themes

Has the United States sent people down here to teach us how to behave?

Desiderio Arias[1]

In April 2015, heads of state of all American republics gathered at the Summit of the Americas held in Panama City, Panama. On his way from the airport, Venezuelan President Nicolás Maduro stopped to lay a wreath at a monument commemorating the 1989 U.S. invasion of the host country. He called the intervention "an unforgivable attack on the people of Panama" and swore to the cheering crowd, "Never again a U.S. invasion in Latin America!"

U.S. President Barack Obama agreed with that last part. "The days in which our agenda in this hemisphere so often presumed that the US could meddle with impunity, those days are over." [2] Calling himself "a student of history," Obama added, "I'm certainly mindful that there are dark chapters in our own history in which we have not observed the principles and ideals upon which the country was founded." At the same time, however, he refused to let the past determine the present: "I'm not interested in having battles that, frankly, started before I was born."[3]

A Short History of U.S. Interventions in Latin America and the Caribbean,
First Edition. Alan McPherson.
© 2016 John Wiley & Sons, Inc. Published 2016 by John Wiley & Sons, Inc.

Was it fair for Maduro to bring up a generation-old invasion? Was Obama dismissive or appropriate? Was it really the case that U.S. interventions were a thing of the past? These questions and more can be answered only by those with a firm background in the history of U.S. military interventions in Latin America and the Caribbean. This book surveys those interventions, from the No Transfer Resolution in 1811 to the drug wars of the 21st century. It narrates a few dozen of the most important interventions among the thousands of military landings by U.S. troops.

The Topic

This book's definition of interventions is broad but not sprawling. It includes all dispatches of large groups of U.S. armed forces by the U.S. government to territories in the Western Hemisphere south of the Rio Grande (now) separating the United States and Mexico and including (now) Florida. It also includes the use of armed non-U.S. citizens funded, trained, and equipped by the U.S. government. These were "proxy wars," in which Washington went to war through a stand-in – usually an army of locals combating their own country's head of state. The definition of intervention also covers declared wars, actions otherwise allowed by the U.S. Congress, and blatantly illegal mobilizations. And it comprises interventions that were requested by heads of state in Latin America and the Caribbean.

The definition does *not* include private U.S. forces landing on Latin American shores without the approval of their government. Chapter 1 does survey private filibustering expeditions, mostly in the 1850s, because they illustrated important motivations and assumptions by U.S. citizens who embraced territorial expansion. But it does not consider them to be official U.S. interventions. It also does not include small military groups sent as part of a diplomatic body, or to train Latin American militaries. Finally, the definition does not include nonmilitary U.S. meddling. Spying, aid, military training, diplomatic arm-twisting, support for dictators, cultural programs, and pressures to open up markets to U.S. trade are common examples of programs that certainly qualify as U.S. pressure on Latin America but nevertheless do not rise to the definition of an intervention. As with small group missions, the book discusses many of these because they provide context. But they are not themselves military interventions.

A host of U.S. military forces carried out interventions in Latin America and the Caribbean. The most frequent were members of the U.S. Marine Corps, who were officially part of the U.S. Department of the Navy after 1834 but largely independent. They made their reputation as a rapid-response amphibious force – traveling by water like a navy, but disembarking and fighting like an army. "Bluejackets," the name given to servicemembers of the U.S. Navy, often accompanied them. In other interventions, such as the land-based Punitive Expedition of 1916–1917, the U.S. Army took the lead. The cavalry, rangers, paratroopers, and pilots have also participated. As in any other military action, some at times displayed uncommon valor. For that courage during actions in Latin America, U.S. servicemembers won 162 Medals of Honor.

Not all Latin American nations have been targets of U.S. intervention. U.S. hegemony or control yes, but not military intervention. Almost all U.S. interventions took place in Mexico, Central America and Panama, and the Caribbean. These areas had in common that they were (1) geographically close to the United States, therefore easier to get to from U.S. naval bases and more integrated into the U.S. economy; (2) poor, and, with the exception of Mexico, small, so unable to beat back a force of even a few hundred or a few thousand marines; and (3) strategically valuable, located as they were in the waterways leading to the Panama Canal. Not for nothing did Alexander Hamilton in 1787 call the Caribbean basin "the American Mediterranean."⁴

Interventions occurred not only in American republics with Latin-based languages such as Spanish and French, but also in the English-speaking Caribbean. And, in the nineteenth century, interventions took place in Spanish Florida and elsewhere in what was to become the continental United States.

South America contained some of the problems that might prompt an intervention further north, but U.S. officials deemed South American nations to be too far, too big, and too powerful to warrant interventions. Even in Mexico, where the United States intervened repeatedly, no serious thought was ever given to occupying the whole country. The experiences of fighting Mexicans during the Mexican War of 1846–1848 and the Punitive Expedition were enough to help banish the thought.

Themes: The Five C's

To help readers navigate through the stories in this book, each chapter's introduction will suggest how to fit them within the book's five themes. These themes are easy to remember as the Five C's: causes, consequences, contestation, collaboration, and context. Each should be considered in every intervention.

1. Causes. U.S. officials, usually presidents, ordered interventions in Latin America and the Caribbean for a variety of reasons, and the student of interventions should keep in mind that *variety* is the most important characteristic of interventions. This book focuses first and foremost on the motivations of U.S. policymakers, and it argues that the most prominent cause of interventions – the one that those who ordered interventions most talked about – was the goal of political stability and political cultural change. When Desiderio Arias, the former Minister of War, suspected in 1916 that the United States was in the Dominican Republic to "teach" him and his compatriots "how to behave," he was right on the mark. From spreading U.S. civilization in the nineteenth century, to President Woodrow Wilson's desire to see only constitutional changes of power in Mexico, to fighting fascists in World War II, to keeping communism contained to Cuba in the Cold War, to restoring democracy in the 1990s, U.S. interventions in the region harbored above all political motives.

Interventions also had economic motivations, and these were, in some instances, the dominant impetuses. Some marines landed just to protect U.S. corporations. Some secretaries of state made sure Wall Street got its loans paid off. To be sure, it was and is legitimate for diplomats to want to protect and promote their country's investments and markets abroad. And those concerns often were foremost in their conversations. But U.S. soldiers who managed interventions on a day-to-day basis worried a lot less about economics.

Many interventions also reflected the prevailing culture of those who ordered them. Racism and paternalism were especially prominent in U.S. culture (not to mention Latin American culture), especially in the nineteenth and early twentieth centuries. "Scientific" textbooks taught whites that race was a fixed biological fact and that there existed a limited number of "races" among humans – "Caucasian," "Mongolian," "Ethiopian," "Malay," "Australian," "American," and so on. It also indicated that some races were inferior while others were born to dominate. Biological theories about evolution influenced social scientists to devise Social Darwinism, or the theory that, in society too, some races were more "fit" to "survive." Feelings of racial superiority sometimes led U.S. forces to commit heinous atrocities. Those feelings, however, did not necessarily lead "whites" to want to annihilate those civilizations they thought inferior. Sometimes they felt a paternal obligation to protect or teach so-called uncivilized peoples. Whatever the form culture took, it helped justify interventions again and again.

In some situations, finally, U.S. officials were primarily concerned with geostrategic issues. They looked at a map, pointed to where great empires had overseas possessions, and felt they should have some too. Transportation was often key: ports, railroads, canals, and sealanes always needed protection in order that troops could be moved quickly in case of war. In the Caribbean basin, the major U.S. concern lay with protecting strategic chokepoints such as the Panama Canal. This tended to be the case especially in times of global war.

But political behavior was, to Washington, the lynchpin of all other troubles in Latin America and the Caribbean. The region was ripe for economic investment and exploitation, but in U.S. eyes, constant fighting among aspirants to presidential palaces kept merchants from exporting or workers from even wandering onto highways, where they might be kidnapped into armies. Yes, cultural change – more English or Protestantism, for instance, or an "Americanized" primary education – would also be nice, said U.S. officials, but these officials often found that Latin American politicians were too set in their ways to allow such change. And it was irresponsible debts owed by presidents to European banks that called forth gunboats and thus U.S. marines to prevent those gunboats from landing.

2. Consequences. U.S. military interventions were among the most consequential events in the history of Latin America and the Caribbean. They were the direct cause of dozens of changes in governments, almost all giving way to U.S.-friendly leaders. They sometimes ended periods of economic reform or hardened repression, or ushered in a democratic spring. Some saved lives by separating warring factions or otherwise restoring order; almost all killed Latin Americans, sometimes in the thousands. Most reinforced U.S. economic interests and pulled the region closer to the U.S. orbit, or else they opened up new possibilities for U.S. investment in land and exports. Arguably the greatest consequence was the loss of the northern half of Mexico to the United States in the 1840s. In short, U.S. interventions were a consistent recurrence in the life of the hemisphere, indicating the continuing hegemony of the "Colossus of the North" in the military, commerce, investment, culture, and politics. Consequences tended to reflect causes in that they achieved U.S. goals in the short term. But in the long term, they had a habit of creating problems for the United States, such as massive migration flows.

3. Contestation. Like Desiderio Arias and Nicolás Maduro, Latin Americans (and many U.S. citizens) criticized U.S. interventions, and many Latin Americans resisted. As with causes, resistance occurred for a host of reasons. Some reasons were selfless, others petty. Some reflected grand ideologies, others desires for local autonomy. Before the Cold War (1945–1992), Latin Americans resisted largely for pragmatic reasons – because U.S. troops were shooting at them, or taking their land, or torturing them, or getting drunk in their cantinas. Directing much of this resistance were politicians. To be sure, many truly loved their nation and were protective of its sovereignty and ready to take up arms for *la Patria*. But even they usually also had concrete motives, such as wanting a government job or even to be president once the intervention ended. The Cold War was a particularly ideological phase in Latin America's resistance, when revolutionaries such as Fidel Castro and Ché Guevara were imbued with a potent cocktail of nationalism, anti-imperialism, some version of socialism, and a personal desire for power. The end of the Cold War brought down not only the number and intensity of interventions but also the ideological fervor of their resisters. Resistance went back to being local and concrete, but no less justified or even heroic.

Latin American and Caribbean peoples who met U.S. troops were astoundingly diverse – here is that word again – in their affiliations. In a few instances of traditional confrontations (Mexico in the 1840s, Cuba in 1898 and 1961, and Grenada in 1983 among others), U.S. intervention forces clashed with government soldiers. Some military resistance came from unpaid soldiers – volunteers or forcibly enlisted men (and, on a few occasions, women). These made an important difference, for instance, in ending the Mexican War in 1848. More commonly, marines fought insurrectionary rural guerrillas, whose techniques the marines found to be similar to those of Native Americans in the nineteenth century and who preceded the better-known guerrillas of the 1960s. Finally, on occasions such as Panama in 1903, there was no armed resistance at all.

Every chapter in this book addresses Latin American responses, and Chapter 5 does only that.

4. *Collaboration.* One Latin American response that arose to some extent in every U.S. intervention was to collaborate with the invader.

In some cases, local governments invited U.S. forces to intervene, usually to prop them up against a political enemy. Others did not invite intervention but welcomed it, sometimes in the hopes that they and their friends could benefit personally, for instance by moving up the political ranks or securing a job. Other Latin Americans were sincere and eager students of U.S. ways of life and government. A final group accommodated rather than collaborated, meaning that they played along with U.S. invaders so as to avoid the consequences of not playing along.

In most interventions, how many resisted versus how many collaborated will never be known. Beware of those who claim that either everyone resisted or everyone collaborated with a specific intervention.

5. Context. Finally, this book provides context to episodes of military intervention. Sometimes it references global events that drove U.S. or Latin American interests, such as an economic crisis or a larger war. Other times, it explains ideologies or concepts that justified or restrained interventions. These included racism, paternalism, the No Transfer Principle, the Monroe Doctrine, Manifest Destiny, gunboat diplomacy, the Roosevelt Corollary, Dollar Diplomacy, the Good Neighbor Policy, continental defense, anti-communism, democracy promotion, and fear of immigrants.

In an effort to inform the reader, for every intervention it looks at, this book discusses, whenever relevant and available, not only the Five C's but also the number of and kind of troops involved, casualties suffered on all sides, and the legality – or lack thereof – of the intervention. By doing so, it helps to disseminate often forgotten knowledge, to spark debate, and to promote independent, critical thinking.

Notes

1   Cited in Frederic M. Wise, Col. USMC, *A Marine Tells it to You: As told to Meigs O. Frost* (J. H. Sears & Co., 1929), 143.
2   "Stark Differences as Obama and Maduro Head for Panama Encounter," *The Guardian*, 10 April 2015, available at www.theguardian.com/world/2015/apr/11/obama-venezuelan-president-nicolas-maduro-regional-summit

3   "Remarks by President Obama at the First Plenary Session of the Summit of the Americas," The White House, 11 April 2015, available at www. whitehouse.gov/the-press-office/2015/04/11/remarks-president-obama-first-plenary-session-summit-americas

4   Cited in Rubén G. Rumbaut, "The Americans: Latin American and Caribbean Peoples in the United States," in *Americas: New Interpretive Essays*, ed. Alfred Stepan (Oxford University Press, 1992), 281.

1

Expanding the Continental Republic, 1811–1897

> Growing and spreading out into unoccupied regions, assimilating
> all we incorporate.
>
> U.S. Secretary of State John Calhoun,
> describing his country's goal[1]

Throughout the nineteenth century, U.S. citizens grabbed land from those beginning to call themselves "Latin Americans," whether they lived in present-day Texas, California, or Florida. The nineteenth was the century of continental expansion – of taking and settling in what would later form the 48 contiguous states of the Union. What distinguished the nineteenth century's expansion from the twentieth's was the idea of settlement. U.S. settlers were intent on building their homes and plantations on these new lands. They were also determined to form a majority that would dominate the political system and render original inhabitants second-class citizens. The leading *cause* examined in this chapter, therefore, was land hunger.

The leading *consequence*, logically enough, was the more than doubling of the size of the United States between 1811 and 1897 and the corresponding loss of land for the Spanish or Latin Americans.

A Short History of U.S. Interventions in Latin America and the Caribbean,
First Edition. Alan McPherson.
© 2016 John Wiley & Sons, Inc. Published 2016 by John Wiley & Sons, Inc.

Peoples in Mexico, the Caribbean, and the still-Spanish empire paid a permanent price for U.S. land hunger.   *lang huge*

Spaniards, Latin Americans, and Native Americans mostly *contested* this naked expansionism. It usually began with significant violence against their persons and property, and the U.S. intention to keep the land also drew resistance. The war that Mexico fought against the United States from 1846 to 1848 was the greatest instance of contestation.

Given the brashness of continental expansion, *collaboration* was rare. Certainly, some Floridians or Mexicans acquiesced to U.S. power since they were powerless to resist it. More active collaboration marked filibusterism, since some filibusterism had Latin Americans seeking to annex their lands to the United States.

Contexts for land expansion were many and crucial. Accelerating the westward movement of U.S. settlers was the struggle between slave states and nonslave states in the Union, which would lead to the U.S. Civil War of 1861–1865. U.S. policymakers also saw themselves competing – and winning – against other empires in North America, including the French, Spanish, and Russian, but especially the British. Also buttressing westward expansion was an ideology that combined racism, religious fervor, and nationalism. These trends reinforced the U.S. sense that military interventions were *defensive*: if the United States failed to take territory to its south, such failure would somehow endanger the growth – even the survival – of U.S. democracy.

The First Ever Landing: *Sally* and the *Sandwich*, 1800

The first ever landing of U.S. marines outside of war anywhere came in Latin America as early as 1800. The U.S. Navy looked to weaken French forces in what was known as the "Quasi-War" with France from 1798 to 1800. On May 12, the U.S. sloop *Sally*, a small, square-sailed ship, reinforced by men from the larger USS *Constitution*, landed outside Puerto Plata, in the Dominican Republic, at the time still a colony of the supposedly neutral Spanish. The *Sally's* target was the *Sandwich*, a speedy British packet or mail ship recently commandeered by the French. While men from the *Sally* boarded the *Sandwich*, marines and sailors drove metal spikes into the touch-holes of not so neutral Spanish cannons so that their charges could not ignite. The takeover lasted five minutes.

The "audacious, but clearly illegal" capture of the *Sandwich* signaled the growing assertiveness of U.S. forces against European powers in the Americas.[2] There were several more such landings in the nineteenth century. But this first landing did not qualify as a full-blown intervention, nor was it meant to help spread U.S. power through the North American continent.

The No Transfer Resolution, 1811

What was arguably the first true U.S. intervention in Latin America can be traced to a few words from the U.S. Congress.

The sparks were the revolutions against Spanish rule, begun in 1810–1811. France had taken over Spain, and creoles, or Spanish elites born in the colonies, revolted against Spanish officials. The second-strongest power in the Americas after Spain was not the United States but Great Britain, which had by far the most powerful navy in the world and in 1808 shipped 40 percent of its exports to Latin America. So if U.S. politicians feared any people taking advantage of Spanish-American weakness, it was the British.

Since the Louisiana Purchase of 1803, the Founding Fathers also had wanted Florida. Spain still owned the colony, divided at the time between West Florida and East Florida, because ports such as St Augustine helped protect Spanish ships against pirates. The British had ceded both to Spain after it lost the American Revolution, but the value of West Florida, which today makes up the coasts of Mississippi, Alabama, and parts of Louisiana, remained high.

President Thomas Jefferson resisted calls to occupy Florida and negotiate later. But when the British attacked a U.S. ship, he reconsidered, especially since he figured he could also wrest Cuba away from Spain.

U.S. officials encouraged U.S. citizens in Florida to revolt against Spanish authority and then to ask for U.S. intervention. Jefferson wished "to exclude all European influence from this hemisphere."[3] Here, then, was imperial competition laid bare.

On September 23, 1810, U.S. settlers in West Florida between the Mississippi and Pearl rivers overtook the small Spanish garrison at Baton Rouge and soon applied to become part of the United States. The president was now James Madison, who feared that an intervention could be seen as an act of war, something only Congress could declare, and only in a crisis. So he thought up the *potential* takeover of West Florida by the British as such as crisis. On October 27, not waiting for Congress, Madison proclaimed West Florida to be annexed.

But the president still longed for a congressional stamp of approval, and he feared British designs on East Florida, which, he wrote, "is also of great importance to the United States."[4] So in early 1811, congressional leaders secretly debated what to do about Florida. Secretary of State James Monroe asked for a joint resolution by the House and Senate and, on January 15, 1811, they delivered, proclaiming

that the United States, under the peculiar circumstances of the existing crisis, cannot without serious inquietude see any part of the said territory [West Florida] pass into the hands of any foreign Power; and that a due regard to their own safety compels them to provide under certain contingencies, for the temporary occupation of the said territory …

Embracing those few words, Madison sent U.S. troops to take over West Florida. Occupation was swift and painless.

The public justification for this No Transfer Resolution was not land hunger. It was that troops were there to safeguard the "security, tranquillity [*sic*], and commerce" of the United States. General Andrew Jackson and his troops had invaded Spanish Florida to strike back against bands of Seminole Indians and free blacks who attacked a U.S. ship and killed about 30 people. Such raids went both ways, with U.S. settlers assaulting Seminoles, but Jackson was not interested in balance. Incursions into foreign territory such as Jackson's were, to Senator Henry Clay, a matter of "self-preservation" for the United States and totally justified if Spain let chaos reign in its colonies.[5]

Spaniards, among others, contested this deluded U.S. interpretation. "While [U.S. leaders] give to the Spanish government the most positive assurances, that they will never permit any American citizen to commit an act of hostility against the territory of Florida," wrote a Spanish diplomat in 1812, pointing out U.S. hypocrisy, "[they] give orders not only for the invasion of that province, but … to join the insurgents, and to bring the torches of revolution, plunder, carnage, and desolution [desolation?]."[6]

The consequence of the No Transfer Resolution was momentous. It evolved quickly into the No Transfer Principle, which held that the passing of any Western Hemisphere territory – not just Florida, and not just land adjacent to the continental United States – from the hands of one European power into those of another would be seen as a threat to U.S. security.

The First Seminole War, 1814–1819

The year after the No Transfer Resolution, the United States and Great Britain went to war. After that conflict ended in 1814, the British failed to protect Native American tribes of the Northwest and the South as they had promised, so thousands fled from Georgia and Alabama into Florida, where they hoped they could live undisturbed by U.S. covert agents, settlers, and other unsavory characters. Florida towns of "several hundred fugitive [sic] slaves from the Carolinas & Georgia" irritated slave owners.[7]

For these reasons, Andrew Jackson was at it again in the Southeast, dispossessing Creeks, Choctaws, Chickasaws, and Cherokees of their land. In early 1817, claiming "self-defense," President Madison sent a military expedition to Florida's Amelia Island, just south of Georgia, where pirates, privateers, free blacks, and Native Americans tended to hide. Meanwhile, Jackson's forces attacked Georgia Seminoles, one of whose chiefs complained that "the white people have carried all the red people's cattle off."[8] The Seminoles fought back. The First Seminole War was already on, and within it, the second U.S. intervention into Latin America began in March 1918 when James Monroe, now president, allowed Jackson to pursue the Seminoles into Florida. Jackson's 3500 men burned Seminole villages, took animals, destroyed crops, and chased fleeing survivors.

Told not to attack Spanish forts or settlements, Jackson still took all of Florida. He occupied Pensacola, declared martial law, and applied U.S. revenue laws and customs duties. He even took over posts from Spanish soldiers, who, instead of resisting or collaborating openly, bought time by asking for instructions from their superiors in Cuba, another Spanish colony at the time.

The No Transfer Resolution had declared that West Florida would "remain subject to a future negotiation." But a common pattern in U.S. expansionism set in: concessions of land only whetted U.S. appetites for more land. Throughout the 1810s, U.S. citizens moved into not only West Florida but also East Florida, bringing along military incursions and diplomatic pressure.

The pressure to annex all of Florida finally grew too intense. Though Congress investigated Jackson for his unconstitutional war there, public opinion was with him. Secretary of State John Quincy Adams wrote that Jackson acted out of the "purest patriotism" and, not incidentally, Adams appreciated how conquering Florida gave him leverage in talks with Spanish minister Luis de Onís.[9] The resulting 1819 Adams–Onís Treaty gave the United States the ownership of all Florida and firmed up the border with Spanish Texas. The U.S. government assumed $5 million in claims against Spain and agreed not to recognize – for the moment – the independence of rebellious South Americans. The Spanish caved in because they were weak and because Adams promised to demand no additional territory. Many wanted to take Texas too, but Jackson himself wrote to Monroe that "for the present, we ought to be content with the Floridas."[10]

With obvious satisfaction, Adams wrote in his diary that these were victories not over Spain but rather over the most powerful European power:

> Great Britain, after vilifying us twenty years as a mean, low-minded, peddling nation, having no generous ambitions and no God but gold, had now changed her tone, and was endeavoring to alarm the world at the gigantic grasp of our ambition.[11]

There would be Second (1835–1842) and Third Seminole Wars (1855–1858), but by then Florida was U.S. territory – no longer "Latin America."

The Monroe Doctrine and Manifest Destiny

The Monroe Doctrine and Manifest Destiny were not U.S. interventions; they were ideological constructions that justified them, and therefore important contexts. Together, they expressed much of the geopolitical, economic, and cultural motivations of taking continental territory from Latin Americans.

The Monroe Doctrine began as a simple statement by President Monroe in his annual message to Congress on December 2, 1823. The context for the message was that the South American revolts against Spain had run their course, and most of South America and the Spanish Caribbean and all of Mexico and Central America were free of Spanish control.

What will happen to these lands?, U.S. observers wondered. Lasting independence was not a sure thing. Spain could reclaim Venezuela, for instance. France could invade any of these new republics, as it would Mexico in the 1860s. Even the Russians could move in, as they did in Alaska and California (not yet U.S. territories).

The British, who might also have been a threat to U.S. land hunger, were more worried about other Europeans moving in on their trade. Also, they were mending fences with the United States after the war of 1812. In September 1822, their Foreign Secretary suggested to the U.S. minister in London that both countries issue a joint declaration against European intervention in the New World. Secretary Adams decided instead to go it alone, another pattern in U.S. expansion. He wrote the Monroe Doctrine for his president. Adams wanted to encourage anti-monarchical rule but without appearing to intervene in Europe's affairs. The statement thus included the idea that "the political system of the allied powers [Europe] is essentially different in this respect from that of America," meaning all of the Americas. It also had a warning: "We should consider any attempt on their part to extend their system to any portion of this hemisphere as dangerous to our peace and safety."

The message contained three smaller "doctrines." *Mutual nonintervention* meant that the United States would stay neutral in European wars and that Europe should equally refrain from intervening in wars between hemispheric peoples or otherwise "oppressing them." *No new colonization* meant that no European power could retake a colony it or any other power had lost. *No transfer,* finally, came directly from the 1811 resolution. In sum, Adams and Monroe were saying, if Latin Americans gained independence, they should keep it.

By and large, Latin Americans collaborated with a statement that seemed to engage the most powerful country in the Americas in protecting them against Europe. In 1826 Colombia called the Monroe Doctrine the "gospel of the new continent."[12]

Europeans did not publicly reject Monroe's speech, but neither did they take it too seriously. Not only did France take Mexico a generation later, but also Spain returned as master of the Dominican Republic. And republicanism did not exactly reign in South America since Pedro I and II ruled the independent Empire of Brazil from 1822 to 1889.

But, as they say, it was the thought that counted. The United States had made a sweeping statement of its defense of independence (from Europe) and of republicanism in the hemisphere. In time, the Monroe Doctrine would grow from a defensive to an offensive statement.

A much more offensive doctrine from the get-go was Manifest Destiny, an ideological cluster validating westward continental expansion throughout the nineteenth century. For decades, U.S. citizens had argued that expansion beyond the original 13 states was necessary to preserve democracy. Jefferson himself called the United States an "empire for liberty" in which only tillers of small farms enjoyed the resources and the independence to hold their elected leaders accountable. It was a nice theory, one that increased the moral righteousness of U.S. settlers. In reality, farmers needed land more than liberty, and the more U.S. citizens there were, the more land they would need. The cause of westward expansion was often economic in nature but cloaked in political rhetoric.

In 1845, newspaperman John O'Sullivan coined the term "Manifest Destiny" to argue for the annexation of Oregon, California, and Texas in order to add more of that land. The word "destiny" meant that the westward movement of Anglo-Saxon peoples was inevitable; "manifest" signified that it was already happening. He praised the United States as the "great nation of futurity" because its main political principle of "equality" was "universal."[13]

Yet in practice as well as in theory, Manifest Destiny excluded and oppressed many. All the Native Americans who lived in the West were not to partake in this civilizing mission. On the contrary, they were to get out of the way. Manifest Destiny did not argue for the annihilation of Native Americans, but rather for their exclusion from citizenship – expressed in the reservations that later sprang up in the West. African Americans and Mexican Americans were essentially in a similar second-class category, though not in reservations. Such racial exclusion made up the first component of Manifest Destiny. It helped O'Sullivan and other Irish Americans, often shunned by British Americans and others, to feel a part of the dominant white majority.

The second component of Manifest Destiny was religious predestination. White settlers' "destiny," after all, was determined by God. O'Sullivan spoke of a "continent allotted by Providence" to whites, and many spoke of westward migrants as the "chosen" people, headed to the "promised land."[14] Many of the first U.S. citizens in Mexican territories were missionaries.

The third component of Manifest Destiny was a relatively new but potent nationalism. Although the United States had been a nation for a half-century, only in the 1840s did its continental territory stretch "from sea to shining sea." It possessed the Louisiana Purchase territory, Florida, and Oregon, and its borders were every year more secure from European powers. Newly arrived immigrants increasingly sought prosperity out west, and railroad promoters happily encouraged national pride.

The takeovers of Latin American territory that followed from these ideological statements helped U.S. citizens believe that they were doing so out of the goodness of their hearts, and if fighting broke out, it was defensive, democratic, and unstoppable.

3 components to Manifest Destiny
① racial exclusion
② religious predestination
③ new but potent nationalism

The Mexican War, 1846–1848

O'Sullivan coming up with "Manifest Destiny" in 1845 was no coincidence. That year, the United States annexed Texas, whose white settlers in 1836 declared its independence from Mexico and stopped being inhabitants of the Mexican state of Coahuila y Tejas, formed in 1824 after Mexico's own war of independence against Spain.

The October 1835 to April 1836 Texas War against Mexico had all the trappings of a U.S. intervention, except that private armies of white settlers against the Mexican government waged it. Its tensions were slow to build, as settlers moved in, many with their slaves, over a matter of years, and declared independence only when they grew into the dominant social group and bristled at how the Mexican government increased taxes and banned slavery from Tejas.

In 1845, too, President James K. Polk invoked Monroe's message of 1823, beginning its transformation into a doctrine. Mexico would not recognize Texas independence, and Polk was reminding Europeans not to mess with Texas. He added that, while Europeans could not transfer territories between one another, the United States was free to transfer Texas from Mexico to itself. Intertwined with the story of Texas was the devastation and depopulation of northern Mexico following decades of raids by the Comanches, Kiowas, Apaches, Navajos, and others. Town after town was emptied and terror reigned in the 1830s and 1840s. Mexico had in fact allowed white U.S. citizens to move to Tejas in the hope that they would control Indian raids. U.S. expansionists, meanwhile, pointed to raids to further justify going to war with a Mexico that was too weak or too neglectful to police its north.

The fracas with Texas and Indian raids led to war with Mexico, the most important U.S. intervention in Latin America before 1898 and the one that, to this day, drew the most resistance and caused the most deaths on both sides.

A dispute over a strip of land barely 150 miles wide at its eastern end started the war. Mexico said that its border with Texas ran along the Nueces River, while U.S. citizens countered that it was at the Rio Grande, further south. In the background was the annexation of Texas, which many in Congress warned might lead to war with Mexico.

Fearing British incursions into the shakily administered northern areas of Mexico, Polk sent negotiator John Slidell to Mexico City with instructions to buy some of those areas – California for $25 million and New Mexico for $5 million – and to settle the Texas border. Moderate Mexican president José Joaquín de Herrera might have taken the money, but conservatives refused, and General Mariano Paredes y Arrillaga overthrew Herrera in December 1845. The new government said "no deal" to Slidell, who wrote to Polk that "a war would probably be the best mode of settling our affairs with Mexico."[15]

The Mexican army reflected the country's disunity: it was decentralized and poorly trained, equipped, and paid. In contrast, the U.S. army had a well-educated, professional officer corps, plenty of horses, and a modern artillery that moved more quickly, shot farther, and killed more people. By war's end, 26,922 regular U.S. soldiers and 73,260 temporary volunteers would serve in the Mexican War.

The immediate cause of the Mexican War was a U.S. military incursion over what Mexicans considered the border. In spring 1846, Polk ordered General Zachary Taylor, nicknamed "Old Rough and Ready," to take a small force across the Nueces toward the Rio Grande.[16] Mexican Major General Pedro Ampudia told Taylor to move back, otherwise "it will clearly result that arms, and arms alone, must decide the question."[17] Taylor refused to leave. On April 25, a Mexican cavalry killed 16 U.S. dragoons or cavalrymen and captured the rest. On May 11, Polk asked Congress for a declaration of war because Mexico had "invaded our territory and shed American blood upon the American soil."[18] Two days later, Congress obliged him.

On June 14, led by frontiersman John Frémont, settlers in California revolted against Mexican authorities there and proclaimed the "Republic of California." The Pacific Squadron seized Monterey, California – still Mexican territory – and raised the U.S. flag.

Some spoke against the war, mostly Whig Party members who opposed the expansion of slavery into the West joined by those who wished to abolish all slavery. Philosopher Henry David Thoreau was jailed after refusing to pay a tax for a war that would surely expand slavery, leading to his classic essay *Civil Disobedience.* Decades after the conflict, then-former president Ulysses S. Grant called it "the most unjust war ever waged by a stronger against a weaker nation."[19]

But most U.S. citizens caught war fever. Twenty thousand assembled in New York City to hear the following song:

The Mexicans are on our soil,
In war they wish us to embroil;
They've tried their best and worst to vex us,
By murdering our brave men in Texas.

The song went on to swear vengeance against "those half-savage scamps."[20] Even poet Walt Whitman, usually known for his compassion, wrote "Yes: Mexico must be thoroughly chastised!"[21]

After Polk expanded the war beyond northern Mexico, most of the fighting took place in Mexico's Gulf coast and interior. López de Santa Anna and other Mexican officers faced powerful onslaughts from Taylor, Colonel Alexander Doniphan, and General Stephen Kearny. With orders from Polk to take Mexico City, General Winfield Scott laid siege to the coastal city of Veracruz throughout March 1847. After half a million pounds of artillery rained on them, the citizens of Veracruz surrendered. In spring and summer, U.S. forces occupied half a dozen cities.

On September 13, Scott ended his march toward the capital by storming Chapúltepec Castle. Contestation came from Mexican teen-age military cadets, who resisted bravely, and six of them perished and became *los Niños Héroes,* commemorated by a national holiday. But, the next day, U.S. marines entered the "Halls of Montezuma," meaning inside the castle, a feat that would make its way into the first line of their hymn.

Figure 1.1   The Battle of Chapúltepec, September 13, 1847. Painting by Sarony & Major, 1848. Library of Congress Prints and Photographs Division, Washington, D.C.

The peace agreement expressed the map-shifting consequences of the Mexican War. Signed on February 2, 1848, the Treaty of Guadalupe Hidalgo gave the United States almost half of Mexico, including Texas – all told, 530,000 square miles. Washington paid Mexico City $15 million and assumed $3.25 million in U.S. citizens' claims. The "All Mexico Movement" to annex the entire country failed, among other reasons because Senator John C. Calhoun advanced that "more than half of Mexicans are Indians, and the other is composed chiefly of mixed tribes. I protest against such a union as that! Ours, sir, is the Government of a white race."[22] Still, the United States now added to its population some 80,000 Mexicans and Spaniards, nearly three-fourths of them in what became New Mexico. Guadalupe Hidalgo also stipulated that the United States was to "restrain" the "savage tribes" – or *indios bárbaros* to the Mexicans – from attacking remaining Mexican territory or capturing and selling Mexicans.

About 15,000 Mexican fighters were killed along with 1000 civilians, versus 1773 U.S. soldiers killed and 13,271 dead from diseases – the highest death rate in U.S. history. Many fought after endless, excruciating walks through deserts. Most of the dead on both sides, however, perished from disease – including the *vómito*, as Mexicans called yellow fever. Fighting the war also cost Washington $100 million.

The war provided several opportunities for mutual hatred to fester. Before it began, Texas volunteers and their followers – many of them gamblers, liquor sellers, and prostitutes – occupied Matamoros. An officer described them as "cursing, swearing[,] fighting, gambling and presenting a most barbarous sight … Murder[,] rapine and vice of all manner of form prevails and predominates here … It is a disgrace to our country; for our own citizens are much worse than the Mexicans who are mixed up with them."[23] U.S. propaganda explicitly promised plunder to volunteers.

Mexicans were horrified at this behavior and wounded in the violation of their sovereignty and Catholic values. "The American nation makes a most unjust war to the Mexicans," wrote Juan Soto, governor of Veracruz. "Liberty is not on the part of those who desire to be the lords of the world, robbing properties and territories which do not belong to them and shedding so much blood in order to accomplish their views, views in open war with the principles of our holy religion."[24] Poor and middling Mexicans held off the U.S. army for two days when Santa Anna abandoned Mexico City. Guerrilla warfare by rural, mixed-race Mexicans lasted long after the war and helped convince U.S. forces not to occupy all of Mexico. The consequences of the Mexican War even went beyond redrawing the map of North America. In late 1848, U.S. voters chose Taylor for president, while López de Santa Anna went into exile. The year after Guadalupe Hidalgo, California, now with 100,000 inhabitants – of whom only 8000 were Mexicans – enjoyed a gold rush unprecedented in world history. Over the following decade, U.S. politicians would brawl, and Kansas would descend into warfare over whether the former Mexican territories were to join the Union as free or slave states, leading to the Civil War. In Mexico, the humiliating defeat led to decades of political fighting and widespread anti-U.S. sentiment. President Porfirio Díaz was surely inspired by the Mexican War when he apparently quipped, "Alas, poor Mexico! So far from God and so close to the United States!"[25]

Filibusters, 1850s

The Mexican War helped spark several other U.S. interventions in Latin America and the Caribbean, known as the filibuster expeditions. None of these involved U.S. armed forces, nor did Washington pay for them or explicitly back them. But almost all expressed the U.S. desire, widespread especially in the South, to add slave states to the Union so as to tilt the balance of power away from free states. As the *New Orleans Delta* linked the issues, "The fate of Cuba depends upon the fate of Nicaragua, and the fate of the South depends upon that of Cuba … We must do or die."[26]

The term "filibuster" came from the Spanish *filibustero*, derived in turn from the Dutch *vrijbuiter*, itself a corruption of "freebooter" – someone who takes booty or loot. At mid-century, it denoted members of private military expeditions that invaded countries at peace with the United States, in violation of the Neutrality Acts of 1794 and 1817.

As early as 1812, private U.S. citizens helped Spaniards try to liberate Mexican territory from Spain. The 1819 Adams–Onís treaty's "surrender" of the Texas border inspired James Long, who briefly took the small settlement of Nacogdoches. In 1820 he tried again, on Galveston Island. Long was arrested, and then shot by a Spanish prison guard.

Filibusters multiplied after the Mexican War, fueled by the racist triumphalism of Manifest Destiny and by the Texas model. "The fever of Fillibusterism [*sic*] is on our country," observed the *New York Daily Times*. "Her pulse beats like a hammer at the wrist, and there's a very high color on her face."[27] The *Daily Times* and other papers filled their pages with filibustering exploits. U.S. citizens, in the North as well as the South, held rallies, bond drives, lectures, and parades in celebration.

Cuba was a prominent target, with many causes leading filibusters to choose it. It was close to the United States and Jefferson and others had identified it early on as desirable. Also, by seizing the Spanish-controlled island, U.S. citizens would deal a blow to monarchy in the Americas. Mostly, Cuba's slave-based sugar economy was attractive to Southerners. Up to 1898, there were over 70 filibusters to Cuba. The most important was that of Venezuela-born Narciso López, who fled Cuba for the United States in 1848 and recruited U.S. supporters, among them John O'Sullivan. Because López broke the law, in 1849 the U.S. Navy put an end to his 2000-man expedition at Round Island, Mississippi. In 1850, López and 600 men tried again and made it to Cuba. But Spanish resistance forced them to Key West, Florida. The following year, López attempted a final time with 400 men, but he and many under his command were captured and executed.

Many in the United States were outraged at the executions and called on the government of Millard Fillmore to exact vengeance from Spain. In 1854, European newspapers published the Ostend Manifesto, an attempt by Franklin Pierce's administration to buy – and, failing that, to seize – Cuba. The manifesto outlined why Cuba belonged "naturally" to the United States: "From its locality it commands the mouth of the Mississippi," where much U.S. commerce flowed. Adding politics to its justifications, it also denounced "the tyranny and oppression which characterized its immediate rulers." If Spain rejected the eventual U.S. offer of $120 million, Cubans would probably rise up in revolt, it added, and "no human power could prevent the citizens of the United States and liberal-minded men of other countries from rushing to their assistance." The Ostend Manifesto stopped just short of supporting filibusters. It concluded that the United States would not take Cuba without Spain's consent … "unless justified by the great law of self-preservation."

The most infamous filibuster of all was William Walker, who called himself "the Grey-Eyed Man of Destiny." In 1849, the diminutive Tennessean joined the California Gold Rush, imbibing its heady brew of expansionism. In October 1853, he led 45 disappointed gold diggers into northwestern Mexico. After taking La Paz, in Baja California, he declared himself president of the "Republic of Lower California" and imposed on Baja the Civil Code of Louisiana, which legalized slavery. California papers celebrated Walker's adventures as "another advance toward that manifest destiny of the Anglo Saxon race."[28] Growing his army but without setting foot in neighboring Sonora, in early 1854 he founded "the Republic of Sonora."

Mexicans saw in this pattern echoes of the Mexican War's beginnings. To avoid losing even more land, on December 30, 1853, they agreed to the Gadsden Purchase, the sale of almost 30,000 square miles of northern Sonora for $10 million, negotiated by U.S. Minister to Mexico James Gadsden. But Mexican troops also attacked Walker, who retreated to California. Walker's "presidency" of Baja-Sonora had lasted six months. As a measure of the divisions among U.S. citizens, Walker was tried for violating the Neutrality Act but acquitted by a jury.

Walker was as persistent as Narciso López. In May 1855, with 58 men this time, Walker took advantage of fighting between Nicaragua's Liberals and Conservatives, whose partisanship caused the small

Central American nation to have few professional soldiers and thus little defense against invasion. Walker accepted an invitation from Francisco Castellón to fight alongside the Liberals, who foolishly thought Walker only brought mercenaries uninterested in politics. In the town of Rivas, Walker's defeat was only prevented by his men carrying rifles and Colt revolvers against the Central Americans' flintlock muskets. On October 13, 1855, Walker took the Conservative town of Granada. Enjoying military control, Walker had a few top Nicaraguan politicians killed and named himself "general-in-chief" of the army. The Pierce administration, though it had not backed his adventure, recognized his puppet government. Many U.S. cities held rallies in celebration of Walker.

But Walker's luck ran out. He was caught in a corporate tussle. When he first took Nicaragua, the Accessory Transit Company, which had a charter to run its ships through Nicaragua, paid Walker a $20,000 "loan" in gold. But Transit's directors, Charles Morgan and Cornelius Garrison, were battling for control of it against another Cornelius – Vanderbilt this time. Vanderbilt wrested the company from Morgan and Garrison. Meanwhile, Morgan secretly revoked its charter while his associate, Walker, approved a new one for Morgan's new company.

This all meant that Walker now had as an enemy Cornelius Vanderbilt, maybe the richest man in the Americas.

Walker had other enemies. When he took over Nicaragua, President José María Estrada and Colonel Tomás Martínez exiled themselves to Honduras and denounced those who allied with Walker. Two months later, Liberal José Trinidad Cabañas of Honduras proposed an anti-Walker alliance with the Conservatives of Guatemala, Honduras, and Costa Rica, who feared that "all the [offices] and emoluments of office would be absorbed by North Americans."[29] In other words, powerful Latin Americans contested Walker in part because they feared losing government jobs and the access to the treasury that went with those jobs. London also saw in Walker an obstacle to British commerce.

On March 1, 1856, Costa Rica declared war on Walker, who ordered 350 men to ride southward. Costa Rican forces pursued them back into Nicaragua, taking the towns of La Virgen and then Rivas on April 11. In June, Walker had himself elected president. Few Nicaraguans outside of Walker's base of Granada voted; U.S. citizens voted again and again.

In September, Walker decreed that anyone not actively looking for work could be sentenced to forced labor for up to six months. Such legislation took its cue from the 1850s United States, where slave owners looked to enslave free blacks by labeling them as vagrants. The following day Walker decreed unlimited labor contracts, or indentured servitude. He made English an official language of Nicaragua. He also forced all lands to be registered, and all those owned by Walker's enemies were sold at auction. "These several decrees," wrote Walker, "were intended to place a large portion of the land in the hands of the white race."

If anyone had any doubt about Walker's ultimate purpose, he annulled the abolition of slavery. Funds from the South started flowing to him.

In Central America, Walker's radical decrees mobilized day laborers, artisans, and indigenous tribes to join multinational armies against the Tennessean. Politicians set aside old feuds. On September 14, an all-Nicaraguan force led by Colonel José Dolores Estrada defeated 300 of Walker's men at San Jacinto. Guatemalan, Honduran, and Salvadoran troops also closed in from the north. Walker retreated to Granada, to which cholera spread, causing 2–3 percent of Walkerites to die *every day*. Losing his authority, Walker found his officers, as he wrote, in "languor and exhaustion" and imbibing "a great deal of liquor."[30] He ordered them to destroy Granada after he fled. On Christmas Eve 1856, Vanderbilt's envoy assisted Costa Rican troops in cutting off Walker's port of escape. Vanderbilt and the British also helped fund a consolidated Central American army, but on May 1, 1857, Walker surrendered to U.S. Commander Charles E. Davis of the *St Mary*, who would not hand him to the furious Central Americans. It was more a rescue than an arrest. U.S. citizens "surrendering" to

Davis numbered 463; the U.S. dead from battle or disease, 566. Some claimed that thousands of U.S. filibusterers were killed in the Walker affair.

Amazingly, once over the border, Walker remained free to tour the South, declaring he could still spread slavery in Central America. Now U.S. Northerners were clearly opposed to his expeditions. A U.S. navy ship caught Walker in Nicaragua in December 1857. The Tennessean tried yet again in 1860, but his ship sank en route, and the British escorted him back to the United States. His final attempt came in 1860 in Honduras with 70 men. There, the British Navy captured Walker and his men, and this time he would not hitch a ride home. The British handed him to the Hondurans, who promptly tried and executed him by firing squad on September 12, 1860.

It is not clear what the consequences of these unofficial adventurers were. They probably helped to hasten the Civil War by whipping up sectional tensions. Filibusters also caused great anxiety among Spaniards and Cubans loyal to the crown, but may have in fact delayed the liberation of Cuba by reinforcing Spain's desire to hold on to it. And Walker's outings in Central America may have caused enough anti-U.S. sentiment to hurt U.S. commerce. It certainly left a lasting impression in Nicaragua, where children still learn about the infamy of the William Walker invasion.

The Bombing of San Juan del Norte, Nicaragua, 1854

Nicaragua was also the target of the U.S. government. Before Walker's adventures there, the U.S. Secretary of State named Solon Borland, a U.S. senator from the slave state of Arkansas, as minister to Nicaragua. Told to obtain from Nicaragua the right for U.S. citizens "to purchase and hold real estate for any purpose whatsoever," Borland began his year in Central America praising the Monroe Doctrine and the Mexican War. He also denounced the Clayton–Bulwer Treaty of 1850, in which Washington and London had agreed that neither could build a canal in Central America without the other's consent. Borland

Clayton Bulwer Treaty
1850

called Nicaraguans "a people ignorant, undiscriminating, conscious of their feebleness, jealous of their rights, and proverbially suspicious and excitable."[31]

On May 16, 1854, Borland was traveling down the San Juan River on board the steamer *Routh*, led by a Captain T.T. Smith, when it rammed a large canoe called a bongo. When the bongo's owner, Antonio Paladino, chewed out Smith in Spanish, the captain grabbed a rifle and shot Paladino dead. Soon after, the Afro-Nicaraguan marshal of San Juan del Norte, a small Caribbean coastal town of about 60 huts, tried to arrest Smith. Gun in hand, Borland warned the marshal to turn around. Town officials tried to reason with the U.S. minister, but someone in their party threw a bottle that grazed Borland's face, causing a minor cut.

Revenge followed. Borland headed back to the United States, but the Pierce administration sent the warship *Cyane* to demand reparations or obtain satisfaction otherwise. On July 13, the *Cyane* fired over 200 rounds at point-blank range at the hamlet. Forty or 50 sailors went ashore, looted what was left– especially liquor – in what was still standing, and torched the remains to the ground. No one died, but inhabitants of San Juan lost $2 million, which the U.S. government never reimbursed.

Why bomb such an insignificant town so mercilessly? Imbued with his era's racism, President Pierce himself described the mixed-race San Juan as "a pretended community, a heterogeneous assemblage gathered from various countries, and composed for the most part of blacks and persons of mixed blood." For this reason, San Juan was "incapable of being treated in any other way than as a piratical resort of outlaws or a camp of savages."[32] Pierce also wanted to show the British his disdain for Clayton–Bulwer, especially since the British claimed a protectorate over San Juan, which they called Greytown. Also on board was the Transit Company, which owned Smith's ship. One of its directors instructed "that the people of the town should be taught to fear us. Punishment will teach them."[33]

The bombardment of San Juan del Norte spoke to the arrogant spirit of U.S. expansion during the nineteenth century. Along with other U.S. interventions, it also indicated a shift away from British and toward U.S. hegemony over the Western Hemisphere. There were no other interventions on the scale of the Mexican War or even the First Seminole War until the War of 1898. Between 1869 and 1897, however, Washington sent warships into Latin American ports 5980 times. Some of these were friendly enough visits, but most of the time U.S. forces landed to oversee a change in political regimes, to quell riots or a civil war, or to enforce a commercial treaty. In all instances, the intent was to serve the interests of the United States, not those of Latin America, regardless of the spirit of the Monroe Doctrine. "Gunboat diplomacy," as this practice came to be called, became standard in relations between the United States and Latin America. It created resentment in the latter, while in the former it became evidence of the growing hegemony – and to most, superiority – of the United States.

Notes

1   Cited in Albert K. Weinberg, "The Mission of Regeneration," in *The Mexican War: Crisis for American Democracy*, ed. Archie P. McDonald (D. C. Heath and Company, 1969), 55.

2   Willis J. Abbot, *The Naval History of the United States* (Peter Fenelon Collier, 1890), available at www.gutenberg.org/files/22305/22305-h/22305-h.htm#chapter2_2.

3   Jefferson to Governor Claiborne, October 29, 1808, cited in John A. Logan, Jr., *No Transfer: An American Security Principle* (Yale University Press, 1961), 106.

4   Madison to Pinkney, October 30, 1810, cited in Logan, *No Transfer*, 115.

5   Clay cited in Brian Loveman, *No Higher Law: American Foreign Policy and the Hemisphere since 1776* (University of North Carolina Press, 2010), 26.

6   Juan de Onís, cited in Liz Sonneborn, *The Acquisition of Florida: America's Twenty-Seventh State* (Chelsea House, 2009), 34.

7   Unknown author cited in Kenneth Wiggins Porter, "Negroes and the Seminole War, 1817–1818," *The Journal of Negro History* 36: 3 (July 1951), 253.

8   Cited in John Missall and Mary Lou Missall, *The Seminole Wars: America's Longest Indian Conflict* (University Press of Florida, 2004), 32.

9   Cited in Sonneborn, *Acquisition*, 75.

10 Cited in Ed Bradley, "Fighting for Texas: Filibuster James Long, the Adams-Onís Treaty, and the Monroe Administration," *The Southwestern Historical Quarterly* 102: 3 (January 1999), 341.

11 Adams cited in Logan, *No Transfer*, 138.

12 Cited in Harry T. Collings, "Misinterpreting the Monroe Doctrine," *Annals of the American Academy of Political and Social Science* 111 (January 1924), 37.

13 John O'Sullivan, "The Great Nation of Futurity," *The United States Magazine and Democratic Review*, November 1839, 426–30.

14 John O'Sullivan, "Annexation," *The United States Magazine and Democratic Review*, July 1845, 5–10.

15 Cited in Norman A. Graebner, "War Aims," in *The Mexican War*, ed. McDonald, 24.

16 John S. D. Eisenhower, *So Far from God: The U.S. War with Mexico: 1846–1848* (University of Oklahoma Press, 1989), xviii.

17 Pedro de Ampudia to Taylor, April 12, 1846, cited in Ernesto Chávez, *The U.S. War with Mexico: A Brief History with Documents* (Bedford/St Martin's, 2008), 70.

18 Polk cited in James M. McCaffrey, *Army of Manifest Destiny: The American Soldier in the Mexican War, 846–1848* (New York University Press, 1992), 7.

19 Cited in Eisenhower, *So Far from God*, xvii.

20 "Our Jonathan," cited in Chávez, *The U.S. War with Mexico*, 98.

21 "The Mexican War Justified," June 6, 1846, in *The Mexican War*, ed. McDonald, 24.

22 Calhoun speech, January 4, 1848, cited in Chávez, *The U.S. War with Mexico*, 119.

23 Volunteer officer cited in Paul Foos, *A Short, Offhand, Killing Affair: Soldiers and Social Conflict during the Mexican-American War* (University of North Carolina Press, 2002), 99.

24 Soto cited in Foos, *Killing Affair*, 106.

25 Cited in Eisenhower, *So Far From God*, 374.

26 Cited in George Black, *The Good Neighbor: How the United States Wrote the History of Central America and the Caribbean* (Pantheon, 1988), 6.

27 March 4, 1854, cited in Robert E. May, "Young American Males and Filibustering in an Age of Manifest Destiny: The United States Army as a Cultural Mirror," *Journal of American History* 78: 3 (December 1991), 857.

28 Cited in Joseph A. Stout, Jr., *Schemers and Dreamers: Filibustering in Mexico 1848–1921* (Texas Christian University Press, 2002), 35.

29 U.S. Minister to Nicaragua John H. Wheeler cited in Karl Bermann, *Under the Big Stick: Nicaragua and the United States since 1848* (South End Press, 1986), 62.

30 Bermann, *Under the Big Stick*, 69.

31 Bermann, *Under the Big Stick*, 41, 42.

32 Bermann, *Under the Big Stick*, 45.

33 T. J. Stiles, *The First Tycoon: The Epic Life of Cornelius Vanderbilt* (Knopf, 2009), 244.

2

The Cuban Crucible

Experiments in Overseas Empire, 1898–1922

None of us thought that [the U.S. war against Spain] would be
followed by a military occupation of the country by our allies,
who treat us as a people incapable of acting for ourselves.

Cuba's Máximo Gómez, 1899[1]

A crucible is a container in which metals or other materials are
melted and reshaped. More abstractly, it's a difficult experience
out of which emerges something novel. The year 1898, when the
United States went to war with Spain in part over Cuba, was such a
moment when old forms of empire, pent-up rebellion, and new ambitions melded to create a new empire.

The *causes* of U.S. designs on Cuba stemmed at least from 1823,
when Secretary of State John Quincy Adams called Cuba a "natural
appendage" of the United States:

> There are laws of political as well as of physical gravitation; and if an
> apple, severed by the tempest from its native tree, cannot choose but
> fall to the ground, Cuba, forcibly disjoined from its own unnatural
> connexion with Spain, and incapable of self-support, can gravitate

A Short History of U.S. Interventions in Latin America and the Caribbean,
First Edition. Alan McPherson.
© 2016 John Wiley & Sons, Inc. Published 2016 by John Wiley & Sons, Inc.

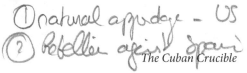

only towards the North American Union, which, by the same law of nature, cannot cast her off from its bosom.[2]

Another cause was that, in 1898, Cuban rebels were involved in a decades-long fight for independence from Spain. Otherwise, the United States intervened for a variety of reasons, ranging from economic to cultural. But their primary motivation, as Adams foresaw, was political gravitation. Especially as U.S. involvement deepened over the next decades, U.S. policymakers wanted to make of Cuba a political dependency and a model of how to benefit from empire without taking full responsibility for it.

The *consequences* of intervention in Cuba were that, compared to nineteenth-century U.S. expansion, the twentieth-century edition presented three new elements. First, it would exist beyond the continental borders of the United States. Second, it would not include settler colonialism, whereby U.S. whites moved in large numbers to overtake native populations permanently. And third, it would not result in the legal admission of these territories to the status of States of the Union. The subjects of the new empire, however, would remain very much beholden to U.S. hegemony.

Many Cubans, especially those who had fought so hard for liberation from Spain, *contested* their subordination to the United States, and rightly suspected the self-interested economic motivations of many Yankees. Others, however, *collaborated* in both the war of 1898 and in what followed – the so-called civilizing mission of U.S. occupiers. Almost every U.S. intervention in this period followed from an invitation by Cubans.

Finally, the *context* of Cuba's subjection to U.S. desires in the first decades of the twentieth century was the continuing imperial race among Great Powers, from which Washington did not want to be excluded. That race partly led to World War I, which deeply affected the island. Cuba was also the victim of ideas shared among the Great Powers about how nonwhites were unfit for self-government. In summary, Cuba's timing was poor: it sought liberation just as imperialism peaked.

The White Man's Burden (and Other Justifications for Empire)

In 1897, British poet Rudyard Kipling penned "The White Man's Burden." It began:

> Take up the White Man's burden
> Send forth the best ye breed
> Go bind your sons to exile
> To serve your captives' need;
> To wait in heavy harness,
> On fluttered folk and wild
> Your new-caught, sullen peoples,
> Half-devil and half-child.

The poem communicated the main justification for both British and U.S. imperialism at the turn of the century: conquest was a difficult, honorable sacrifice undertaken *only* for the good of the colonized ("to serve your captives' need"). The poem was a morale booster in an age when many of the white man's actual actions did not seem so moral.

The "burden" reasoning also papered over several other motivations for U.S. empire in Cuba.

First among these motivations was the desire for markets for U.S. exports. In 1893, the most severe economic crisis to date hit the United States, sending unemployment to about 18 percent within a year. The U.S. economy was producing too much and not paying its workers enough to buy its products. To U.S. leaders, the solution was not to hike salaries but rather to seek more buyers abroad. Cuba, with a population of 1.8 million, was the natural place to enlarge U.S. commerce. In 1894, the United States bought 90 percent of the island's exports and produced 40 percent of its imports. Cubans were used to consuming U.S. goods, and the wealthy spent part of their lives stateside.

A second motivation for taking Cuba was geostrategic. Compared to other European empires, Spain appeared decrepit, barely holding on to not only Cuba but also neighboring Puerto Rico and the faraway

Philippines. U.S. leaders concluded that rival powers such as Germany or Japan were champing at the bit for these islands. U.S. naval strategist Alfred Thayer Mahan spent the 1890s calling for new U.S. Navy and coal refueling stations in the Pacific Ocean and in the Caribbean if Washington was to be a player in the imperial game. "Whether they will or no," he urged, "Americans must now begin to look abroad."[3] "I do believe that we may dominate the world, as no nation has dominated it in recent time," agreed Theodore Roosevelt, then assistant secretary of the Navy.[4] Roosevelt felt that U.S. citizens, without a war since the 1860s, had lost "the fighting edge" and "virile virtues" and suffered "a gradual failure of vitality."[5]

A third motivation was cultural. U.S. empire was partly fueled by a racist paternalism, a replication of sentiments felt toward Native Americans and African Americans. Kipling's reference to "sullen peoples, half-devil and half-child" communicated much of the superiority that white U.S. citizens felt toward nonwhites, whom they saw as biologically lazy, unintelligent, impulsive, and capable of great evil. U.S. citizens called Latin Americans, whether white or not, "niggers" and "Indians." Racism intersected with imperialism to produce paternalism, the idea that whites should act toward colonized peoples as fathers toward children: protective and nurturing but also authoritarian and punitive.

Closely related to this paternalism was the U.S. feminization of Cuba. Like a young male on the make, Roosevelt was eager to test his nation's "virile virtues" against other nations that he considered analogous to women – pretty and fertile, but in need of protection and domination. As with race, such gendered images allowed U.S. policymakers to imagine Cuba as unfit to govern itself.

A fourth motivation for empire was the desire to change the political culture of subject nations. U.S. policymakers wanted to foster not so much democracies, which they considered beyond the abilities of nonwhites, but rather stable, peaceful regimes where power passed from one leader to another in constitutional ways. Cuba seemed particularly ripe for U.S. guidance since it was still a colony and so had no experience with self-rule.

Political reform would smooth out all the other motivations. It would facilitate trade, since office-holders in Latin America would lower tariffs and other trade barriers to let in U.S. goods, tax their citizens more equally and actually collect those taxes, and spend budgets on roads, sewers, and hospitals instead of stealing them. Those same men would refrain from overthrowing opponents through violence and from taking out high-priced loans from European banks – both acts that invited, say, French or German gunboats to Caribbean shores. Finally, politicians interested in stability would foster a more "civilized" culture, for instance by building more schools (or encouraging attendance in the schools that did exist) in which young Latin Americans could learn not only European-style poetry and history but also U.S.-style practical skills such as arithmetic, engineering, and animal husbandry.

The War of 1898

In early 1898, all these motivations lay dormant, waiting for a cause. Then came the sinking of the *Maine*.

The explosion of this U.S. warship in Havana's harbor on February 15 killed 266 crewmembers and ignited U.S. passions for helping Cuban rebels against the Spanish crown. These patriots had fought a Ten Years' War from 1868 to 1878 and launched a second rebellion, led by José Martí, in 1895. Martí gathered almost every social class in Cuba against Spain, including former slaves and other Afro-Cubans, long neglected by other white patriots. Martí had also spent years in the United States as a journalist. "I lived in the monster and I know its entrails," he claimed.[6] He welcomed U.S. sympathies but also feared that, if U.S. citizens ever fought Spain, they would try to annex Cuba. "Cuba must be free of Spain and the United States," he told a colleague.[7] Martí died in his first battle in Cuba in 1895. Nevertheless, the rebels scored several victories by 1898, arguably coming within striking distance of defeating the Spaniards. In response to demands for self-government, Spain made concessions, but not enough to satisfy the rebels.

The U.S. business community was split on the issue of war with Spain. To be sure, U.S. investors in Cuba saw some of their $50 million in plantations, railroads, and other businesses damaged by the rebellion, and President William McKinley, a pro-business Republican, wanted to protect U.S. interests.

Yet Colorado's beet sugar producers, who feared lowered prices against Cuban cane sugar exports, were opposed. The American Federation of Labor also feared competition from cheap Cuban laborers. Others thought the war would cost too much. "We will have this war for the freedom of Cuba despite the timidity of the business world and of financiers," Teddy Roosevelt had to promise journalists.[8]

The Congress was similarly divided, sometimes along party lines, sometimes along geographic ones. Many in the press warned that a war would benefit only Cuban rebels, or, as the *San Francisco Chronicle* called them, "negroes and half-breeds."[9] Others still argued that a war against Spain would mark the United States as an empire, contrary to national identity.

Few swam against the tide, however, after journalists from the "yellow" or sensationalistic press, led by William Randolph Hearst's *New York Journal*, began to cover Spanish atrocities against Cubans. Their favorite target was the "reconcentration" policy of Spanish General Valeriano Weyler y Nicolau that forced 1.6 million Cubans into fortified towns, where some 240,000 perished of starvation and disease. The yellow press called Weyler a "butcher."

In a concrete example of the feminization of Cuba, Hearst homed in on the tribulations of Evangelina Cosio y Cisneros, a young white Cuban jailed by Spaniards, using her as a stand-in for the nation and positioning Uncle Sam to come to her rescue.

Six days before the sinking of the *Maine*, the *Journal* also published a private letter by Enrique Dupuy de Lôme, the Spanish minister in Washington, which called McKinley a "weak," "would-be politician" who catered to "the jingoes in his party."[10] Hearst so successfully whipped up war frenzy that he referred to the conflict as the "*Journal's* war."[11]

The U.S. public seethed with thoughts of revenge after the USS *Maine* blew up. Hearst and other publishers immediately concluded

Figure 2.1 The wreck of the *Maine* in Havana Harbor. Photo by Underwood & Underwood, 1903. Library of Congress Prints and Photographs Division, Washington, D.C.

that the Spanish were to blame, even though the evidence was scant. (In 1976 a report concluded that a spontaneous fire inside the coal bins probably caused the explosion.) Hearst offered $50,000 "for the detection of the perpetrator of the *Maine* outrage."[12]

"The taste for Empire is in the mouth of the people even as the taste of blood is in the jungle," observed the *Washington Post*.[13]

McKinley certainly felt pressure to "Remember the *Maine*!," especially in an election year. But the president remained opposed to war. On March 17, 1898, Vermont Senator Redfield Proctor, fresh from Cuba, argued that the United States should go to war if for no other reason than the suffering of innocent Cubans under "the worst misgovernment of which I ever had knowledge." Proctor's speech, wrote one reverend, "swept away the ethical restraints and let the elemental passions loose."[14] On April 11, McKinley made his strongest case for war "in the name of humanity" and "in behalf of endangered American interests."[15]

As business and religious leaders argued for war, Congress acted. In March, both houses voted unanimously for $50 million "for the national defense."[16] On April 19, Senator Henry Teller of Colorado shepherded through Congress the Teller Amendment, a promise that the United States would not annex Cuba after the war. This mollified some U.S. opponents as well as some Cuban rebels. "It is true that they have not entered into an accord with our government," wrote General Calixto García in an example of collaboration, "but they have recognized our right to be free, and that is enough for me."[17] The amendment accompanied a resolution signed by McKinley demanding that Spain withdraw and authorizing the president to use force to help Cuba gain independence. The next day, Spain broke relations with the United States and the U.S. Navy instituted a blockade of Cuba. War had begun.

McKinley made this the first war run directly from the White House, where he had installed 15 phone lines running to executive departments, the House, and the Senate. The military portion of the Spanish-Cuban-American War took place from April 21 to August 12, when the United States and Spain signed a Protocol of Peace. The war in Cuba had two theatres: a land war and the Battle of Santiago.

The Cuban land war began April 30, 1898, when a Spanish fleet under Admiral Pascual Cervera y Topete left Portugal's Cape Verde Islands toward the U.S. east coast. The U.S. military enacted a naval blockade of Cuba while the Navy hunted the Spanish ships. Rear Admiral William T. Sampson's Atlantic Squadron and his Flying Squadron under Commodore Winfield Scott Schley were fooled when the Spaniards slipped into Santiago, Cuba's second biggest city, on the other end of the island from Havana on May 19. Nine days later, Schley brought the USS *Brooklyn*, USS *Texas*, USS *Massachusetts*, and USS *Iowa* close to Santiago. With the USS *Oregon* on the way around South America from California, he had Cervera surrounded.

Schley bombarded Santiago on June 6, but the Navy decided that going into Santiago's narrow harbor was too risky. On June 10, 150 men from the First Marine Division landed at Guantánamo Bay and took the city easily. Four days later, General Rufus Shafter left Tampa, Florida, with an armada of about 15,000 men and 2300 horses and mules.

This would not be a fair fight. Shafter shelled the town of Daiquirí, only to find it abandoned by the Spanish. Siboney was the same. On June 24, U.S. forces finally fought retreating Spaniards, suffering 16 dead and 52 wounded in their first foreign land battle since the Mexican War.

Now all that separated them from Santiago was a fortified ridge called the San Juan Hills where hundreds of Spaniards waited for U.S. troops, who could only charge up the hills. Army Lieutenant Colonel Theodore Roosevelt of the 1st American Volunteer Cavalry, otherwise known as the Rough Riders, got ashore before other units and became part of a larger force, including the African American 9th Cavalry and 10th Cavalry whose white officers included Lieutenant John J. Pershing. Black units actually took Kettle Hill on the far right of the ridge rather than San Juan Hill on the left, although Roosevelt did lead a group of Rough Riders to help the regulars after his first objective was taken. The 500 reporters covering the war nevertheless fed the myth that Roosevelt led the charge up San Juan Hill, which, according to his biographer, "sounded like a better name, a more Spanish name, a more romantic and exotic name."[18] The Spanish withdrew to Santiago. The United States lost 205 dead and 1180 wounded at San Juan while Spain lost 215 dead and 376 wounded. Many more died of disease.

The naval battle of Santiago began on June 24, when Cervera was ordered to leave its bay. He could not run the U.S. blockade, so he told his captains to fight as long as possible and then scuttle their own ships. On July 3, the Spanish fleet left Santiago in single file and tried to escape down the coast, but it was hopelessly outgunned and easily run aground. The United States lost one man killed and no wounded to Spain's 323 dead and 151 wounded.

On July 17, the Spanish forces in Santiago surrendered. Spain's days as a naval power had come to an end.

The war in and around Cuba led to more U.S. Medals of Honor than any other Latin American conflict by far: 27 for the Army – including one for Roosevelt – 12 for the Marine Corps, and 55 for the Navy. Almost half were given for a single incident near Cienfuegos on May 11, when crews on the USS *Marblehead* and the USS *Nashville* tried to cut three underwater telegraph cables used by Spain while under constant fire from Spanish ships.

The United States took advantage of the war to take Puerto Rico, where Spain still had 8000 regular troops and 9000 local militias. A U.S. bombardment on May 12 killed a dozen Spaniards and one U.S. soldier, followed by a two-month blockade. On July 21, General Nelson Miles landed 3314 men at Guánica on the southeast coast and marched into Ponce without resistance. By August 15, there were 15,000 American troops in Puerto Rico, and Miles marched toward San Juan, but the war ended before he met significant resistance. Some Puerto Ricans were heartened by Miles's promise to bring "protection" and "enlightened civilization" to the island.[19] The Teller Amendment had never promised not to annex Puerto Rico, so McKinley demanded that Spain cede it and one of the Marianas Islands as payback for U.S. investment losses in Cuba.

On December 10, U.S. and Spanish negotiators – no Cubans or Filipinos were invited – signed the Treaty of Paris, in which Spain gave Cuba its formal independence and the United States purchased the Philippines for $20 million. Spain also ceded Puerto Rico, its possessions in the West Indies, and the island of Guam in the western Pacific. Ratification in the United States was not without debate, with many senators arguing that colonies were un-American, expensive, immoral, and conducive to race mixing. But after war broke out with Filipino rebels, the Senate ratified the treaty.

The consequences of what the U.S. ambassador to Great Britain John Hay called the "splendid little war" in Cuba were tremendous, especially for Cuba and for other interventions in Latin America.[20] After the Mexican War of 1846–1848, Cuba was only the second, but also the last, declared U.S. war in Latin America. The U.S. dead numbered only 224 while fallen Spaniards totaled 3429. U.S. occupiers ruled Cuba until 1902. Puerto Rico's cloudy status set off a decade of U.S. Supreme Court decisions, and in 1917, the Jones Act gave Puerto Ricans U.S. citizenship and made them eligible for the military draft. U.S. capital flowed into Puerto Rican sugar, which caused peasants to overcrowd cities and eventually to move to the United States. Puerto Ricans on the continent, concentrated in New York City, grew from 12,000 in 1920 to 888,000 in 1960. Finally, Cuba became a blueprint for interventions in the United States in the Caribbean area. The new control over additional territory convinced many in the United States, Spain, and Latin America that the Colossus of the North was now an empire like many others. Many saw nothing wrong with that.

The First Cuban Occupation, 1899–1902

Beginning January 1, 1899, and ending May 20, 1902, the first Cuban occupation was, in U.S. eyes, where the real work of changing Cuban politics began. Yet U.S. occupiers did not truly believe that Cubans could govern themselves. "Self-government!" Major General Shafter harrumphed to a reporter about Cubans. "Why, those people are no more fit for self-government than gunpowder is for hell."[21] Prewar pity for Cubans morphed into contempt.

> This city and island is a pesthole, and the army does not have much sympathy for the Cubans. All the Cubans we have met here are dirty nasty niggers who eat our rations, will not work and will not fight.[22]

And that's how he described Cubans to his own mother!

A U.S. military governor ran the island. The first, U.S. Army Major General John Rutter Brooke, took control from the last Spanish governor. Brooke immediately disbanded the Cuban Revolutionary Army and implemented U.S.-supervised elections in which only men over twenty who had property valued at more than $250 or were literate or had served in the Army could vote. President McKinley hoped that an electorate of the elite and the middle class would bring about a stable pro-U.S. government. Brooke also attempted to reform the customs and postal services.

In late 1899, Major General Leonard Wood replaced Brooke and vowed to modernize Cuba. Havana's death rate was a staggering 166 per thousand, half from poor sanitation. U.S. Army doctor Walter Reed confirmed the hunch of a Cuban doctor that yellow fever was spread by one kind of mosquito, *Stegomyia fasciata*. The Army Medical Corps undertook to eradicate mosquitos, and from before the war to 1901, cases of yellow fever in Havana dropped from 1232 to 18, and smallpox from 1404 to zero. Wood also supervised the dredging of Havana harbor and the building of thousands of public schools and of many hospitals, railroads, roads, harbors, and bridges. Of the $55 million spent by the military government, $22 million went to such public works.

By the end of the occupation, U.S. capitalists had doubled their investment, to $100 million. By 1905, U.S. individuals and corporations owned 60 percent of rural Cuban land, while Cubans owned only 15 percent. (Spaniards owned the rest.) U.S. interests also dominated sugar, mining, public utilities, railroads, and even cigars.

Wood enjoyed less success in preparing Cubans for independence. In two elections in 1900, voters chose candidates whom Wood considered to be "political radicals" and "agitators." He believed that the majority of the constitutional assembly were "adventurers, pure and simple," and not "safe leaders." Wood and U.S. cartoonists now portrayed Cubans as black or dark-skinned children rather than as light-skinned adults to suggest how their lack of compliance was irrational. The Cuban Army, wrote Wood to bring home the point, "is made up considerably of black people, only partially civilized, in whom the old spirit of savagery has been more or less aroused by years of warfare."[23]

Before leaving, occupiers guaranteed the protection of U.S. interests. In January 1901, U.S. Secretary of War Elihu Root, annoyed at the costs of occupation, outlined preconditions to Cuban independence and asked Senator Orville Platt to present his proposal to the

Figure 2.2   A rare reversal of imagery, in which Cubans accuse the United States of "infantile diplomacy." Cuban Minister to the United States Gonzalo de Quesada holds a "potpourri" filled with "trade reciprocity," "American aspirations," and "general political treaty." By the Cuban-American Reciprocity Bureau in Washington, D.C., 1902. Library of Congress Prints and Photographs Division, Washington, D.C.

U.S. Congress. On March 2, Congress approved what would become the Platt Amendment, which stated that Cuba could not sign away its independence through a treaty; could not contract a public debt it could not repay; promised to pursue sanitation projects; allowed the leasing of land to the United States for coaling or naval stations; and, most important to future interventions, gave the United States "the right to intervene for the preservation of Cuban independence, [and for] the maintenance of a government adequate for the protection of life, property and individual liberty."[24]

Wood admitted that "the Platt amendment has left Cuba with little or no independence."[25] Cubans in the constitutional assembly knew this also, but U.S. forces would stay until the Cubans caved in to Platt's conditions. By a margin of one vote, therefore, the assembly collaborated and added the Platt Amendment to the Cuban Constitution on June 12, 1901. "It is either annexation or a Republic with an Amendment," reasoned one Cuban. "I prefer the latter."[26] Cuba became a virtual protectorate of the United States, and Guantánamo Bay a valued naval station.

Five months after the end of the occupation, the Navy established the Caribbean Squadron, a permanent group of ships whose mission was to maintain law and order through what was fast becoming the "American lake."

The Roosevelt Corollary

The occupation of Cuba overlapped with Theodore Roosevelt's arrival in the Oval Office. Roosevelt was a true believer in empire. Born to a prominent and wealthy New York family but a sickly boy, he transformed himself into a boxer, a Harvard graduate, New York's police commissioner, and an accomplished patriotic historian. Before the conflict with Spain, Roosevelt welcomed "almost any war."[27] His media-distorted charge up "San Juan Hill" catapulted him to the governorship of New York in 1899–1901, then to the vice presidency in 1901, from which he rose to the presidency when an assassin took McKinley's life later that year.

Toward Latin America, Roosevelt adopted a more aggressive policy than his predecessors, transforming the Monroe Doctrine from a defensive, verbal opposition to new European colonization in the Americas into an aggressive, military right of the United States to intervene in the affairs of any nation that appeared too unstable to withstand a European attack.

Two crises helped Roosevelt unfurl what came to be known as his "corollary" to the Monroe Doctrine. (A corollary is an addition to something from which it follows logically.) In 1902, when Venezuela stopped paying its debts to European nations, Germany and Britain, later joined by Italy, blockaded Venezuela's ports and seized or sank several of its ships. Roosevelt sent some 50 ships, and the Europeans agreed to sit down and talk. The resulting Washington Protocols lifted the blockade, reduced the debt, and arranged for a schedule of payments. Roosevelt was not doing this for Venezuela – he called its president "an unspeakably villainous little monkey" – but against Europe.[28] Imperial competition was the order of the day.

By 1904, the Dominican Republic owed to various European nations $32 million, an enormous sum. A private U.S. firm, the San Domingo Improvement Company (SDIC), had started buying some of that debt and then getting Dominicans to export so they could earn foreign currency and pay back the loan. Roosevelt and others saw in the SDIC an instrument for stabilizing small Caribbean nations. In 1903 and 1904, the U.S. government arranged for the SDIC to control directly some Dominican ports and take in the customs taxes on imports.

In the midst of these changes, Roosevelt made a December 6, 1904, speech to Congress. "It is not true that the United States feels any land hunger or entertains any projects as regards the other nations of the Western Hemisphere save such as are for their welfare," began its key passage. "All that this country desires is to see the neighboring countries stable, orderly, and prosperous." So far, well in line with the White Man's Burden.

"Chronic wrongdoing," Roosevelt continued, "or an impotence which results in a general loosening of the ties of civilized society, may in America, as elsewhere, ultimately require intervention by some civilized nation, and in the Western Hemisphere the adherence of the United States to the Monroe Doctrine may force the United States, however reluctantly, in flagrant cases of such wrongdoing or impotence, to the exercise of an international police power."

There it was. Roosevelt divided the world into "civilized" nations and others, only to add that the United States would arrogate for itself a "police power" much like a cop walking a beat. "It will show those

Dagos that they will have to behave decently," explained Roosevelt, applying to Latin Americans a common slur for Italians, Spaniards, or Portuguese.[29] In 1905, his government took direct control of Dominican customs receipts. In a sharp departure from the nineteenth century, intervention now excluded annexation, or transforming conquered territories into U.S. States. As Roosevelt said of the Dominican Republic, "I have about the same desire to annex it as a gorged boa constrictor might have to swallow a porcupine wrong-end-to."[30] To be fair, Roosevelt was not the warmonger he often seemed in speeches. During his presidency, he sent no troops into action and none died in combat.

The Second Cuban Occupation, 1906–1909

Meanwhile, Cuban politicians tested – and contested – the Platt Amendment. After a rigged election in December 1905, opponents accused President Tomás Estrada Palma of fraud. Their leader, General José Miguel Gómez, found no friendly ear in the United States. So his 24,000 men pillaged towns, looted their treasury, and took their horses.

Estrada Palma played his last card – asking for intervention from the United States "because he cannot prevent rebels from entering cities and burning property," cabled a U.S. diplomat to Washington. "Probably about 8000 rebels outside Habana. Cienfuegos also at mercy of rebels. Three sugar plantations destroyed."[31] On September 13, 1906, a U.S. commander on the scene feared that "low negro and lawless elements" might take over the uprising, and he landed troops in Havana.[32] Roosevelt eventually agreed with him and ordered gunships to Cuba, but disembarked sailors little by little, hoping warring parties would reconcile. Instead, Estrada Palma and his vice president resigned, and 2000 marines under Colonel Littleton W. T. Waller went in to protect the treasury. Secretary of War William Howard Taft became provisional governor of Cuba and the opposition laid down its weapons. Roosevelt still claimed to be a reluctant colonizer: "I loathe the thought of assuming any control over the island such as we have over Puerto Rico and the Philippines."[33] Yet the second occupation of Cuba was on.

Brigadier General Frederick Funston commanded the eventual force of 6500, made up of infantry regiments, cavalry squadrons, artillery batteries, and engineers and hospital workers. The Army of Cuban Intervention (later Pacification) occupied big cities, practiced military drills, spied, and developed maps. The occupation also dredged harbors and built or repaired hospitals, jails, lighthouses, railroads, telephone lines, and 478 miles of roads.

Real efforts at reform came with Charles Magoon, who took over the governorship on October 13, 1906. He decreed laws, collected taxes, multiplied public works, and encouraged agriculture. Magoon also placed 60 U.S. officers in the Cuban government to "advise" Cubans. One way of "Americanizing" Cuban politics was to establish a spoils system that rewarded winners of elections with jobs for their supporters and friends, thus institutionalizing corruption and encouraging relative stability in government. Magoon established the Advisory Law Commission, made up mostly of Cubans, to prepare for democratic politics and fraud-free elections. He created a Rural Guard of 5000 Cubans and combined it with the militia and standing army into the Armed Forces of Cuba. It was the first of many military forces or constabularies that the United States would create in the Caribbean.

The winner of the August 1908 election was the same Gómez who had revolted against Estrada Palma. After his inauguration, the provisional U.S. government withdrew from Cuba.

The Cuban Intervention of 1912

After 1909, U.S. officials wanted to prevent another intervention. They worked with Gómez to limit corruption, but with little success. In the end, they defended him against greater instability.

Trouble began when veterans of the war against Spain argued that Spaniards and all Cubans who had supported Spain should be removed from their jobs. In January 1912, Gómez saw these demands as opportunities both to comply with the veterans and to reward friends with government jobs. By mid-year, the opposition was literally up in arms – but quickly repressed. Soon after, Afro-Cubans under the Independent Party of Color led a greater revolt demanding jobs and claiming discrimination against veterans of color. As many as 5000 died in the uprising.

White Cubans panicked, rumors spreading that *los negros* were out to destroy all property and block trade. Taft, now U.S. president, ordered three gunboats to Guantánamo and Nipe Bays. A few marines landed, to protect, for instance, the sugarcane fields of the Cuban-American Sugar Company and the Spanish-American Company. Mostly, U.S. forces stayed in their ships.

Before the year was out, the leader of the Afro-Cuban revolt was dead, the government amnestied its enemies, and an election ousted Gómez. "This orderly transmission of authority is most gratifying," U.S. President Woodrow Wilson congratulated Gómez's replacement, Mario Menocal, "and seems to indicate that the Cuban people have successfully undergone one of the severest tests of republican government."[34]

The intervention was short, lasting from May 31 to mid-July.

The Third Cuban Occupation, 1917–1922

The final – and longest – U.S. intervention under the Platt Amendment again followed a breakdown of politics in the midst of armed conflict and electoral fraud. The U.S. government was more than ever interested in protecting its investment, which had grown past $1 billion, or more than a quarter of all U.S. assets in Latin America.

The Cuban election of 1916 did not go well. Opponents accused President Menocal of intercepting the ballots when Liberal Alfredo Zayas was about to win. U.S. officials urged peace, but once again Cubans – this time the opposition – urged Wilson's intervention in elections planned for early 1917. Wilson did as his predecessors and backed Cubans already in power, selling Menocal arms and ammunition. On February 11, former president Gómez kicked off yet another revolt, and another three U.S. ships steamed toward the island. Wilson also had the context of the coming U.S. intervention in World War I on his mind: "so many things are happening we cannot let Cuba be involved by G[erman] plots."[35] Over 2500 troops would eventually land, mostly to protect cane fields, which rebels tended to burn. Menocal's troops retook Santiago in March and another amnesty freed the opposition.

Unlike in 1912, the U.S. minister and the State Department meddled in the election planned for 1920 by providing an electoral commission. Its head was General Enoch Crowder, who had chaired the Advisory Committee during the 1906–1909 occupation and whose main task was to eradicate ballot stuffing. The United States also took a census, so that Cubans would actually know how many of them there were. Cuba passed his reforms, but Menocal refused to have Crowder himself supervise the presidential election.

A financial crisis due to the end of World War I hit most of the Caribbean, and Cuba, a large exporter, felt the pain of plummeting sugar prices. Gómez and the Liberals withdrew from the planned election of 1921, so Zayas found himself in the presidency. Crowder came back to Cuba, and was now in control. He gave Zayas detailed reforms to follow and even approved his Cabinet.

By January 6, 1922, all U.S. forces had left Cuba, except for those in Guantánamo Bay. As in 1906–1909 and 1912, U.S. forces did no fighting. By the end of the occupation, the United States sold Cuba 73 percent of the island's imports and bought 84 percent of its exports. Two years later, U.S. investments in Cuba were up to $1.2 billion.

In many ways Cuba became the blueprint of the *Pax Americana* in the Caribbean. The Latin term, meaning "American peace," was a reference to a long period of British domination of the seas called *Pax Britannica*, and indicated the further shifting of imperial power away from Great Britain and toward the United States. The cocktail of motivations for intervention not only in Cuba but also in surrounding lands was one part competition with Europe, one part protection of investments, one part political reformism, and a generous splash of racist paternalism. Occupations themselves aimed to centralize and modernize small nations with national militaries, clean elections, disarmament, and public works. But Cubans, like other Caribbean basin peoples, were not so willing to be pacified, modernized, centralized, or controlled in any way.

Notes

1   Cited in Louis A. Pérez, Jr., *Cuba between Empires, 1878–1902* (University of Pittsburgh Press, 1983), 211.
2   Cited in Louis A. Pérez, Jr., *Cuba in the American Imagination: Metaphor and the Imperial Ethos* (University of North Carolina Press, 2008), 30.
3   Cited in Stephen Kinzer, *Overthrow: America's Century of Regime Change from Hawaii to Iraq* (Henry Holt, 2006), 33.
4   Cited in George Black, *The Good Neighbor: How the United States Wrote the History of Central America and the Caribbean* (Pantheon, 1988), 3.
5   Cited in Gerald F. Linderman, *The Mirror of War: American Society and the Spanish-American War* (University of Michigan Press, 1974), 93, 92.
6   Martí cited in Robert Holden and Eric Zolov, eds., *Latin America and the United States: A Documentary History* (Oxford University Press, 2000), 63.
7   Cited in Ivan Musicant, *Empire by Default: The Spanish-American War and the Dawn of the American Century* (Henry Holt, 1998), 47.
8   Cited in Max Boot, *The Savage Wars of Peace: Small Wars and the Rise of American Power* (Basic Books, 2002), 140.
9   Cited in Piero Gleijeses, "1898: The Opposition to the Spanish-American War," *Journal of Latin American Studies* 35: 4 (November 2003), 704.
10 Cited in Mark Gilderhus, *The Second Century: U.S.-Latin American Relations since 1898* (Scholarly Resources, 2000), 17.
11 William Randolph Hearst cited in Jon Knetsch and Nick Wynne, *Florida in the Spanish-American War* (History Press, 2011), 13.
12 Cited in Black, *The Good Neighbor*, 2.
13 Cited in Black, *The Good Neighbor*, 3.
14 Proctor and Reverend Washington Gladden cited in Linderman, *Mirror of War*, 45, 37.

15 Cited in Gilderhus, *Second Century*, 19.

16 Cannon Emergency Bill cited in Musicant, *Empire by Default*, 158.

17 Cited in Kinzer, *Overthrow*, 38.

18 David McCullough cited in Black, *The Good Neighbor*, 4.

19 Miles cited in Kinzer, *Overthrow*, 45.

20 Cited in Black, *The Good Neighbor*, 17.

21 Cited in Pérez, *Cuba between Empires*, 218.

22 Cited in Alice Wexler, "Pain and Prejudice in the Santiago Campaign of 1898," *Journal of Interamerican Studies and World Affairs* 18: 1 (February 1976), 60.

23 Cited in Linderman, *Mirror of War*, 138.

24 Cited in Alan McPherson, ed., *Encyclopedia of U.S. Military Interventions in Latin America*, vol. 2 (ABC-CLIO, 2013), 748.

25 Cited in Black, *The Good Neighbor*, 22.

26 Enrique Villuendas cited in Pérez, *Cuba between Empires*, 327.

27 Cited in Howard Zinn, *A People's History of the United States*, available at www.historyisaweapon.com/defcon1/zinnempire12.html

28 Cited in Boot, *Savage Wars of Peace*, 136.

29 Cited in Richard Collin, *Theodore Roosevelt's Caribbean: The Panama Canal, the Monroe Doctrine, and the Latin American Context* (Louisiana State University Press, 1990), 411.

30 Cited in Boot, *Savage Wars of Peace*, 137.

31 Consul-General Frank Steinhart cited in David A. Lockmiller, *Magoon in Cuba: A History of the Second Intervention, 1906–1909* (University of North Carolina Press, 1938), 41, 42.

32 Commander Colwell of the *Denver*, September 13, 1906, cited in Richard D. Challener, *Admirals, Generals, and American Foreign Policy, 1898–1914* (Princeton University Press, 1973), 164.

33 Cited in Boot, *Savage Wars of Peace*, 138.

34 Cited in Louis A. Pérez, Jr., *Intervention, Revolution, and Politics in Cuba, 1913–1921* (University of Pittsburgh Press, 1978), 3.

35 Cited in Pérez, *Intervention*, 79.

3

Monopolizing the Central American Isthmus, 1903–1926

> The inevitable effect of our building the Canal must be to require us to police the surrounding premises.
>
> Secretary of State Elihu Root, 1905[1]

While U.S. policymakers tried to make Cuba politically stable and predictable, they had an additional goal for the Central American isthmus, or the strip of land that today runs from Guatemala in the north to Panama in the south: to build a canal between the Pacific and Atlantic, or at least to keep others from doing so. The *cause* of this goal was *geo*political, meaning that it took account of geography in international relations. The waterway was not primarily about Central America, but about U.S. competition with the rest of the world – an omnipresent *context* in early twentieth-century U.S. interventions.

Within the Central American isthmus, canals could be built in several places, but the narrowest point on the isthmus was in Panama, a province of Colombia. The struggle for a canal had *consequences*: it set off not only one intervention to separate the two but several more to shelter the canal from the instability of Panamanian politics. Securing the canal was also the primary reason for the 1912 U.S.

A Short History of U.S. Interventions in Latin America and the Caribbean, First Edition. Alan McPherson.
© 2016 John Wiley & Sons, Inc. Published 2016 by John Wiley & Sons, Inc.

intervention in Nicaragua's civil war. That intervention lasted until 1925, and U.S. troops returned a few months later.

Another consequence of deepening U.S. involvement in the isthmus was the growing instability of its politics. Part of that instability was due to Dollar Diplomacy, a strategy ironically meant to stabilize. Identified most closely with Theodore Roosevelt and William Howard Taft, Dollar Diplomacy was a loan collection scheme that went hand in hand with building and securing a canal in the greater effort by Washington to control Central America and the Caribbean.

U.S. ambitions, finally, fed off visions of Central America as an untapped land of riches inhabited by unworthy peoples. As journalist Richard Harding Davis wrote of the subregion, "It has great forests, great pasture-lands, and buried treasures of silver and iron and gold. But it is cursed with the laziest of God's creatures, and the men who rule them are the most corrupt and the most vicious ... It is time that they ... made way for their betters."[2]

Central Americans who actually toiled on the Canal and harvested the bananas of U.S. plantations *contested* being called "lazy." Workers resented interventions for defending corporations, political leaders loathed U.S. marines for backing their political opponents, while intellectuals balked at the U.S. lack of respect for their nation's sovereignty. *Collaborators,* meanwhile, tended to come from the elite, whose property and political power U.S. interventions tended to protect and who, as in Cuba, at times invited interventions.

Panama 1903

Panama held geopolitical value for the United States and for others long before its independence from Colombia in 1903. After 1513, when Spanish explorer Vasco Núñez de Balboa crossed the isthmus to become the first European to reach the Pacific from the New World, Panama became a hub of transportation. After gold rush fever hit California in 1848 and Panama became one of the easiest ways to reach San Francisco from the east coast, the fever spread to the tiny isthmus.

The United States could not yet outpace other great powers. In 1850, it signed with Great Britain the Clayton–Bulwer Treaty, which stated that neither nation could "obtain or maintain" exclusive control over any canal in the isthmus. In the following five years, U.S. investors build a 42-mile railroad that carried gold eastward and gold diggers westward.

This was already an intervention of sorts because U.S. citizens were brutal in enforcing security along the railroad, known as the "Yankee Strip." The first real U.S. intervention in Panama followed the Watermelon Riots of April 15, 1856, when a U.S. traveler refused to pay a black Panamanian vendor 10 cents for what he deemed a sour slice of watermelon. Things escalated, knives and guns came out, and a full-scale riot killed 16 U.S. citizens and two Panamanians. U.S. officials cried "massacre," and, in September, 160 U.S. troops occupied the railroad station in Panama City until Colombia agreed to compensate the United States to the tune of $412,394. From 1860 to 1873, the United States intervened six more times in Panama. Additional interventions followed in 1885, 1895 and 1901, even when the French tried and failed to build their own canal. Causes were diverse: sometimes, soldiers protected the railroad or other U.S. property. One time, they crushed a strike against a U.S.-owned banana plantation. Another, they restored political order when partisans grew violent.

After the war of 1898 and the ascension of Roosevelt to the White House in 1901, ardor for a U.S. waterway burned hot. During the war, it took nearly ten weeks for the cruiser *Oregon* to steam from San Francisco to Cuba. Had there been a canal, the ship would have shown up in about three weeks. In 1901, the Hay–Pauncefote Treaty muscled the British out of any canal. And in August 1903, when the Colombian senate refused to ratify the Hay–Herrán Treaty that would have finally given the United States the right to build the waterway because Colombia would likely lose $50 million in revenue, Roosevelt was furious at Bogotá's "homocidal corruptionists."[3] "I do not think the Bogotá lot of jack rabbits should be allowed permanently to bar one of the future highways of civilization," he fumed.[4] He switched from preventing Panama's separation from Colombia to encouraging it.

Private individuals schemed behind the scenes of this secession. French engineer Philippe Bunau-Varilla, whose canal-building company had gone bankrupt, conspired with Wall Street lawyer William Nelson Cromwell, whose firm would benefit from canal contracts, and with U.S. military officials to support the Panamanians. Washington, however, was not yet sold on Panama. It considered canal routes also in Mexico, Nicaragua, and elsewhere in Colombia. Although the Nicaragua route was at first arguably easier and cheaper, it was longer and less accessible for laborers and had no strong lobbyist in Congress. Allies of Bunau-Varilla and Cromwell, meanwhile, put on the desks of all U.S. senators Nicaraguan stamps that featured an erupting volcano, misleading them to fear for the safety of a Nicaraguan canal.

Knowing that a revolt was coming, and without getting consent from his Cabinet, the Congress, or the U.S. public, Roosevelt put the wheels in motion. "You don't have to foment a revolution," he explained. "All you have to do is take your foot off and one will occur."[5]

The day before the revolt, the USS *Nashville* arrived in Colón, on the Atlantic side, to prevent its repression by Colombian troops. On November 3, 1903, Panamanian insurrectionists scored a quick, near bloodless victory – the only dead were a shopkeeper and a donkey fired upon by mistake – which depended on preventing the 500 Colombian soldiers in Colón from crushing the rebels in Panama City at the other end of the railroad. The U.S. superintendent of the railroad lied that there were only enough cars to take their general and his staff, who arrived in Panama City only to be captured. On November 5, the USS *Dixie* landed 400 marines in Colón under Major John Lejeune, and the Colombian colonel there took an $8000 bribe from Panamanian bankers to sail back to Cartagena with his men. On November 6, Washington recognized the new nation of Panama and sent more warships. The Colombians got the message, but they were enraged, and they complained until 1921, when Washington paid them a $25 million indemnity.

When President Roosevelt asked his Attorney General, Philander Knox, to mount a legal defense for the brazen revolution of 1903,

Knox responded, "Oh, Mr. President, do not let so great an achievement suffer from any taint of legality."[6] Panamanian leaders learned that no Great Power would grant them independence for nothing. In fact, Washington gave Panamanians a worse deal that they would have received under the Hay–Herrán Treaty offered to Colombia. The agreement that gave the United States forever a 10 mile-wide swath of land on which to build the canal was known as the Hay–Bunau-Varilla Treaty. To Panamanians, this was "the Panamanian treaty that no Panamanian signed." When Panamanian negotiators stepped off their train in Washington, D.C.'s Union Station to join the talks, Bunau-Varilla showed them the pact that he had negotiated in a hurry, and Carlos Amador nearly fainted on the platform. Although Panamanians contested "the manifest renunciation of sovereignty" in the 1903 Treaty, Bunau-Varilla cabled Panama to warn that, if they did not ratify it, the United States would give Colombia free rein to punish Panama.[7]

In 1911, when now former President Roosevelt boasted, "I took the Isthmus [and] started the Canal," he was pouring salt on an open wound. Just as the Platt Amendment had done in Cuba, Article 136 of the 1903 Treaty gave the United States the right to intervene militarily in Panama to restore order.[8] A U.S. "protectorate" over Panama, which lasted until 1939, shielded the small nation from external enemies but mostly safeguarded U.S. interests, the canal being first among them. Starting in 1904, the United States mobilized tens of thousands of engineers, medical staff, and especially manual workers from around the world to build what was then arguably the greatest engineering feat ever. The Panama Canal opened to global traffic in 1914.

Again, World War I mattered to interventions. The opening of the canal coincided with the outbreak of violence in Europe, and in early 1918 the U.S. military occupied Punta Paitilla and parts of Taboga and other islands to protect the waterway from German submarines. Washington claimed it could occupy land outside the Canal Zone because the 1903 Treaty gave it "eminent domain" rights. In June 1918, the Panamanian president's death led to disorder, and U.S.

troops moved into Panama City and Colón and even shut down bars, gambling dens, and brothels, to the displeasure of U.S. soldiers and Panamanian business owners. One month later, U.S. troops took over much of Chiriquí Province to help U.S. corporations exporting Panama's fruit, tobacco, and manganese. Their managers complained that Panamanians threatened and attacked them and their property. One U.S. citizen had died, and Panamanians had accused another of killing the governor of Chiriquí. In late 1920, border skirmishes between Panama and Costa Rica in the Coto region of Chiriquí led U.S. President Warren Harding to order the battleship USS *Pennsylvania* to land marines to force President Belisario Porras to accept U.S. arbitration. But Porras felt intense pressure from nationalists in Panama's first ever conflict with another country. The fighting stopped, but Panamanians did not accept U.S. terms until the 1940s.

Another U.S. intervention, however, did the Panamanian elite a favor when it opposed poor Panamanians strikers. In 1925, the wealthy owners of apartment buildings, backed by President Rodolfo Chiari, raised rents, and this after years of rising unemployment and poverty and stagnating wages in the cities. The poor took to the streets. Some looted and burned property, some rioted, and several died. Chiari had no response because the United States had, years earlier, taken rifles away from his police so as to minimize fights with U.S. soldiers in the red-light districts. The Panamanian president did the only thing he could: he requested U.S. help. Six hundred U.S. Army troops rushed into Panama City, and some marines landed. As a result, Panamanians increasingly saw the Panamanian wealthy and the Yankees as one and the same.

The rent riots intervention was the last of the protectorate era, which ended in 1939. The United States had intervened for a variety of reasons, ranging from keeping the Germans out to helping corporations against workers to keeping Panamanian presidents in power. Always, the Panama Canal was foremost among their concerns. Its commercial value to the United States was as high as it would ever be. Its military value would peak in World War II.

Dollar Diplomacy

Poorer nations in Central America and the Caribbean had a problem – and thus a cause for U.S. intervention – different from Panama's: the loans they contracted got them in deep trouble with creditors. The policy of sending marines to secure the repayment of loans was called "Dollar Diplomacy," which marked U.S.–Central American relations since the Roosevelt Corollary of 1904.

Refined mostly by Secretary of State Philander Knox under the Taft administration, Dollar Diplomacy used private bank loans to get foreign governments to accept U.S. financial advisers who would make sure that Latin American presidents would not waste or steal loans or otherwise default on them. Knox feared that failure to repay European bankers would cause French, German, British, or other gunboats to land on Caribbean shores to collect the money by force. The scheme of Dollar Diplomacy was to have Wall Street repay the loans to Europeans, give its own loans to Caribbean governments, and have the U.S. marines occupy customs houses, where import taxes came in, and thus guarantee the repayments. Wall Street thus scratched the back of the State Department by providing the money, while the State Department scratched Wall Street's by having the marines collect it and letting Wall Street earn a sweet commission. Knox, however, cautioned that no loan should be "unconsciously profitable" for Wall Street.[9]

For Knox, Dollar Diplomacy's stated goal was to *avoid* intervention – a peaceful imperialism that stabilized Latin American politics, benefiting all. In the same spirit, in 1907 his predecessor Elihu Root had led Costa Rica, El Salvador, Guatemala, Honduras, and Nicaragua to agree on a peacekeeping machinery at the Central American Peace Conference, including a Central American Court of Justice. But these failed to stop wars. "There should be some conventional right to intervene in Central American affairs promptly," wrote Knox in frustration in 1909, "without waiting for outbreaks and with a view to averting rather than quelling disturbances."[10] Where Roosevelt had sought joint interventions, Taft preferred Washington to act alone.

In a December 3, 1912, message to Congress, Taft defined Dollar Diplomacy as "substituting dollars for bullets." It "appeals alike to idealistic humanitarian sentiments, to the dictates of sound policy and strategy, and to legitimate commercial aims." It was also caused by more than a desire to help U.S. corporations – "We are after bigger game than bananas," said diplomat Alvey Adee.[11] Dollar Diplomacy flowed from the Monroe Doctrine, whose intention was to keep Europeans from intervening in the affairs of the Americas.

Intentions were one thing, unintended consequences another. Dollar Diplomacy often ended up prompting U.S. interventions and resulting in destabilizing violence. As Taft himself said about Central Americans to a Mexican diplomat, he wanted "the right to knock their heads together until they should maintain peace between them."[12]

In the Caribbean islands, the U.S. government used Dollar Diplomacy in Haiti and the Dominican Republic. In 1905, the Roosevelt administration assumed all Dominican debts and took over customs duties, which gave it the right to decide how much of them to use to pay back the debt and how much to give back to the Dominicans. Out of this came the General Customs Receivership, which survived in some way until 1941. The United States would use this agreement to justify their 1916 occupation of the whole country.

Domini Republic

Nicaragua, 1909–1925

In Central America, Nicaragua lived through a long intervention directly caused by Dollar Diplomacy and the Panama Canal.

Nicaraguan–U.S. relations deteriorated after the United States failed to build a canal there. José Santos Zelaya, president of Nicaragua since 1893, long praised the United States as a model of development, and he welcomed foreign investors. But starting in 1903, after Washington opted for the Panama route, he no longer tolerated abuses of contracts by U.S. corporations. He turned to France, Japan, Germany, and Great Britain either for loans or to see if *they* would build a canal through Nicaragua. This annoyed the State Department no end.

Worse for Washington, Zelaya sought to dominate Central American politics. In 1906 he supported an invasion of Guatemala by El Salvador and Mexico. Washington asked him to stop. Instead, the following year, he invaded Honduras after Honduran soldiers pillaged a border town.

In 1909, Washington backed a rebellion against Zelaya with the excuse that his men had captured and executed two U.S. mercenaries who mined the San Juan River. Knox blamed the Nicaraguan, and U.S. warships moved to blockade the port of San Juan del Norte, which helped the rebels. To avoid invasion, Zelaya left office. The new president, José Madriz, tried himself to blockade remaining rebels in the Caribbean coast town of Bluefields, but a U.S. naval leader blocked the blockade and the insurgents overthrew Madriz in 1910.

Civil war was the consequence. This was not exactly Taft's hoped-for "dollars for bullets."

In 1912, more bullets flew and the United States began a 13-year occupation. The immediate cause was fighting between Nicaraguan Liberals and Conservatives, made far worse by Dollar Diplomacy. In 1910, U.S. agents had backed Juan J. Estrada for the presidency, but only on the condition that he take out a loan from U.S. bankers. The State Department brokered deals in which Nicaragua got $2.25 million in loans from Brown Brothers and J. & W. Seligman, and in return the banks received 51 percent of the national railway and the country's steamers and wharves. Throughout the following decades, Washington pursued a special Dollar Diplomacy in Nicaragua by insisting that the Central American country's financial advisers be Wall Street bankers rather than U.S. government officials.

"It is obvious that the Monroe Doctrine is more vital in the neighborhood of the Panama Canal and the zone of the Caribbean than anywhere else," explained President Taft to Congress. "Hence the United States has been glad to encourage and support American bankers" to help "remove at one stroke the menace of foreign creditors and the menace of revolutionary disorder."[13]

On August 3, 1912, in the midst of yet another civil war, the Conservative Nicaraguan minister of foreign relations warned of danger to U.S. lives and property and asked for an intervention. The following day, 100 bluejackets or U.S. Navy sailors aboard the USS *Annapolis* disembarked in the Pacific port of Corinto and headed for Managua. Ten days later, 354 marines joined them from the U.S.-controlled Panama Canal Zone. Within a few more weeks, there were 2350 U.S. forces in Nicaragua. The State Department explained that the intervention was "to take the necessary measures for an adequate legation guard at Managua, to keep open communications, and to protect American life and property."[14] The fighting was all over by December, when the force was reduced to 120 after 2–5000 Nicaraguans died in the civil war and the U.S. intervention.

Heightening the hatred between Liberals and Conservatives, U.S. invaders openly sided with the latter. Liberals and even many Conservatives detested Dollar Diplomacy. In 1911 the U.S. minister had found "an overwhelming majority of Nicaraguans ... antagonistic to the United States" because of the loans. During the civil war, Nicaraguans insulted one another by yelling, "Yankee pigs!"[15]

Faced with the 1912 U.S. intervention, the head of the rebels, General Luis Mena, surrendered quickly, but General Benjamín Zeledón took a stand. He bombarded Managua in mid-August, then retreated to two fortified, never-taken hills some 15 miles north of Managua, which overlooked the railroad. Since the U.S. priority was to secure the U.S.-owned track, Zeledón had to go. While on the hills, he called the United States a nation "that I admire and respect for its size and power; but that I do not wish as my country's conqueror." By invading Nicaragua repeatedly, he added, Washington acted "outside accepted norms of civilization." He wrote to his wife that "we lack everything: provisions, arms and munitions, we are surrounded by cannons and thousands of men ready to pounce. It would be madness to expect a fate different from death."[16] The following day, he met that fate at the hands of Nicaraguan troops as he tried to flee.

Ordinary Nicaraguans also fiercely resisted U.S. intervention. As one train with U.S. troops rolled into Masaya, a man on horseback thundered toward the train and six or seven others "started to blaze away," followed by "everybody shooting in every direction."[17] In the

Figure 3.1 President Theodore Roosevelt collecting debts and patrolling Central America and the Caribbean with his "big stick." By William Allen Rogers, 1904.

Liberal town of León, one U.S. captain wrote how "all along the streets they showed their hostility, even women spat at us, many women were armed with rifles and machetes, it was a crazy mob." Other Nicaraguans forced a commander and his men to get off their train and walk the 55 miles back to Managua in pouring rain. "Oh, you don't know that crowd," said the commander. "They're bloodthirsty."[18]

Much of the hostility came from Liberals, who were fighting the friends of their enemies, the Conservatives. But many were Nicaraguans independent of any party. Liberal chiefs who surrendered warned a U.S. commander that "they could not control all their soldiers as many had refused to give up their arms and had decided to fight us to the bitter [end should] we attempt to disarm them and take over the city."[19] Others complained that marines stole their water, wood, and cattle.

U.S. invaders, simplifying this constellation of resistance, judged Nicaraguan violence to be merely a result of their race. Smedley Butler, an iron-willed commander of many U.S. interventions who held Latin Americans in low esteem, said Nicaraguans reminded him of his son Tommy "playing Indian." Years after the intervention, Nicaraguan mothers quieted their children by saying, "Hush! Major Butler will get you."[20]

The U.S. intervention in the Nicaraguan civil war gave way to the "100-man occupation," named after the number of soldiers who guarded the legation in Managua. Their job was not only to secure U.S. diplomats but also to remind Nicaraguan warring parties that a larger force could come back anytime to enforce the peace. Politically, the marines kept the Conservatives and their president, Adolfo Díaz, in power. They also imposed martial law so as to prevent another civil war. "Even if we stop fighting and establish the present Government in power," said one U.S. lieutenant colonel during the 1912 war, "the same thing will break out again after our troops leave the country."[21] So the troops stayed.

Meanwhile, the canal issue remained foremost in the minds of State Department officials. In 1914, Secretary of State William Jennings Bryan penned the Bryan–Chamorro Treaty, which gave the United States the exclusive right to build a canal in Nicaragua. This meant Washington could choose not to build one and thus nix any competition with Panama. The treaty also handed the United States 99-year renewable leases on the Corn Islands in the Caribbean and a naval base in the Gulf of Fonseca. In one of the most egregious instances of collaboration, President Díaz even asked that Cuba's Platt Amendment be tacked on to the Bryan–Chamorro Treaty. In return, Nicaraguans received $3 million with which to pay off loans. To Bryan, this was "money well spent if it does nothing more than remove from the arena of discussion the possibility of sale [of a canal] to other countries."[22]

The U.S. Senate ratified the treaty in 1916, but only after stripping it of the Platt Amendment clause and assuring Costa Rica, El Salvador, and Honduras that none of their rights would be affected. Still,

Nicaragua's neighbors asked the Central American International Court of Justice to declare the treaty null and void. Salvadorans said it might lead to a U.S. naval base in its Gulf of Fonseca, while Costa Rica wanted its own canal. They won the case. But the United States said it was not under the court's jurisdiction, Nicaragua withdrew from the organization, and the court itself soon fell apart.

Many Nicaraguans never saw the occupying marines, who stayed in the capital from 1912 to 1925, and several others seemed satisfied that they brought peace between political parties. In 1923 a marine major assessed that "the majority [of Nicaraguans] are very glad of American intervention and would like to see it continued indefinitely."[23] The occupation also introduced a stable currency in 1913, fought graft, outlawed forced labor, and reduced the military budget to a fraction of that of its neighbors. But, unlike in Cuba, the Nicaraguan occupation planned no major public works project. It built no road, ran no school, and did nothing to improve farming or sanitation.

When the marines did try reforms, they usually failed. They founded a constabulary – a half-army, half-police force called the National Guard that was supposed to follow whoever was the president rather than a party leader. But training did not start until the eve of the marines' departure in 1925. The Nicaraguan Congress also wanted to hold on to its old army, which it could better politicize. Potential new guards assumed that officers would steal their salaries as they did in the old army. Finally, the budget was too small. For all these reasons, the Guard collapsed in 1926–1927.

Compounding these failures was the humiliation of being occupied. Many Nicaraguans were outraged at the news of the Bryan–Chamorro Treaty, which killed the Zelayan dream of a canal in Nicaragua. One Nicaraguan recalled that marines "when off duty caused a ruckus in the cantinas of Managua, sometimes assaulting peaceful Nicaraguan citizens, without any authority daring to stop them." "Prostitution and vile liquor are cheaply obtainable," agreed a Navy captain. Nicaraguan police, soldiers, and artisans made less money than prostitutes, he added, which added to their embarrassment. Officials began to provide a canteen, dancehall, movie theater, and other buildings "with a view to keeping the marines from visiting Managua."[24]

Others objected to the spread of Protestantism and to the transformation of middle- and upper-class women into Nicaraguan "flappers," or "modern" women who wore short hair and sleeveless blouses, smoked in public, and sought jobs as clerks or even lawyers. What concerned U.S. officials most was the apparent inability of Nicaraguan politicians to change their ways – not to have perfect democracy, but at least to allow other parties a voice in government, to stop stealing treasury funds, to have a reasonably free press, and to stop grabbing power through violence. After six years of occupation, Dana Munro of the U.S. legation bemoaned that Nicaraguans still joined political parties because of "petty prejudices and loyalty to individuals rather than political principles."[25]

Nicaraguans, meanwhile, wanted Dollar Diplomacy to end. One economist in 1924 calculated that Washington's forced loans had cost Nicaraguans more than $33 million, of which more than $8 million were Wall Street profits and sky-high salaries for U.S. officials.[26]

Occupiers also made democracy more difficult. In 1922, a Navy captain wrote that the U.S.-friendly Conservatives were elitist and divided and only represented a third of the country. So, instead of pressing the Liberals not to run in elections as U.S. officials had done in 1916 and 1920, when the Nicaraguan president died in 1923 and his vice president tried to replace him, the State Department judged that unconstitutional and backed a bipartisan ticket. The election of 1924 attracted only minimal accusations of fraud and force.

The marines knew they were leaving behind a weak government, but the hundred-man guard left anyway in August 1925. "Seldom if ever has a nation," wrote Harold Denny in the *New York Times*, "having full knowledge of the danger, taken deliberately a step whose disastrous results were more thoroughly a mathematical certainty than the United States took in ordering this withdrawal."[27]

The chancy 1925 withdrawal from Nicaragua was an anomaly. The purpose of U.S. interventions in early-century Central America was usually to minimize risk. Roosevelt backed rebels in Panama so as to assure U.S. control over a waterway. Taft sent marines to collect its Dollar Diplomacy loans so as to make sure they'd be paid back. And the military intervened again and again in Panama and Nicaragua to minimize losses to U.S. corporations and political friends. Throughout it all, the goal – though rarely the consequence – was to stabilize the politics of the isthmus of Central America.

Notes

1   Cited in George Black, *The Good Neighbor: How the United States Wrote the History of Central America and the Caribbean* (Pantheon, 1988), 74.
2   Cited in Black, *The Good Neighbor*, 9.
3   Cited in Max Boot, *The Savage Wars of Peace: Small Wars and the Rise of American Power* (Basic Books, 2002), 133.
4   Cited in Richard Collin, *Theodore Roosevelt's Caribbean: The Panama Canal, the Monroe Doctrine, and the Latin American Context* (Louisiana State University Press, 1990), 239.
5   Cited in Walter LaFeber, *The Panama Canal: The Crisis in Historical Perspective* (Oxford University Press, 1978), 32.
6   Cited in Boot, *Savage Wars of Peace*, 134.
7   Panamanian government cited in LaFeber, *The Panama Canal*, 38.
8   Cited in Francisco Escobar, *"I Took the Isthmus": Ex-President Roosevelt's Confession, Colombia's Protest, and Editorial Comment by American Newspapers on "How the United States Acquired the Right to Build the Panama Canal"* (M. B. Brown, 1911), n. p.
9   Cited in Boot, *Savage Wars of Peace*, 139.
10 Cited in Richard D. Challener, *Admirals, Generals, and American Foreign Policy, 1898–1914* (Princeton University Press, 1973), 288–9.
11 Cited in Boot, *Savage Wars of Peace*, 139.
12 Cited in Challener, *Admirals*, 289.
13 Cited in Karl Bermann, *Under the Big Stick: Nicaragua and the United States since 1848* (South End Press, 1986), 153.
14 Cited in Bermann, *Under the Big Stick*, 163.

15   Elliot Northcott cited in Ivan Musicant, *The Banana Wars: A History of United States Military Intervention in Latin American from the Spanish-American War to the Invasion of Panama* (Macmillan, 1990), 143; Michel Gobat, *Confronting the American Dream: Nicaragua under U.S. Imperial Rule* (Duke University Press, 2005), 103–8.

16   My translations, Zeledón to Southerland, Masaya, September 19, 1912, E-001, C-002, 000109, and Zeledón to "Estercita," Masaya, 3 October 1912, E-001, C-002, 000082, both in Collección BZ (Benjamín Zeledón), Centro de Historia Militar, Managua, Nicaragua.

17   Butler, Granada, September 23, 1912, folder Transcripts of Nicaraguan letters, 1912, box 5, Papers of Smedley Butler, Marine Corps Archives and Special Collections, Gray Research Center, Quantico, Virginia.

18   Entry for August 20–21, 1912, Vulte, "Expedition to Nicaragua," August 10, 1912 [through September 23], folder Nicaragua-1912, Nicaragua, Geographical Files, Reference Branch, Marine Corps Archives and Special Collections, Gray Research Center, Quantico, Virginia; cited in Smedley Butler, *Old Gimlet Eye: The Adventures of Smedley D. Butler as told to Lowell Thomas* (Farrar & Rinehart, 1933), 141.

19   Frank F. Zissa, cited in Robert Zissa, "Nicaragua – 1912," *Leatherneck*, July 1984, 28.

20   Butler, aboard USS *Annapolis*, August 28, 1912, folder Transcripts of Nicaraguan letters, 1912, box 5, Papers of Smedley Butler, Marine Corps Archives and Special Collections, Gray Research Center, Quantico, Virginia; no title or author, *The Nation*, 278.

21   Long, October 3, 1912, folder 7, box 1, Papers of Joseph H. Pendleton, Marine Corps Archives and Special Collections, Gray Research Center, Quantico, Virginia.

22   Cite in Bermann, *Under the Big Stick*, 171.

23   Marine Major Marston, Managua, September 30, 1923, folder Nicaragua Intell. Summaries (1921–1925), box 7, General Correspondence, 1907–1936, Record Group 127, National Archives and Records Administration, Washington, D.C.

24   My translation, José Francisco Borgen, *Una vida a la orilla de la historia* (Dilesa, 1979), 68; Taylor to secretary of the navy, Managua, January 27, 1922, roll 30, OCNO/OSN; "Asks Marines' Withdrawal," *New York Times*, February 6, 1922, 15.

25 Munro, *The Five Republics of Central America: Their Political and Economic Development and their Relationship with the United States* (Russell & Russell, 1967), 73.

26 Bermann, *Under the Big Stick*, 179.

27 Cited in Bermann, *Under the Big Stick*, 184.

4

Wilsonian Interventions, 1913–1919

[handwritten: contradictions between causes and consequences during the Wilson Period]

> Intervention must be avoided until a time comes when it is inevitable, which God forbid!
>
> Woodrow Wilson to his wife, August 1913[1]

The Latin American and Caribbean interventions ordered by Woodrow Wilson were steeped in contradictions, sometimes between *causes* and sometimes between causes and *consequences*. He promised never to grab land in the region, yet he did so more often than any of his predecessors. He claimed to protect the area from the Germans, yet Germany never tried to invade. Finally, Wilson was especially dedicated to "improving" the politics of the area. As early as 1902, he wrote that it was "our peculiar duty" as U.S. citizens to teach colonial peoples "order and self-control" and to "impart to them, if it be possible … the drill and habit of law and obedience."[2] But he ended up doing next to no follow-through. To be fair, Wilson's interventions overlapped with World War I, a *context* that might have driven any U.S. president to fear "losing" Latin America. Regardless, by the end of the war, the priorities of interventionists had shifted from keeping Europeans out to changing the political culture of the invaded. Wilson, perhaps more than anyone, was focused on the political causes and consequences of intervention.

A Short History of U.S. Interventions in Latin America and the Caribbean, First Edition. Alan McPherson.
© 2016 John Wiley & Sons, Inc. Published 2016 by John Wiley & Sons, Inc.

In a 1913 speech, Wilson expressed his contradictory morality toward Latin America. He criticized his predecessor's Dollar Diplomacy as unfair because bankers forced Latin Americans to take loans and then marines forced them to pay back those loans. "The United States will never again seek one additional foot of territory by conquest," the new president promised.[3] But at the same time, Wilson called for the United States to recognize only governments who grabbed power by following their own constitution, a departure from recognizing governments as long as they controlled their country.

All the while, Wilson surrendered the region to hacks. His first Secretary of State, William Jennings Bryan, was a party boss more than a specialist in international affairs, and he used his tenure at State to replace almost all of William Howard Taft's ministers to the region with political appointees who had no experience in Latin America and did not speak the language.

Such dismissive attitudes and policies from Washington engendered much *contestation* from Latin Americans. Mexicans, for instance, were incensed that the United States saw sharing a border with them as justification enough for massive interventions, especially during the already violent and transformative Mexican Revolution. Haitians and Dominicans, meanwhile, also protested their loss of sovereignty as well as the loss of government jobs and private armies that marine takeovers of their nations meant. In both Haiti and the Dominican Republic, too, many *collaborated* with intervention forces, sometimes because they blamed their countrymen for bringing on the intervention, sometimes out of resignation, and sometimes out of the same desire for a government job, even under a foreign occupier.

Veracuz, 1914

The first test of Wilson's contradictions came in the Caribbean port city of Veracruz, Mexico, occupied by the United States from April to November 1914.

The occupation grew out of the Mexican Revolution, which began in 1910 with long-time dictator Porfirio Díaz's replacement by the democratically elected Francisco Madero. But, on February 22, 1913, General Victoriano Huerta had Madero shot, and he transformed the presidency into a harsh dictatorship. Wilson worried that Huerta could not maintain order in Mexico or safeguard U.S. lives and property.

Alongside this struggle for national power were major class tensions tearing apart Mexicans. The gap between rich and poor was cavernous, and peasants and workers felt exploited. One of their major demands was the redistribution of land. In 1910, about half of the peasants toiled on the plantations of either rich Mexican families or foreign corporations, who, already in 1894, owned a fifth of Mexico's soil.

The United States owned much of that land. In 1910, foreign investments in Mexico were worth well over a billion dollars, most of them from the United States. Railroads accounted for 70 percent of U.S. capital in 1902, and Mexico City began buying tracks to reduce this imbalance. Other U.S. funds rested mostly in mining, agriculture, and petroleum. By 1910, too, Mexico exported and imported nearly a quarter of a billion dollars per year, two-thirds with its northern neighbor. During the decade that followed, about one million Mexicans crossed the U.S. border as the demand for their labor increased during World War I.

What Wilson really hated was how Huerta used nonconstitutional means in taking power. "I am going to teach the South American republics to elect good men!" Wilson apparently said when faced with Huerta-like regimes.[4]

However, it was, to say the least, awkward that, during the William Howard Taft administration that preceded Wilson's, Huerta had overthrown Madero with the connivance of U.S. Ambassador to Mexico Henry Lane Wilson. *Ambassador* Wilson was neither related to nor appointed by *President* Wilson. Yet the new president was enraged at his representative's intervention in Mexican politics, especially an intervention that, while it involved no U.S. troops, encouraged violence. Despite Wilson's goal of "constitutionalism" for Mexico, in the eyes of Mexicans, the overthrow of Madero set an ugly pattern for U.S. intervention in the revolution.

So, despite his own reticence against intervening, Wilson saw an opportunity to influence Mexican politics when three Mexican armies moved south against Huerta's troops.

On April 9, 1914, in what became known as the Tampico Incident, Huerta's shore patrol arrested nine U.S. sailors picking up gasoline in a restricted area close to Huerta's line of defense. It was a minor error, and the "dumbfounded" military governor, Morelos Zaragoza, apologized profusely for having arrested U.S. citizens aboard their own ship and marched – "paraded," huffed U.S. newspapers – them through town.[5] Unsatisfied, Rear Admiral Henry T. Mayo demanded not only an apology but also a 21-gun salute to the Stars and Stripes.

President Wilson backed Mayo. "The salute will be fired," he promised grimly, and sent the Atlantic and Pacific Fleets toward Mexico.[6] Huerta, citing "a mistake of subordinate officers," offered that both countries salute each other, but Wilson again refused.[7] He instead asked Congress for a blank check to use force, and while Congress deliberated, on April 21 Wilson woke up to the news that the German ship *Ypiranga* was steaming toward Veracruz with arms for Huerta. (It would arrive weeks later, too late to save the Mexican.) "There is no alternative but to land," said Wilson.[8] The Navy Secretary radio-grammed Rear Admiral Frank Friday Fletcher: "Seize custom house. Do not permit war supplies to be delivered to Huerta government or to any other party."[9]

Wilson predicted no resistance from a Mexican population "struggling toward liberty."[10] But when the USS *Florida* landed 787 marines and sailors, Mexican soldiers, civilians, and prisoners released and armed by General Gustavo Maass surrounded the customs house. "No! It cannot be!" was Maass's reaction upon hearing of the approaching intervention.[11]

Maass got orders to withdraw. But he commanded 1000 regular infantry plus over 300 volunteers from the "Society of the Defenders of the Port of Veracruz," and he had already sent many into the Avenida de Independencia and the Avenida Cinco de Mayo.

Stores began closing. Children hurried home from school. Mexican soldiers quietly lined up along Independencia. Just before noon, an unknown Mexican soldier squeezed his trigger and killed a U.S. Navy signalman, and the battle for Veracruz was on.

Firing from the Veracruz Naval Academy invited counter-fire from the USS *Prairie*, then from the USS *San Francisco* and USS *Chester* the following day. Ships kept coming. The USS *Utah* sent 1000 more forces, until 6000 marines and sailors were in Veracruz. After ferreting out snipers for three days – during which 19 were killed and wounded on the U.S. side and over 400 Mexicans, mostly civilians, died – U.S. troops took Veracruz. They raised a U.S. flag over the Terminal Hotel, where Fletcher set up his headquarters.

In resisting intervention, heroes were made. José Azueta, the son of a commodore, was one of 15 cadets from the Naval Academy killed while shooting from behind mattresses and pillows. A U.S. consul explained how Azueta was "extolled in the same category as the Chapultepec cadets who fought against the Americans in 1847."[12]

On the U.S. side, Chief Boatswain John McCloy, whose detachment came under fire, took three small boats and fired their one-inch guns against the school building where snipers were active, and the returning fire gave away the Mexican position for the *Prairie* to blast.

Naval pilots flew over the harbor, looking for mines and bombarding the Mexican Army. Some pilots left from warships, and Lieutenant Patrick Bellinger became the first U.S. military aviator to fly a combat mission. Fifty-five U.S. servicemembers won Congressional Medals of Honor – more than in any other single engagement. Major Smedley Butler, who had also landed in Nicaragua in 1912, was one of them. Casualties were 17 dead and 63 wounded on the U.S. side, and probably 126 dead and 195 on the Mexican side.

Upon hearing of the ferocity of the fighting, Wilson was characteristically ambivalent: "It was right. Nothing else was possible, but I cannot forget that it was I who had to order these young men to their deaths."[13]

Mexicans, driven apart by the Revolution, almost united against the taking of their sovereignty. "Vengeance! Vengeance! Vengeance!" demanded *La Patria*, while *El Imparcial* condemned the "pigs of *Yanquilandia*."[14] Pancho Villa, the leader of a redoubtable group, called on all Mexicans to rally against the invasion. In Mexico City, one group tied a U.S. flag to the tail of a donkey to sweep the streets. Anti-U.S. riots exploded in several cities, aimed often at U.S. properties, which prompted the fleeing of many of the 50,000 U.S. citizens in Mexico City. All 2600 *gringos* from Tampico evacuated. Some lost everything they owned. Mexico City broke diplomatic relations with Washington. Latin Americans demonstrated against U.S. embassies in most large cities. Argentina, Brazil, and Chile – known as the ABC powers – offered to mediate, and U.S. and Mexican negotiators met at Niagara Falls, Canada, but never came to an agreement.

On April 30, General "Fightin' Fred" Funston led the Fifth Infantry Brigade of about 4000 in occupying Veracruz for seven months. As in Cuba, the U.S. occupiers made sanitation a priority. They cleaned the market, the prison, and the water supply, built modern sewers, and imported 2500 garbage cans. Deaths dropped by a quarter. After Veracruz's city officials left, citing a Mexican law that punished anyone serving a foreign government, Funston's men also took over city hall, collected customs and taxes, declared martial law, and raised the U.S. flag. Funston called himself "Military Governor of Vera Cruz."

But Wilson limited the occupation to Veracruz and refused to declare war against Mexico, and Huerta also refrained from fighting beyond the occupied city. Reflecting the confusion of most U.S. military leaders, Rear Admiral Mayo called this undeclared war a "decidedly strange ... state of affairs."[15] Funston also itched for a fight, telling superiors, "Merely give the order and leave the rest to us." Mexicans also warned of war, with the *Independiente* newspaper predicting, "Federal bullets ... will perforate blonde heads and white breasts swollen with vanity and cowardice."[16]

Wilson, however, got what he wanted: after 10 weeks without Veracruz's customs revenue, Huerta resigned in July 1914.

Haiti, 1915–1919

Wilson's ordering of troops into Haiti flowed from some of the same causes as Veracruz: anti-German fears, economic self-interest, and frustration with revolutionary violence. Added to the mix was a particularly strong racism toward descendants of Africans shared throughout his administration. "Dear me," exclaimed Secretary Bryan, when briefed on Haiti, "think of it – niggers speaking French!"[17]

Six presidents ruled Haiti from 1911 to 1915 as the country struggled to repay debts to France. In 1825, its former colonial power had forced Haiti to pay France 150 million francs as "compensation" for revolting in 1791–1804 against French slaveholders. Haitians had retreated to small family farms, neglecting their roads, ports, education, and health care. In 1915, Haiti's foreign debt was still $21.5 million, gobbling up 80 percent of revenues.

Wilson's military and diplomats also kept a close eye on German plotting in the Caribbean after the Panama Canal opened in August 1914. The water between Haiti and Cuba, known as the Windward Passage, was where ships going through the canal sailed, so U.S. military men feared that Germany coveted Haiti. There were only 200 Germans in the country, but they were bankers and merchants, many sympathized with their homeland, and other Germans in Latin America did aim to terrorize the United States or at least keep it out of World War I.

Haiti also was a target of Dollar Diplomacy. In 1910, the State Department supported the National City Bank of New York in controlling the Banque Nationale d'Haïti. When Wilson came into the White House, he supported businessman Roger Farnham's rickety National Railway, forcing the Haitians to accept it. Farnham also drew up a plan under which the United States would take over the customs receivership along with the Môle Saint-Nicolas, the perfect site for a naval base overlooking the Windward Passage.

Haitians, however, hated the Farnham plan. They wanted no U.S. troops in their customs houses and promised not to give away the Môle to any foreign power. They even wanted to discuss giving free land to U.S. corporations. Bryan was insulted: "While we desire to encourage in every proper way American investments in Haiti, we believe that this can be better done by contributing to stability and order than by favoring special concessions to Americans."[18] In other words, Washington had political rather than commercial priorities.

In July 1914, U.S. warships began spying on Haitians, assessing their military. By November, the Navy Department had a plan for occupying Port-au-Prince. In December, fearing that the government would raid its own coffers, marines walked out of the Banque Nationale with $500,000 in gold and brought it to Wall Street. As with Veracruz, the marines were waiting for an excuse to land.

They got it on July 27, 1915. President Jean Vilbrun Guillaume Sam had wanted to end violent overthrows – and went about it through violence. He ordered 167 of his political prisoners shot and bayoneted through the bars of their cells. In retaliation, Sam's enemies chased him out of his palace. The mob found him in the French Legation, hiding behind a bathroom dresser. They dragged him into the street, and literally tore him to pieces, parading the body parts on spikes. *President torned into piece by a mob*

U.S. officers cabled the White House, and on July 28, Wilson ordered 330 marines into Port-au-Prince. While marines described Haitians welcoming them with "relief and joy," a palace guard expressed the more common fatalism of Haitians. "Everyone fled. Me too. You only had to see them, with their weaponry, their massive, menacing appearance, to understand both that they came to do harm to our country and that resistance was futile."[19] Some Haitians dumped their waste from second-story dwellings onto U.S. curfew patrols. The Haitians who did welcome the occupation force hoped it would rid Haiti of its violence. They also assumed the Americans would leave after six months as they had in Veracruz.

U.S. forces secured the foreign legations, then took over other ports and the national bank. Saving foreigners and avoiding starvation were an "excuse," Secretary of State Robert Lansing said. His immediate goal was to "conserve the customs and prevent their receipt by irresponsible persons."[20] His *primary* goal, however, was "to terminate the appalling conditions of anarchy, savagery, and oppression which had been prevalent in Haiti for decades." Wilson agreed, his own goal being to "put men in charge of affairs whom we can trust to handle and put an end to revolution."[21]

With their usual racism, U.S. officials blamed Haitian problems on "the failure of an inferior people to maintain the degree of civilization left them by the French, or to develop any capacity of self government." One marine concluded that "these people are no more fitted to govern themselves than a tribe of apes," to which the solution was "a white man's government." Diplomats similarly recommended "complete forcible intervention" for 33 years, followed maybe by another 33.[22]

Wilson agreed to a "long programme" of legislative and treaty changes to legalize this illegal intervention.[23] Rosalvo Bobo, who controlled maybe 500 men, wanted to be president. He said of U.S. citizens, "There is no people whose genius and industrial activity I admire more than theirs." But, he added: "To turn over to them our custom houses and our finances, to put ourselves under their tutelage, never, never, NEVER."[24]

Admiral William Caperton, who headed the landing force, instead chose Philippe Sudre Dartiguenave because the Haitian agreed to U.S. oversight. In August, the Haitian legislature "voted" in Dartiguenave as president, Caperton's men took the customs houses, and almost all government employees resigned. Marines installed their own provost courts to try anyone resisting the occupation. In 1916, the State Department presented to Haiti a treaty of occupation for 20 years, during which marines would, as in Nicaragua, create a constabulary, called in Haiti the Gendarmerie. The following year, a U.S.-written constitution removed the Haitian law against foreigners owning land in Haiti, which led to at least 43,000 acres passing into U.S. hands. Reflecting a fear common among descendants of a people who had fought the whites who once owned them, *Le Nouvelliste* suspected that the peasant, "no longer enjoying a hearth and plot of land, will return to slavery."[25] When the Haitian legislature refused to ratify the Constitution, Smedley Butler – now in his third Latin

American intervention – dissolved the body. U.S. officials committed massive voter fraud to pass a plebiscite approving the constitution, 98,225 to 768.

The period right after the landing witnessed the first war against the *cacos* or the rural armed Haitians. While Bobo accepted exile, some of his followers declared an "international war" against "the invaders."[26] Poorly trained and armed with swords or with muskets that barely worked, the *cacos* had no chance against the mighty marines. Most chiefs accepted bribes and formally surrendered on October 1, 1915. On November 17, 27 marines cornered the remaining *cacos* at Fort-Rivière. Butler and two marines snuck into a four foot high ditch and popped out into the courtyard. "Sixty or seventy half-naked madmen, howling and leaping, poured down upon us," recalled Butler.[27] The rest of the marines followed, and a 10-minute hand-to-hand combat ended with 50 dead Haitians. This daring won Butler his second Medal of Honor.

Once the *cacos* were defeated, Butler set about building 470 miles of roads, using an unenforced law called the *corvée* that compelled Haitians to build roads a few days a year without pay. Some gendarmes and marines abused the law, even after the occupation abolished it. In contrast to their hatred of the *corvée,* Haitians generally welcomed the new airports and railroads, and the occupation cleaned up the jails and the book keeping.

Throughout, anti-black racism influenced U.S. treatment of Haitians. Some, such as Butler, infused their disdain with some affection for "my little chocolate soldiers." Others were incredibly brutal, killing and otherwise treating Haitians no better than slaves. "I know the nigger and know how to handle him," crowed Colonel Tony Waller, a descendant of slave owners.[28]

Some urban Haitians who were against the occupation founded an opposition newspaper the day after Dartiguenave's "election." Newspapermen and lawyers formed the Patriotic Union and held courses that denounced land seizures, corporate abuses, unfair laws, and violence against Haitians. To silence such contestation, Caperton declared martial law and muzzled the press.

Dominican Republic, 1916–1919

In the Dominican Republic, the marines also landed to control the country's loans, keep the Germans out, and put an end to revolutions. Also as in Haiti, longer-term goals soon arose, such as reforming the country's institutions and, more than in Haiti, dragging its farmers and merchants into the world economy. The whole enterprise was wrapped in a disdain for Dominicans, although nothing as racist as in Haiti.

As in Haiti, however, a political breakdown provided the spark for intervention. Desiderio Arias, the Minister of War, was a classic regional strongman – a *caudillo*. The days of the *caudillos* were passing in richer, more centralized Latin American countries such as Venezuela and Argentina, but in the Caribbean, these men controlled private armies that could challenge the president's.

Trouble came when Arias competed against two other *caudillos*, Horacio Vásquez and Juan Isidro Jimenes. Jimenes took the presidency in December 1914 and began to collect taxes only from political enemies. Arias got Senate friends to charge the president with misuse of funds, illegal imprisonment, and abuse of power. Jimenes arrested Arias's aides. The House and Senate, in turn, impeached Jimenes in early May 1916.

Arias took advantage of the weakened president to take the capital, Santo Domingo. This prompted a first landing of 150 marines off the *Prairie* on May 4 to protect foreigners but not take the city. Jimenes resigned three days later, refusing to be protected by "foreign bullets."[29] Admiral Caperton was on the scene, landing more marines. While Arias pretended to consider Caperton's offer to surrender, he packed up his army of 300 and headed north to Santiago, the country's second biggest city. Six hundred U.S. troops now occupied the capital.

President Wilson saw the occupation as "the least of the evils in sight in this very perplexing situation." "The United States was tired of revolutions," recalled a marine officer. The French minister in Santo Domingo thought that this intervention "could last, given that Mr. Russell [the U.S. minister] and Admiral Caperton refuse to authorize presidential elections as long as there are in the country armed revolutionaries who could affect the result."[30]

Marines noted "very few cases of hostile feeling displayed" in Santo Domingo, but incorrectly concluded there was no opposition. Dominican newspapers instead saw a "silent protest."[31] Only men, servants, and dogs roamed the streets. Stores, social clubs, and theatres closed, and Dominicans flew their flags at half-mast or covered them with crepe. Less silently, town councils organized "Patriotic Commissions" and sent one to warn marines of an "international war" – the same term Haitians had used.[32]

Also as in Haiti, however, some accepted the occupation as just punishment for chronic infighting. One Dominican argued that, with the marines in charge, government employees could finally count on steady salaries, and widows could rely on pensions.

After taking Santo Domingo in the south, the marines set their sights on Arias in Santiago and landed on the north shore. The governor of Puerto Plata province vowed "he would kill all Americans" if they landed. On June 1, 1916, U.S. gunboats were met with "a storm of bullets, coming from the water front, and streets in town, and practically every house near the water front."[33] Captain Herbert Hershinger died that day, the first marine killed in the Dominican campaign. As with the *cacos*, however, the marines had superior firepower, and they defeated the Dominicans in three hours.

On June 24, Colonel Joseph Pendleton, who commanded the U.S. march toward Santiago, explained to his men that "our work in this country is not one of invasion." Marines were there to "support the Constituted Government," to "restore and preserve peace and order, and to protect life and property." "We are not in an enemy's country," he added, "though many of the inhabitants may be inimical to us." He counseled "minimum force" at all times, "but armed opposition or attack will be sharply and firmly met and suppressed with force of arms."[34]

That armed opposition soon came from some 80 Dominicans entrenched on two hills blocking the road to Santiago. On July 3, these men, ranging in age from 14 to 80, kept up single-shot fire against the automatic weapons of marines before the marines drove them off. The resisters were almost all peasants. One of them explained that he fought because no one wanted "another cock in his henhouse, right?" When asked if it mattered that the invaders were from the United States, another said, "Oh no, no, no, no, that did not matter to me at all; that they be American, no matter who they were."[35] After the battle, one Dominican even showed up at the marines' sickbay to have his wounds dressed!

With his supporters defeated, Arias surrendered on July 5 in exchange for being pardoned. Then he opened a cigar store in Santiago and called himself "a Dominican friend of the United States."[36]

Next, invaders turned to disarming the Dominicans, who, more than Haitians, were attached to their guns. Fathers tended to give sons revolvers when they reached puberty. U.S. officials seized 53,000 firearms, 200,000 rounds of ammunition, and 14,000 knives and swords. Street brawls resulted. On October 24, marines crossed the Ozama

Figure 4.1 Marines patrolling around a Dominican hut. U.S. National Archives RG 127-G Photo 515012.

river to arrest Ramón Batista, whose job it was to collect weapons but who instead harbored them. When they grabbed Batista, dozens of men with guns suddenly appeared out of nowhere, blasting away at the marines. One woman took a marine bullet to protect a sniper. Marines killed Batista but escaped by boat while bullets plopped into the water around them.

Politicians in Santo Domingo also made life for the marines difficult. After Jimenes resigned, they somehow agreed on a replacement, Francisco Henríquez y Carvajal. "Don Pancho," as he was called, seeing himself as representing not the invaders but his compatriots, refused to do as instructed by the marines.

Caperton was livid. "The only thing for these Republics, is a strong United States Military government," he wrote. "They will never be able to govern themselves, that is, not for several generations, if ever."[37] Since he controlled the customs houses, Caperton kept Don Pancho from paying government employees.

On November 29, 1916, a frustrated Captain Harry Knapp issued a "Proclamation of Occupation" that decreed an indefinite military government headed by Knapp himself as military governor. The Knapp Proclamation dissolved the presidency and suspended the Congress, appointed U.S. officials to head all government departments, and imposed martial law. This went further than the occupation of Haiti, which kept a Haitian president and legislature. Knapp also banned firearms and imposed censorship. The proclamation said he was repressing these Dominican freedoms "with great forbearance and a friendly desire to enable Santo Domingo to maintain domestic tranquility." President Wilson authorized it "with the deepest reluctance."[38]

One consequence of the Knapp Proclamation was the loss of government jobs for Dominicans. The Cabinet resigned en masse and Don Pancho boarded a ship to Cuba. Dominican diplomats denounced the Knapp Proclamation as violating international law, if only because there existed no state of war between the two nations.

Armed with the notion that Dominicans were "a backward people who need an object lesson in modern ideas and ideals," the military government moved swiftly with several decrees.[39] The occupation inoculated the masses, built sewers and telegraphs and 395 miles of roads, and raised the number of pupils in school from 18,000 to 200,000. For merchants, it developed ports and lighthouses. A new land tax was to pay for some of these works.

The occupation also eased U.S. access to Dominican resources. In 1919, occupiers slashed 700 tariffs and completely eliminated 245 others, and abolished revenue taxes on imports, thus easing imports from the United States but also harming local producers of shoes, apparel, furniture, hats, shirts, soap, hides, cigarettes, and matches. Hundreds of manufacturers closed shop. The 1920 Land Registration Act intended to make the purchase of land easier and more predictable, but it also opened the door to poor squatters being cheated out of their land – often by U.S.-owned sugar corporations or by richer, more literate Dominicans.

The Punitive Expedition, 1916–1917

Overlapping with the Haitian and Dominican interventions and in the middle of the Mexican Revolution, the United States sent eventually 12,000 men into Mexico to punish revolutionary Pancho Villa. They were south of the border from March 15, 1916 to February 5, 1917.

Mexico was arguably the most important country in Latin America for the United States. U.S. investments were a large part of the reason, and so was the 2000-mile border between the two countries. Washington wanted stability in Mexico also to keep other Latin Americans at bay. As Secretary of State Elihu Root said, "Mexico is worth more than twenty Central Americas, and we should not forget it is the golden chain that links us to Latin America."[40]

At 4.30 am on March 9, 1916, Villa and 400 men threatened to break that chain when they launched a surprise attack on the border town of Columbus, New Mexico. One group attacked downtown, killed nine civilians and wounded several others, burned down a hotel and other buildings, looted stores, and stole horses. Another group attacked nearby Camp Furlong, home of the 13th Cavalry Regiment. Eight U.S. soldiers died while killing over 100 of Villa's army. At the end of the day, Villa was responsible for the first ever Latin American intervention in the United States.

The raid on Columbus was payback for Wilson's recognition of First Chief Venustiano Carranza, a rival of Villa. Wilson had also lifted a prohibition to sell arms to Mexico, but only for Carranza. Villa had responded first by holding 30 U.S. citizens hostage and then killing 17 others in cold blood.

Tragically, Wilson had recognized Carranza because, as Secretary of State Robert Lansing wrote, he wanted "not to intervene to restore order in Mexico."[41] His administration suspected German machinations – "Am sure Villa's attacks are made in Germany," cabled the U.S. Ambassador to Berlin – but, with a U.S. population shunning World War I, Wilson could not afford the distraction.[42]

Still, Wilson faced re-election and could not look like a wimp. He ordered General John J. Pershing, famous from fighting in Cuba and the Philippines, to go after Villa, who had fled back into the Mexican state of Chihuahua. Pershing assembled an impressive group into two brigades of cavalry and one of infantry. The fighting force included 30-year-old 2nd Lieutenant George Patton, who would become a legendary leader in World War II.

Marching through Mexico proved excruciating. Chihuahua was largely a desert, vast and hilly to boot. Keeping a large force of men and horses fed and equipped would not be easy. The expedition took vehicles, but these tended to break down from dust. White alkaline dust forced U.S. troops to wear bandanas and even cover their horses' mouths and nostrils. Days were hot, nights were freezing, and Pershing's troops had not brought warm coats. Where there were no telegraph wires, Pershing had to use mounted messengers. Villa never seemed to be close to railroads, constantly straining the supply chain. The expedition had to carry almost all its food and water. Washington forbade the expedition from seizing supplies from locals; some of the officers spent their own money to feed their men.

Capturing Villa was even dicier. He could be anywhere, and either no Mexican knew where he was, or no one would give him up. A frustrated Pershing compared himself to "a man looking for a needle in a hay stack with an armed guard standing over the stack forbidding you to look in the hay."[43] Villa was seriously hurt early on while fighting against his own government's forces;he convalesced in a cave looking over Pershing's men march through the valley below. They never got close to him again.

Diplomatically, too, things were touchy. Mexico's Carranza had certainly not ordered Villa to raid Columbus, but now Mexicans wanted the First Chief to resist the Punitive Expedition. Wilson and his military also expanded the mission from just capturing Villa to stopping his entire band. Carranza thus sent mixed messages: he was "pained to hear of the lamentable occurrence at Columbus" but would consider "an operating army into Mexican soil … an invasion of national territory."[44]

On April 12, Major Frank Tompkins's 90 cavalrymen rode into the town of Parral, where protesters yelled "Viva Villa!" and "Viva Mexico!" and brandished sticks and rifles at them. Mexican soldiers soon joined them, and Tompkins's men – including Major Charles Young, one of the few African American officers in the army – fought them off from an irrigation ditch. Two U.S. soldiers were killed and six wounded, including Tompkins, versus 40 Mexican dead and many more wounded.

Parral was 516 miles into Mexico. The Punitive Expedition never went further south.

The expedition also used planes to find Villa's men from above, but the result was a disaster. The eight Curtis JN1 Jennys had no machine guns and were too weak to climb above the 5000-foot mountains, and strong winds did not help. Two planes flew all the way to Chihuahua City, but civilians there burned cigarette holes into the fabric of the wings and stabbed the fuselage with their knives.

In early May 1916, Mexican gunmen attacked two more border towns, Glenn Springs and Boquillas, Texas. Some even hatched the Plan of San Diego to regain the territory lost in the Mexican War. Again, this made plain Carranza's inability to control the border.

Carranza and ordinary Mexicans, also observing the Joint Mexican-American Commission that failed, were running out of patience with an intervention that had lasted months without finding Villa. The Mexican head of state ordered that no more U.S. soldiers enter his country.

On June 21, a clash in the town of Carrizal ended the expedition. Pershing sent Captain Charles Boyd of the African American Tenth Cavalry and his 43 men to learn about Carranza's army. But General Félix Gómez and his 400 soldiers told Boyd that, if he wanted to take Carrizal, "you'll have to walk over my dead body."[45]

"Tell the son of a bitch that we're going through!" was Boyd's response.[46] The battle that followed left 12 U.S. forces dead, including Boyd. Gómez also died, along with 44 other Mexicans, but they drove off the U.S. force.

As news of the rout made its way north, anti-Mexican violence in the United States multiplied, some of it from the Texas Rangers. Wilson ordered 112,000 National Guardsmen to the border. However, not wanting to turn a manhunt into a war, Pershing counseled diplomacy. He was also surrounded by admirers of Villa, who had healed from his wound and had marched into Chihuahua City with 1000 men on September 16. As winter settled on northern Mexico, Pershing felt relief to be ordered back home.

After 10 months in Mexico, the Punitive Expedition crossed the border back into Columbus. Two days earlier, Wilson had broken diplomatic relations with Germany. "I do not wish America's energies and forces divided," he said, "for we will need every ounce of reserve we have to lick Germany."[47] The expedition had accomplished practically none of its objectives. It did break up Villa's band, but only temporarily. It mostly increased anti-U.S. sentiment among Mexicans and enhanced the reputation of Villa, who tried to rally Mexicans by denouncing "the unjustified invasion by our eternal enemies, the barbarians of the north."[48]

Despite the failure of the Punitive Expedition, U.S. investment in Mexico only increased, but not without contestation. In 1917, the Mexican Constitution granted the government the ownership of all resources under the Mexican soil – including, of course, petroleum. In the early 1920s, with sky-high prices because of World War I, Mexico pumped out most of the petroleum produced outside the United States. By the early 1930s, it pumped out only a fifth of what it had in 1921. In the mid-1930s, foreign companies controlled all oil production in Mexico and kept laborers from forming unions. Workers struck anyway, which led the Mexican government in 1938 to nationalize the petroleum industry under Pemex.

U.S. anxiety about Mexican attacks also increased in March 1917, when it became public that the German government had sent what came to be known as the Zimmerman Telegram to Mexico proposing that, after the United States entered the war – which it did in April of that year – Mexicans attack the United States and receive as compensation much of the territory lost in 1848. It was a cockamamie scheme and Mexicans quickly concluded that they could not conquer, much less hold, Texas, New Mexico, and Arizona. But the Zimmermann Telegram created a furore up north, where members of Congress debated again, as they had in 1848, whether to invade all of Mexico. They never did, and the Punitive Expedition helped convince many that they never should.

One of the greatest ironies of the Wilsonian interventions was not only their number but also their dubious legality. Unlike Teddy Roosevelt, Wilson, a former lawyer, was obsessed with constitutional procedure. Yet the president never once obtained a declaration of war from Congress for his interventions in Latin America. The United States called Veracruz "enforcing redress for a specific indignity," referring to the Tampico Affair, and Congress did pass a Joint Resolution allowing the use of force.[49] Two years later, the Punitive Expedition hung on the thread of the right of "hot pursuit" between Mexico and the United States. The Dominican occupation was illegal, except that a 1907 Convention had required U.S. approval before increasing Dominican debts. Haiti 1915 had no legal basis whatsoever, as Wilson admitted: "I fear we have not the legal authority to do what we apparently ought to do."

Yet political stability trumped legality. "I suppose there is nothing for it but to take the bull by the horns and restore order," added Wilson.[50]

Notes

1 Cited in Frederick S. Calhoun, *Power and Principle: Armed Intervention in Wilsonian Foreign Policy* (Kent State University Press, 1986), 40.

2 Cited in George Black, *The Good Neighbor: How the United States Wrote the History of Central America and the Caribbean* (Pantheon, 1988), 28.

3 Cited in Alan McPherson, ed., *The Encyclopedia of U.S. Military Interventions in Latin America* (ABC-CLIO, 2013), 751.

4 Cited in Harley Notter, *The Origins of the Foreign Policy of Woodrow Wilson* (Johns Hopkins University Press, 1937), 274.

5 Zaragoza cited in Robert E. Quirk, *An Affair of Honor: Woodrow Wilson and the Occupation of Veracruz* (University of Kentucky Press, 1962), 23, 40.

6 Cited in Max Boot, *The Savage Wars of Peace: Small Wars and the Rise of American Power* (Basic Books, 2002), 150.

7 Huerta cited in John S. D. Eisenhower, *Intervention! The United States and the Mexican Revolution, 1913–1917* (W. W. Norton, 1993), 100.

8 Cited in Eisenhower, *Intervention!*, 108.

9 Cited in Quirk, *Affair of Honor*, 85.

10 Cited in Boot, *Savage Wars of Peace*, 151.

11 Cited in Lester Langley, *The Banana Wars: United States Intervention in the Caribbean, 1898–1934* (Scholarly Resources, 2002), 89.

12 U.S. Consul William Canada cited in Eisenhower, *Intervention!*, 121.

13 Cited in Eisenhower, *Intervention!*, 122.

14 Both cited in Quirk, *Affair of Honor*, 107.

15 Cited in Boot, *Savage Wars of Peace*, 153.

16 Both cited in Eisenhower, *Intervention!*, 135, 129.

17 Cited in Black, *The Good Neighbor*, 14.

18 Cited in Calhoun, *Power and Principle*, 93.

19 Edward Beach, "From Annapolis to Scapa Flow: The Autobiography of a Naval Officer," unpublished manuscript, U.S. Navy, 1941, Hoover Institution Archives, Stanford, California, 254; my translation, Gelin

Choute interviewed in Roger Gaillard, *Les blancs débarquent*, vol. 3, *Premier écrasement du cacoïsme: 1915* (n. pub., 1981), 13.

20   Lansing to Woodrow Wilson, August 3, 1915, 838.00/1275 B, Central Decimal Files Relating to Internal Affairs of Haiti, 1910–1929, Record Group 59, National Archives and Records Administration, College Park, Maryland.

21   Lansing cited in Boot, *Savage Wars of Peace*, 160. Wilson cited in Robert Debs Heinl, Jr., and Nancy Gordon Heinl, *Written in Blood: The Story of the Haitian People 1492–1971* (Houghton Mifflin, 1978), 406.

22   Division of Latin-American Affairs, undated, 838.00/1391, enclosed with July 31, 1915, 838.00/1390, Central Decimal Files Relating to Internal Affairs of Haiti, 1910–1929, Record Group 59, National Archives and Records Administration, College Park, Maryland; William Upshur to his mother, Fort Liberté, March 29, 1916, folder 1914–1916, box 2, William P. Upshur Letters, Southern Historical Collection, University of North Carolina at Chapel Hill.

23   Wilson to Lansing, Washington, August 4, 1915, 838.00/1418, Central Decimal Files Relating to Internal Affairs of Haiti, 1910–1929, Record Group 59, National Archives and Records Administration, College Park, Maryland.

24   Cited in "History of Flag Career of Rear Admiral W.B. Caperton, U.S. Navy Commencing January 5, 1915," available at www.history.navy.mil/research/library/online-reading-room/title-list-alphabetically/h/history-of-flag-career-of-rear-admiral-w-b-caperton.html

25   My translation, "Plus de restriction au droit de propriété pour les Compagnies Etrangères," *Le Nouvelliste*, February 25, 1925, 1.

26   Caperton to Secretary of Navy, USS *Washington*, August [misdated as July] 17, 1915, 838.00/1256, Central Decimal Files Relating to Internal Affairs of Haiti, 1910–1929, Record Group 59, National Archives and Records Administration, College Park, Maryland.

27   Cited in Boot, *Savage Wars of Peace*, 164.

28   Both cited in Boot, *Savage Wars of Peace*, 166.

29   Cited in Bruce Calder, *The Impact of Intervention: The Dominican Republic during the U.S. Occupation of 1916–1924* (University of Texas Press, 1984), 8.

30   Cited in Niall Ferguson, *Colossus: The Rise and Fall of the American Empire* (Penguin Books, 2004), 56; Pendleton to Bishop, Santiago, June 17, 1919, folder 22, box 3, Papers of Joseph H. Pendleton, Marine Corps

Archives and Special Collections, Gray Research Center, Quantico, Virginia; my translation, De Saint-Saud to minister of foreign affairs, Santo Domingo, May 18, 1916, dossier 7, République Dominicaine, Correspondance Politique et Commerciale/Série Nouvelle 1897 à 1918, Archives Diplomatiques, Ministère des Affaires Étrangères, Paris, France.

31   Hall to Caperton, Santo Domingo, May 15, 1916, folder Dominican Republic, Santo Domingo, 1916, Dominican Republic, Geographical Files, Reference Branch, Marine Corps History Division, Marine Corps Base, Quantico, Virginia; Von Zielinski to Lansing, Santo Domingo, May 17, 1916, 839.00/1842, Central Decimal Files Relating to Internal Affairs of the Dominican Republic, 1910–1929, Record Group 59, National Archives and Records Administration, College Park, Maryland.

32   Cited in Caperton to Benson, Santo Domingo, June 15, 1916, folder Correspondence June 1916, box 1, Papers of William Banks Caperton, Manuscripts Division, Library of Congress, Washington, D.C.; Luis F. Mejía, *De Lilís a Trujillo: historia contemporánea de la República Dominicana* (Editorial Elite, 1944), 128; Neici M. Zeller, "The Appearance of All, the Reality of Nothing: Politics and Gender in the Dominican Republic, 1880–1961," (PhD diss., University of Illinois at Chicago, 2010), 52.

33   Henry to Lansing, Puerto Plata, May 18, 1916, 839.00/1836, Central Decimal Files Relating to Internal Affairs of the Dominican Republic, 1910–1929, Record Group 59, National Archives and Records Administration, College Park, Maryland; Hatch to commander cruiser squadron, Puerto Plata, June 4, 1916, folder Dominican Republic, Santo Domingo, 1916, Dominican Republic, Geographical Files, Reference Branch, Marine Corps History Division, Marine Corps Base, Quantico, Virginia.

34   Cited in Captain Stephen Fuller and Graham Cosmas, *Marines in the Dominican Republic 1916–1924* (History and Museums Division, U.S. Marine Corps, 1974), 13–14.

35   My translation, María Filomena González Canalda, *Línea noroeste: testimonio del patriotismo olvidado* (Universidad Central del Este, 1985), various interviews.

36   My translation, Arias to Pendleton, Santiago, September 9, 1916, legajo 27, 1916–1917, Fondo Secretaría de Estado de Interior y Policía, Archivo General de la Nación, Santo Domingo, Dominican Republic.

37   Caperton to Benson, July 9, 1916, Santo Domingo, folder Correspondence July–Dec 1916, box 1, Papers of William Banks Caperton, Manuscripts Division, Library of Congress, Washington, D.C.

38   Wilson to Lansing, Washington, November 28, 1916, 839.00/1951a, Central Decimal Files Relating to Internal Affairs of the Dominican Republic, 1910–1929, Record Group 59, National Archives and Records Administration, College Park, Maryland. The Proclamation is in McPherson, ed., *Encyclopedia*, 751.

39   Snowden, cited in Kenneth J. Grieb, *The Latin American Policy of Warren G. Harding* (Texas Christian University Press, 1976), 62.

40   Cited in Jürgen Buchenau, *In the Shadow of the Giant: The Making of Mexico's Central America Policy, 1876–1930* (Tuscaloosa: University of Alabama Press, 1996), 90.

41   Cited in Cole Blasier, *The Hovering Giant: U.S. Responses to Revolutionary Change in Latin America 1910–1985* (University of Pittsburgh Press, 1985), 106.

42   Cited in Black, *The Good Neighbor*, 29.

43   Cited in Calhoun, *Power and Principle*, 57.

44   All cited in Eisenhower, *Intervention!*, 232–3.

45   Cited in Eisenhower, *Intervention!*, 297.

46   Cited in Boot, *Savage Wars of Peace*, 199.

47   Wilson cited in Blasier, *Hovering Giant*, 106.

48   Cited in Boot, *Savage Wars of Peace*, 201.

49   Cited in Calhoun, *Power and Principle*, 116.

50   Wilson cited by Calhoun, *Power and Principle*, 101.

5

Accommodation and Resistance, 1917–1930

Some cheered, the majority passively looked on with contempt in their eyes for the "gringo invader," and some of the bolder ones even went as far as to hiss at the procession.

One observer of Nicaraguan reactions to landing marines[1]

U.S. interventions in Latin America and the Caribbean prompted reactions from invaded peoples that were about as varied as the motivations of invaders, and this chapter looks almost exclusively at contestation and *collaboration* in their complex forms. In no intervention were Latin Americans completely united for or against. Also, there existed no polls of public opinion in many small countries, so we will never know how many were on each side.

But Latin Americans can be grouped roughly into two, depending on their responses. There were those who accommodated the occupations, by inviting them, welcoming them, or otherwise changing their behaviors so as to benefit from the occupation. Against them were the resisters, those who either joined violent guerrilla armies or raised their voices peacefully in protest. This second category included those who met occupation with passive resistance – noncollaboration, sabotage, and other behaviors.

A Short History of U.S. Interventions in Latin-America and the Caribbean, First Edition. Alan McPherson.
© 2016 John Wiley & Sons, Inc. Published 2016 by John Wiley & Sons, Inc.

Context mattered, as always. Resistance seemed muted during World War I, as the Woodrow Wilson government censored the press at home and abroad where it could. Also important, however, was the growing economic and cultural power of the United States in the hemisphere, which, since 1898, was irritating to many Latin Americans even if their country was not invaded. Uruguay's José Enrique Rodó, for instance, published the 1900 essay *Ariel* calling for Latin Americans to get in touch with their common culture and unite against *nordomanía* or the attraction to North America.

Sympathizers outside countries under occupation often joined in transnational contestations of interventions. Most were in Latin America, while others were in Europe, the United States, and even beyond. These networks of resistance were in touch with the invaded and often enjoyed more success in pressuring Washington to withdraw.

The Dominican Republic, Haiti, and Nicaragua illustrate the gamut of resistance. In each country, resisters perceived the political threat to their ways and defended their autonomy. Some were nationalists, concerned with loss of national sovereignty, but most had a mix of more local and concrete motivations, many no less political.

Dominican Republic, 1917–1924

Although marines occupied the Dominican Republic starting in 1916, the resistance there and in Haiti was dormant for most of World War I. When Harry Knapp's Proclamation of November 1916 forced out President Francisco Henríquez y Carvajal, Dominican diplomats protested in Washington and Havana, but to no avail.

Some Dominicans in the cities hoped at least to get a job out of the occupation. Since almost everyone in the government had quit or been fired in late 1916, promotions to those who remained came quickly. Félix María Nolasco went from a clerk to the chair of the Santo Domingo town council. "Some do not consider me a good

Dominican," admitted Eligio Vidal as he asked for a job, "because, on more than one occasion I have refused to sign protests against the Government." Many who agreed with the occupation in private said the opposite in public. For instance, four Cabinet ministers refused to request a U.S. troop movement, telling Admiral William Caperton that "while they believe and all feel it for the good of the country, that they could not put it in writing and afterwards live in the Dominican Republic."[2]

Meanwhile, the marines in rural areas swept up what they thought were the remnants of insurrection. Dominican bands long existed in the countryside. Some were purely bandits; Dominicans called them *gavilleros* and largely resented them. Others did some looting but also offered political services to party leaders such as Horacio Vásquez. Their motivation could be partly ideological, but usually they sought from those who ordered them to attack political enemies concrete goods and services – money, food, shoes, weapons, maybe a job in the new police force. Marines, however, shared President Wilson's wish for "constitutionalism" and refused to reward insurrectionists. When band leader Salustiano "Chachá" Goicochea gave up his men allegedly for a $500 bribe, the occupation denied him the governorship of a province.

Chachá's replacement as the head rebel was Vicente Evangelista. A *horacista* or follower of Vásquez, "Vicentico" saw family members' property sacked and burned by U.S. soldiers. He kept a huge following in the Dominican east, where years of sugar companies buying up land had left many landless or jobless in the off-season. He once tied to a tree two U.S. engineers surveying land for a sugar company and ordered his men to chop off their heads and hack them to pieces. Peasants either respected or feared Vicentico to the point that, as one marine wrote, they "will not give us information of any value." The Dominican called himself an "avenger of the fatherland," but he hated rival leaders more than the marines and asked U.S. troops to let him rule a few eastern provinces in the strongman tradition. Instead, in June 1917, they tricked him into surrendering, shot him dead while "trying to escape," and jailed all his men.[3]

The disappearance from the scene of Chachá and Vicentico yielded about a year of peace. But from mid-1918 to 1922, a second wave of rural insurrections took place that involved 5–10 larger bands active at one time, some involving 150 men in arms.

This second wave was somewhat politicized, at least among leaders such as Ramón Nateras. Nateras used a rubber stamp on correspondence, wore a red sash, and had his "army," as he called it, hoist the Dominican flag and play the anthem daily. His main demand was "the complete restoration of my Country." Yet the new rebels had no strategic goals, no co-ordination, and no national reach. Also for that reason, these insurrectionists were hard to decapitate. In 1919, the violence in the east forced the marines to triple their force to 1480, then to 2500 in 1921–1922, when the last holdouts surrendered. In 467 battles or "contacts," 1137 rebels died compared to 16 marines. (Forty U.S. sailors died separately when a hurricane wrecked their ship on Santo Domingo's rocky shore.)

By 1922, urban Dominicans were coming close to ending the occupation. The end of World War I in 1918 freed up political space to contest occupations. The exiled President Henríquez lobbied Washington during the war, but got no response. In 1919, however, Dominicans and Cubans in Cuba founded Pro-Santo Domingo Committees. Cubans helped partly out of resentment at the Platt Amendment over their own island, and out of fear that the robbing of Dominican sovereignty could spread. They called Wilson's defense of "self-determination" for nationalities in Europe a double standard. "The hour has come not only for the small nationalities of Europe but also for the Americas; not only for Belgium and Poland but also for Santo Domingo," editorialized the *Diario de Cuba*. Cubans also considered themselves bound to Dominicans by "the powerful ties of blood, religion, and language." On the matter of blood, Henríquez and his colleagues wrote to Wilson that they wanted independence "in behalf of the prevalence of the white race and with the same unswerving will they conserve religion, language, and the racial attributes bequeathed by the Spanish founders."[5]

Dominicans' strategy was to raise money to send Henríquez to the post-World War I peace conference in Versailles, so he could present these arguments to Wilson. He made it to Paris, but a State Department official there told him that no non-European issue would be discussed. Unbowed, Henríquez family members and friends sailed around South America, convincing presidents and ministers of foreign relations to denounce the occupation.

The press throughout Latin America also rose to the defense of the Dominican Republic, publicizing the imprisonment of poets such as Fabio Fiallo and the torture of innocents such as Cayo Báez. Press attention saved Fiallo from a death sentence.

Opposition among ordinary Dominicans grew because of day-to-day abuses by the marines and the Dominican National Guard. In Hato Mayor, Captain Thad Taylor's suspicion of all inhabitants meant that, as a fellow marine wrote, "his policy sooner or later would have found nearly everyone in jail." His colleague Captain Charles Merkel cut off the ear of a prisoner, beat him with a stick, and "did maliciously cause the said prisoner to be cut across the breast and salt to be put in his wounds."[6] Merkel's own men reported him. While under investigation, he blew his brains out when someone slipped him a gun. Dominicans also were subject to *desalojos*, or the evacuation of whole towns to search the area.

Urban Dominicans, meanwhile, were shocked by the "drunk and disorderlies" by marines who would harass or assault women and start bar fights. At least 14 drunken marines once attacked a Dominican who had defended the honor of a woman slapped by one of them. After beating him, they torched a store and some houses, firing shots to prevent anyone from putting out the flames. Dominicans, in contrast, were rarely drunk in public. They also that U.S. citizens were hypocrites since they prohibited the sale of alcohol back in the United States but abused it abroad.

Dominicans resisted in sometimes creative ways. The marines increased the visibility of baseball in the country, and games between them and Dominicans could be friendly enough. But Dominicans loved to see the Yankees get flogged, as one Dominican player recalled: "The crowds were full of this fervor and wanted us to win because we were their team and because we represented the Dominican flag."[7]

The more the occupation interfered with small towns, too, the more resistance emerged. The marines first took armies away from the 12 provincial governors, making revolt impossible. Then, though Military Governor Thomas Snowden realized that centralization was "rather against the Dominican idea and also against the intent of Dominican laws," Executive Order #44 allowed for restaffing of small town councils with those loyal to the occupation. One Dominican touring the countryside reported that rural authorities were illiterate, too numerous, and unaware of their job descriptions. "Entirely incompetent," they often occupied no office, kept no books, estimated no budgets, and stole from fellow villagers. Dominicans also protected their cockfights as "one of the few relics that the Motherland" – Spain – "bequeathed to us."[8] The occupation's many new regulations also baffled Dominicans. Why should bakers need a permit to sell bread? Why make midwives pass an exam? Why inspect pharmacies?

Other big changes sapped support for the occupation from the elite and middle classes. The end of war in Europe spelled economic catastrophe for the Caribbean. The price of sugar plummeted from 22 cents to 1.8 cents per pound. Government revenues shrank. The occupation imposed a land tax on the wealthy. Merchants, who largely had enjoyed the security that the occupation brought, now opposed it because of sweeping tariff reductions that flooded their country with U.S. goods.

In Washington, Dominicans hired U.S. lobbyists, who helped convince the Senate to lead an investigation into the Dominican and Haitian occupations in 1921–1922. It helped that Republican President Warren Harding, elected in 1920, denounced the Democratic Wilsonian interventions during his campaign. When the Senate committee went to Santo Domingo to hold hearings, U.S. friends coached them to focus their arguments on diplomatic and financial problems, not on abuses that other U.S. investigators dismissed as isolated.

Strong nationalists such as writers Fiallo and Américo Lugo, who formed the National Dominican Union, rejected any negotiation with marines and insisted instead on a "pure and simple" withdrawal. Military Governor Snowden did not believe in Dominican independence, however. The ungenerous proposals of Snowden and his successor, Samuel Robison – that there remain a U.S. "military mission" and that Washington oversee a new constitution, for instance – hardened the Dominican resolve in favor of withdrawal. U.S. citizens suddenly were disinvited to social clubs. "The schism between Dominicans and the military government is complete," wrote a French diplomat in April 1920.[9]

Resisters were not united. As party chiefs such as Horacio Vásquez anticipated an end to the occupation, they started to scheme. The first task was to avoid the return to the presidency of Henríquez, who predicted that Vásquez and his ilk were "ready to reengage in their pettiness and despicable acts." The chiefs kept Henríquez out of discussions, spread malicious rumors that he wanted to give away the natural harbor of Samaná Bay to the U.S. Navy, and took a hard line against occupation in public while they secretly negotiated with the State Department. "As much as Dominicans distrust Americans," wrote one U.S. officer, "they distrust one another more."[10]

In spring 1922, a compromise called the Hughes–Peynado Agreement emerged. The Dominicans accepted a loan, a road-building program, and continued U.S. supervision of their finances. In return, a provisional government led by Dominicans would prepare elections for 1924 without marine oversight. Nationalist Lugo criticized Hughes–Peynado as "three or four citizens [the party chiefs] exploiting the personalism of the political parties."[11] Still, in October 1922, Juan Bautista Vicini Burgos was appointed as provisional president, and the voters on March 15, 1924, chose none other than Horacio Vásquez. On July 12, the last of the marines left.

Vásquez ruled until 1930, when Rafael Trujillo, who came up the ranks of the U.S.-controlled constabulary during the occupation, took over in a fraudulent election and intimidated or killed all remaining regional strongmen. His brutal dictatorship over the Dominican Republic lasted until 1961.

Haiti, 1917–1930

When Haitians in government learned that the marines assigned to "advise" them instead intended to order them around, they rebelled. In 1917, the Haitian Congress refused to declare war on Germany. Haitian officials declined to pay for marine projects, or else they promised to do so and then blamed subordinates for inaction. President Sudre Dartiguenave, in office until 1922, protested U.S. control over customs, threats of martial law, and plans to control the postal service, telegraph, public works, and records. Judges and juries tended to acquit any Haitian who claimed that his crime was in defense of his country. Many urban elites even supported guerrillas in the countryside.

Haitian elites were highly educated, often with degrees from Paris, and they blanched at the cultural changes brought about by the Anglo-Saxon occupation. Schools did not teach English, but Haitians interacting with marines had to learn at least some, and one poet apparently drowned himself by hanging a French dictionary around his neck. U.S. occupiers did try to make education more technical and practical – teaching the typical peasant "to count his chickens and pigs and care for his garden, for instance" – and African American educators on a visit suggested similar reforms. But the Haitian elite were "indignant," said one. Even peasants saw schooling only as a way to abandon farming and move to the city.[12]

Ordinary Haitians, meanwhile, suffered a broader array of depredations from occupiers and the gendarmerie or Haitian constabulary. As in the Dominican Republic, individuals and small groups terrified small towns. Marine Freeman Lang's three-month rule over Hinche in 1918 still sent "shudders up the spine of the townsfolk" in the 1970s. In Saint-Marc, a captain was said to have whipped a 75-year-old woman, hanged a 15-year-old boy for petty theft, and seared an innocent man's whole body with hot irons. Women, fearing rape, stopped bathing in rivers. One teenage girl recalled fearing "all foreign men in the neighborhood. Whites, especially, had a bad reputation. When they came to town, we would be hidden out of sight, tucked away in attics."[13]

When criticized, marines often noted that it was Haitian gendarmes, and not they, who committed most abuses. "Immaterial," retorted one Haitian.[14] Marines either ordered gendarmes to commit atrocities, looked the other way, or failed to police them.

Haitians, like Dominicans, also resented economic hardships. Perhaps 400,000 moved to Cuba's sugar plantations during the occupation to escape the low wages in Haiti. In 1919, workers launched the first strike in Haiti's history after the Haitian-American Sugar Company lowered wages and lengthened hours.

The occupation also tried to ban Vodou, the African-descended religion of almost all Haitians, even the supposedly Catholic elite. Marines patrolled villages to destroy the talismans or objects in Vodou ceremonies and to stop its dances, which marines associated with "savagery." U.S. writers falsely portrayed Vodou as little more than cannibalism.

Unlike Dominicans, Haitians largely followed one man during an otherwise similar second wave of guerrilla aimed at the abuses of the occupation. Charlemagne Péralte commanded a garrison during the 1915 U.S. landing, but soon after, President Sudre Dartiguenave fired him. He swore, "I will never remain under white domination."[15]

His comeback came on October 15, 1918, when he attacked Hinche with 300 *corvée* laborers who had not been paid. After bursting into *corvée* camps and recruiting more, Péralte led perhaps 15,000 fighters and sympathizers in the greatest rural resistance movement until Augusto Sandino's in Nicaragua the following decade. From April to October 1919, 1000 U.S. troops along with 2700 gendarmes fought Péralte's *cacos* in 131 battles. In hilly terrain, the *cacos* ambushed marines and combined Catholic symbols such as the crucifix with traditional Haitian drums, smoke signals, and conch shells to call one another. *Caco* leaders and followers shared the belief that, if *blancs* ruled Haiti, slavery would follow.

Other resisters were traditional *cacos* who saw an opportunity to plunder. Decils Defilise admitted he "heard stealing was going on and that he came to Hinche to steal because it was in his heart to steal." Many gave food or shelter to the rebels out of sympathy or fear. At the height of the insurrection, the Vatican's chargé d'affaires noticed that peasants in the countryside, "ordinarily very calm and hospitable, appeared fearful and fled at the sight of strangers. The *cacos* threaten to massacre all those who helped the Americans."[16]

But the weapons and training of *cacos* were as ineffective as during the first wave in 1915, dooming their resistance. On October 31, 1919, a few daring marines – including Sergeant Herman Hanneken, who would also serve in Nicaragua – smeared their faces with lamp black, fooled guards in Péralte's camp, and when they were miraculously brought before him, whipped out their pistols and shot him dead. Marines then tied Péralte's body to a door, took a photo, and distributed it to show all insurrectionists that their leader was not immune to bullets as he claimed. After Péralte's death, engagements were rarer, and the war ended after the killing of his successor in May 1920. In the entire *caco* war, only 13 U.S. soldiers died versus 1861 Haitians.

With a shorter rural insurgency than the Dominican one, Haitians soon depended completely on urban groups to end the occupation, but they found fewer friends abroad, especially among white U.S. citizens and Latin Americans. The Haitian elite was also poorer and smaller than the Dominican one, so raising funds for travel abroad was challenging. While the Dominicans gathered donations of $115,000 in one week, Haitians raised less than $10,000 in several months.

In the United States, African Americans largely led Haitian solidarity movements. In 1919, Addie Hunton founded the International Council of Women of the Darker Races, which investigated the lot of Haitian women and children. Madam C.J. Walker, the Oprah Winfrey of her time, allied with A. Philip Randolph to form the International League of the Darker Peoples to oppose the occupation. Many wrote to Haitians, who told them of abuses and sent them newspaper clippings. Back then, New York had only about 500 Haitians, but many were active on behalf of their homeland and through their churches.

Mostly, it was the National Association for the Advancement of Colored People (NAACP) that publicized Haiti's cause. As early as 1915, co-founder W.E.B. DuBois urged Wilson to send blacks instead of whites to occupy Haiti. In 1920, musician, diplomat, and writer James Weldon Johnson, the NAACP's first black field secretary, traveled to Haiti for two months and returned with tales of racism, atrocities, and economic exploitation that he published in *The Nation* and in his own *Crisis* magazine. By 1920, the majority of U.S. publications had swung from pro-occupation to anti-occupation.

The U.S. Senate investigation that helped end the Dominican occupation argued that Haiti, in contrast to its neighbor, was not ready for self-determination. Partly, Haitians had not been good witnesses, bringing up old grievances, exaggerating other ones, and convincing senators that all Haitians were liars. But mostly, U.S. officials let their racism win the day. The Latin American Division, or alleged experts in the region, urged the State Department

> to distinguish at once between the Dominicans and the Haitians. The former, while in many ways not advanced far enough on the average to permit the highest type of self-government, yet have a preponderance of white blood and culture. The Haitians on the other hand are negro for the most part, and, barring a very few highly educated politicians, are almost in a state of savagery and complete ignorance. The two situations thus demand different treatment.[17]

The outcome was that, in 1922, the State Department took control of the Haitian occupation away from the military but appointed a military man, Brigadier General John Russell, as the "high commissioner" for what was turning into a colony of the United States. Louis Borno became the new president of Haiti, and he ruled with a Council of State whose members he appointed.

With the *caco* war over and atrocities toward peasants diminishing, elite resistance shifted from anti-U.S. to anti-Borno. The new president was petty and arrested anyone who criticized him. He also had few jobs to give to allies. "The governing élite have been ousted from their natural function in the state," complained Constantin Mayard, indicating that politicians on the "outs" couldn't imagine doing anything but government jobs. They opposed almost every

Borno initiative – a new loan, a reorganization of the national railroad, new lands for the Sinclair Oil Company, a contract with the Haitian Pineapple Company, and a tax on the manufacture of rum and tafia, a crude local alcohol. What the opposition most wanted was the departure of Borno and the return of elections. Some traveled to Washington – Joseph Jolibois Fils even toured Latin America for two and a half years – but Dana Munro of the Latin American Division refused to hold elections because "at least 95% of the people are not only illiterate but absolutely ignorant of the first principles of representative government."[18]

Through most of the 1920s, Haitians saw little hope of an end to occupation.

Nicaragua, 1927–1928

The rebellion led by Augusto Sandino against the marines in Nicaragua was unique in many ways. Sandino was its undisputed leader from beginning to end. He was the most clearly nationalistic of guerrilla leaders while also expressing the specific grievances of many. He had the most collaborators and sympathizers, perhaps in the tens of thousands. His followers included peasants and workers, artisans and lawyers, and indigenous, mixed-race, and European-descended Nicaraguans. As a consequence of its force, the rebellion drew more marines: about 5692 at their most numerous, and the marines never killed him or forced him or his army to surrender. Most noteworthy, and a good part of the secret of his success, was that Sandino drew the admiration and the support of people all over the world. His struggle embodied both violent, rural insurrection and urban, peaceful resistance; both the national and the international.

When the marines left Nicaragua in August 1925, they suspected they would return. They did so in May 1926, landing in Bluefields to again quell a war between political parties. By January 1927, when they occupied Managua again, they had no idea they would soon be fighting Sandino. The U.S. intervention of 1926–1927 was in response to a Conservative Party invitation to help put down the Liberals. President Calvin Coolidge hesitated to embroil his troops in Nicaragua again, but the war had killed a U.S. citizen and was pressing taxes on U.S. firms. To further justify the intervention, Coolidge accused Mexico City of furnishing weapons to the Liberals and Bolsheviks of endangering the Panama Canal. The response from Russia's actual Bolsheviks? "The Soviet Government has no more interest in factional political squabbles in Nicaragua than it has in the mountains of the moon."[19]

Recognizing the error in siding with the minority Conservatives, Washington sent diplomat Henry Stimson to Nicaragua to mediate. On May 4, 1927, Stimson had Liberals accept Díaz as president in return for government jobs and U.S.-supervised elections in 1928 and 1932, which Liberals were sure they would win. The "peace of Tipitapa," after the town in which it was signed, also disarmed Nicaraguans and re-established the constabulary or National Guard. President José María Moncada signed the agreement, along with all 13 Liberal generals.

All, that is, but one. Augusto Sandino was born poor, the product of a middle-class landowner's sexual liaison with his indigenous servant. Augusto grew up ostracized, having to eat with the help. In his mid-twenties he shot a man and fled Nicaragua, and spent a few years taking odd jobs, including for U.S. fruit and sugar corporations in Honduras and Guatemala and in Mexican oil fields. There he learned about the radical ideologies of the Mexican Revolution, including communism and anarcho-syndicalism. In May 1926 he returned to Nicaragua and took a job in a U.S.-owned gold mine. When the civil war erupted later that year, he took his $300 in savings, some guns and men, and became a "general" for the Liberals.

The peace of Tipitapa enraged Sandino because it was achieved under Yankee rule. "They want to install a Yankee as president," he told supporters, considering Díaz a puppet of Washington, "and in my opinion it should be a son of the nation, be he Liberal or Conservative, but a son of the nation – but a Yankee, never." Sandino's determination and courage were immediately evident. Retreating to a

Figure 5.1   Augusto Sandino, center, and generals, 1929. National Archives.

small town, with all his men before him, he slammed a bullet on a table and told them to choose sides. "From here to there, Yankees; from here to *there*, Sandino." Nine of every 10 deserted. Still, Sandino defied his former boss and now President Moncada, who instructed him to surrender: "I don't know why you keep ordering me around … I DO NOT SELL OUT, I DO NOT SURRENDER, you must defeat me."[20]

On July 16, 1927, the first major battle of the rebellion took place in a small town near Honduras called Ocotal. Sandino attacked the 87 marines and guards with 400–500 men. Big mistake. Marines won the 16-hour battle by calling in planes to bomb the "sandinistas," killing about 60. The defeat convinced Sandino that he should avoid taking marines head-on in towns and should instead hide his men in mountains and adopt guerrilla hit-and-run tactics. Both the U.S. squadron commander who flew threw a tropical storm to reinforce the marines and the commander of the Ocotal garrison won the Navy Cross. Ocotal may have seen the first organized dive-bombing raid ever.

To put pressure on Washington and attract money and supplies, Sandino also learned that he needed public opinion on his side.

Sandino was popular with his followers and throughout the world because he represented several groups at once. Perhaps a majority of the four departments in Nicaragua's Segovia mountains supported Sandino – not necessarily fighting, but providing food and keeping secrets from marine patrols. He denounced the unfair working conditions of miners who worked for "thirty cents a day, thirty lousy cents," as one said. Sandino occupied gold mines and minted his own coins. He sympathized with indigenous Nicaraguans who feared the disappearance of their communal lands. He fought against regulations and the wage economy that threatened peasants – nine-tenths of *segovianos*. And the inhabitants along the Nicaragua-Honduran border resented the marines, who insisted on patrolling a place where the central government had rarely been. Because of the occupation, merchants became smugglers, and regular people, outlaws. One Nicaraguan guard at the border explained "the intense hatred that people, rich and poor, express toward the guardia … and the marines." "Every home has a picture of Sandino," added a Navy official. "In the movies, they play Sandino's song and everyone is speaking about him as the national hero."[21]

Mostly, Sandino tapped into the fear of foreign troops on Nicaraguan soil. "No, no, I didn't know what *la patria* meant at the time," said Sandino follower Eudiviges Herrera Siles years later. But to him and others, marines in villages were a concrete threat, more concrete than Wall Street loans. Sandino's most consistent demand, therefore, was the withdrawal of the "Yankee invaders." Sandino declared "his intention of cutting the throat of every American and other foreigner with whom he came in contact." He called marines "blonde beasts," "degenerate pirates," "paid assassins," "hired thugs," "morphine addicts," "murderers," "criminals," and "the enemy of our race and language."[22]

Sandino helped to spread tales of abuse by marines, especially the M Company of the National Guard, whose First Lieutenant William Lee allegedly assassinated and mutilated Nicaraguans, including children, and killed animals for pleasure. In these stories, Lee was either subhuman or superhuman. His commander, the legendary Captain

Lewis "Chesty" Puller, recounted how, during an ambush, the sandinistas shot Lee in the arm and head and concluded he was dead. Fellow marines also thought so – for 20 minutes. But then Lee stumbled to his feet and took over a Lewis machine gun "with telling effect." When the battle was over, he marched for six days, during which guerrillas attacked the M twice more. "No joy ride," summarized Puller with understatement.[23]

Torture was especially prevalent on the Caribbean coast, where a British consul reported that marines "used unnecessary violence in dealing with the Indians and negroes of that region." A U.S. doctor in Bluefields charged "all sorts of inhuman beatings and unmentionable tortures by our marines, in which an electric chair figured." When they suspected that a farmer knew more than he let on about hidden weapons,

> He was struck in the face and on the head and body repeatedly by the clenched fists of four marines … his hair was pulled, his head forced back and his throat choked by the hands of these beasts until he spat blood … his head was forced into a barrel of water and held there until he thought he would strangle; water was dashed into both ears, forcefully, from full buckets; he was given the "water cure"; ropes were twisted about his wrists … and his testicles were grasped and twisted until he nearly fainted from pain.

The doctor estimated that such cases occurred "by the hundred right along the Atlantic Coast to-day."[24]

Sandino countered atrocities with atrocities. When his men captured marines, they might break their necks or chop off limbs with machetes. The most fearsome sandinista was Pedro Altamirano. With a barrel chest, tousled hair, thick eyebrows, a large mustache, a hoarse voice, a cigar at his lips and a scar on his face, "big Pedro" spent his nights on a leather hammock with a .44 Winchester by his side, his black dog under him, and a wooden board over his chest in case someone tried to machete him while he slept. He had over 60 severed heads to his name.

At the same time, however, Sandino promoted love and brotherhood among his followers. He prohibited drinking while on duty, selling alcohol, or stealing animals from peasants. A man could be killed for raping a woman.

The different kinds of contestations to U.S. interventions – rural and violent, urban and peaceful, and transnational – had, logically enough, different consequences. Rural insurrections under Péralte, Sandino, and others could be effective at whipping up propaganda against the marines, but held out little hope of military success. Diplomats, lawyers, and others in the cities were more effective at challenging the legality of the occupations, expressing nationalist fervor, and finding sympathetic allies abroad. Those allies turned into networks that most directly communicated the grievances of the invaded with policymakers in Washington. None of these groups, therefore, can be fully discounted when explaining the coming of the end of U.S. occupations in the 1920s and 1930s. Also important were changes within U.S. society and the U.S. government.

Notes

1 Dom Pagano, *Bluejackets* (Meador, 1932), 74.

2 My translation, Vidal to Robison, Neyba, September 22, 1921, folder 34, 26–50 Miscellaneous, box 40, Military Government of Santo Domingo, Record Group 38, National Archives and Records Administration, Washington, D.C.; Caperton to Benson, Santo Domingo, June 19, 1916, folder Correspondence June 1916, box 1, Papers of William Banks Caperton, Manuscripts Division, Library of Congress, Washington, D.C.

3 Davis to regimental commander, 3rd Prov. Rgt, San Pedro de Macorís, June 1, 1917, folder Dominican Republic 1917, Dominican Republic, Geographical Files, Reference Branch, MCH; my translation, Perroud to Ministry of Foreign Relations, Santo Domingo, June 10, 1917, dossier 7, République Dominicaine, Correspondance Politique et Commerciale/ Série Nouvelle 1897 à 1918, Archives Diplomatiques, Ministère des Affaires Étrangères, Paris, France.

4   Nateras to managers of sugar estates, September 30, 1921, legajo 37, 1921–1922, Fondo Gobierno Militar, Archivo General de la Nación, Santo Domingo, Dominican Republic.

5   My translation, "La Soberanía Dominicana," *Diario de Cuba*, February 18, 1919, U.S. vice consul in Cuba to secretary of state, Antilla, Cuba, June 24, 1919, 839.00/2140, Central Decimal Files Relating to Internal Affairs of the Dominican Republic, 1910–1929, Record Group 59, National Archives and Records Administration, College Park, Maryland; my translation, Comité Pro-Santo Domingo de la Provincia de Oriente, communiqué, Santiago de Cuba, December 30, 1918, legajo 72 and 117, 1918–1921, Fondo Gobierno Militar, Archivo General de la Nación, Santo Domingo, Dominican Republic; Tulio Cestero to Wilson, Washington, April 1, 1920, legajo Papeles 1919–1920, Tomo 1, Archivo de Tulio Cestero, Fondo Antiguo, Universidad Autónoma de Santo Domingo, Santo Domingo, Dominican Republic.

6   Thorpe to brigade commander, May 30, 1918, folder 20, box 2, Pendleton Papers; Kingsbury to brigade commander, Santo Domingo, September 30, 1918, folder Dominican Republic, Santa [sic] Domingo, 1918, Dominican Republic, Geographical Files, Reference Branch, Marine Corps History Division, Marine Corps Base, Quantico, Virginia.

7   Báez Vargas cited in Rob Ruck, *The Tropic of Baseball: Baseball in the Dominican Republic* (University of Nebraska Press, 1998), 26.

8   Snowden to Rowe, Santo Domingo, March 2, 1920, folder unmarked, box 30, Military Government of Santo Domingo, Record Group 38, National Archives and Records Administration, Washington, D.C.; my translation, Lora, June 8, 1917, legajo 1157, 1918, Fondo Secretaría de Estado de Interior y Policía, Archivo General de la Nación, Santo Domingo, Dominican Republic; Carbonell et al. to ayuntamiento of San Pedro de Macorís, San Pedro de Macorís, November 28, 1917, legajo 5527, 1917, Fondo Municipio, Archivo General de la Nación, Santo Domingo, Dominican Republic.

9   My translation, Barré-Ponsignon to minister of foreign affairs, Santo Domingo, April 3, 1920, dossier 2, République Dominicaine, Amérique 1918–1940, Correspondance Politique et Commerciale 1914–1940, Archives Diplomatiques, Ministère des Affaires Étrangères, Paris, France.

10 My translation, Henríquez y Carvajal to Henríquez García, Washington, December 9, 1920, in Enriquillo Henríquez García, *Cartas del Presidente Francisco Henríquez y Carvajal* (Sánchez, 1970), 11; Kilgore, Santo

Domingo, June 30, 1921, folder Santo Domingo – Intell. Summaries May–Aug. 1921, box 5, General Correspondence, 1907–1936, Record Group 127, National Archives and Records Administration, Washington, D.C.

11 My translation, Américo Lugo, *El Plan de Validación Hughes-Peynado* (La Cuna de América, 1922), 4.

12 Transcript of interview with George Freeman, Port-au-Prince, March 13, 1930, folder Courts, 1929–30 & Undated, box 1069, President's Commission for Study & Review of Conditions in Haiti, Herbert Hoover Library, West Branch, Iowa; Perceval Thoby to Borah, Port-au-Prince, May 29, 1929, folder Haiti 1928–1929, box 271, Papers of William E. Borah, Manuscripts Division, Library of Congress, Washington, D.C.

13 My translations, Roger Gaillard, *Les blancs débarquent*, vol. 6, *Charlemagne Péralte le caco, 1918–1919* (n. pub., 1982), 32, 35.

14 Angell, statement, U.S. Congress, Senate, *Hearings before a Select Committee on Haiti and Santo Domingo*, 67th Congress, 1st and 2nd sessions, vol. 2 (U.S. GPO, 1922), vol. 2, 1514.

15 My translation. Christophe cited in Roger Gaillard, *Les blancs débarquent*, vol. 3, *Premier écrasement du cacoïsme: 1915* (n. pub., 1981), 40.

16 Doxey to chief of the Gendarmerie, Hinche, March 17, 1919, folder Operations Against Hostile Bandits 1919 + 1920, box 1, Special Correspondence of the Chief of the Gendarmerie d'Haiti, 1919–1920, Record Group 127, National Archives and Records Administration, Washington, D.C.; my translation, Delage to minister of foreign affairs, Port-au-Prince, October 12, 1919, dossier 9, Haiti, Amérique 1918–1940, Correspondance Politique et Commerciale 1914–1940, Archives Diplomatiques, Ministère des Affaires Étrangères, Paris, France.

17 Mayer to Hughes, July 30, 1921, 839.00/2451, Central Decimal Files Relating to Internal Affairs of the Dominican Republic, 1910–1929, Record Group 59, National Archives and Records Administration, College Park, Maryland.

18 Mayard cited in Donald B. Cooper, "The Withdrawal of the United States from Haiti, 1928–1934," *Journal of Inter-American Studies* 5: 1 (January 1963), 85; Munro to White, March 16, 1929, folder Elections, 1929–30 & Undated, box 1069, President's Commission for Study & Review of Conditions in Haiti, Herbert Hoover Library, West Branch, Iowa.

19   Cited in George Black, *The Good Neighbor: How the United States Wrote the History of Central America and the Caribbean* (Pantheon, 1988), 42.

20   My translation, Joseph O. Baylen, "Sandino: Death and Aftermath," *Mid-America*, April 1954, 403; my translation, Sandino, "Una digna respuesta al traidor Moncada," [May?] 1927, E-001, C-004, 000201, Collección ACS (Augusto César Sandino), Centro de Historia Militar, Managua, Nicaragua.

21   Eudiviges Herrera Siles, interview with Shroeder, Estelí, October 1990, in Michael J. Schroeder, "'To Defend Our Nation's Honor': Toward a Social and Cultural History of the Sandino Rebellion in Nicaragua, 1927–1934," 2 vols (PhD diss., University of Michigan, 1993), 133; Cuadra to Matthews, March 11, 1932, folder Misc. Confidential Data, box 1, Correspondence of the Intelligence Department (GN-2), 1932, Record Group 127, National Archives and Records Administration, Washington, D.C.; Navy to Morgan, Washington, September 27, 1928, 817.00/6006, Central Decimal Files Relating to Internal Affairs of Nicaragua, 1910–1929, Record Group 59, National Archives and Records Administration, College Park, Maryland.

22   Schroeder, "'To Defend,'" 141; Linton Wells, "Marine Planes Again Targets in Sandino Attack," *New York Herald Tribune*, July 21, 1927, Franklin Delano Roosevelt Library, 1; cited in Jeffrey M. Paige, *Coffee and Power: Revolution and the Rise of Democracy in Central America* (Harvard University Press, 1997), 170.

23   Captain L. B. Puller, Commanding Officer, Company "M," memo to Jefe Director, October 3, 1932, folder [unlabeled] 2 of 3, box 1, Selected Correspondence of the Intelligence Department (GN-2), 1928–32, Record Group 127, National Archives and Records Administration, Washington, D.C.

24   Marchand to Borah, Bluefields, March 12, 1928, file A4574, reference 12746, Foreign Office 371, Public Record Office, Kew, UK.

6

From Occupier to Good Neighbor, 1921–1936

In the American Continent there are neither big brothers nor
little brothers. They are all of the same age from the spiritual
and political point of view.[1]

Herbert Hoover in Argentina, 1928

This is the Bizarro chapter of this book because it traces the
opposite Five C's of U.S. interventions and identifies those that
related to the *end* of interventions from the 1920s to the 1930s.
The U.S. abandonment of direct armed intervention to fulfill policy
goals in Latin America and the Caribbean came largely as a result of
economic and political pressure, and not as a sudden desire for moral
redemption. It also came gradually since it took three Republican
presidents and one Democrat to commit fully.

Such a momentous change had many such *causes*. The most
important was the constant activism by occupied peoples and their
allies around the world. But the *context* of world events and the Great
Depression also convinced many U.S. citizens that interventions were
counterproductive, expensive, and immoral.

Inside the State Department, *collaboration* with ending interventions
came when new officials, more attuned to Latin American opinions and

A Short History of U.S. Interventions in Latin America and the Caribbean,
First Edition. Alan McPherson.

more confident in the region's self-governing abilities, avoided potential interventions and ended long-running occupations. These diplomats often had to contend with military men on the ground, who were doing the hard work of implementing political change and *contested* what they saw as the hurried end of occupations. Events in Nicaragua, Haiti, Cuba, and Panama in the 1930s showed that putting an end to the era of U.S. interventions in Latin America and the Caribbean would be a long, hard slog.

The *consequences* – some unintended, others not – were even harder. After 1934, Latin America for a half-decade had practically no U.S. troops on its shores. But it did suffer murderous dictators, many of whom had either risen to power during U.S. interventions or took advantage of institutions that those interventions had created.

Nonintervention from Harding to Roosevelt

The adoption of nonintervention by the U.S. government followed trends brewing among not only violent and peaceful resisters in occupied countries but also a larger Latin American public and U.S. public opinion.

First, for a generation, Latin America had made nonintervention the cornerstone of its participation in inter-American diplomacy. Even while they welcomed foreign trade and took out large loans, Latin Americans resented Europeans backing up their economic might with gunboats. In 1868, Argentine jurist Carlos Calvo challenged the European position that governments could send navies to enforce the claims of their own citizens, such as a French gunboat landing in Colombia so that a French plantation owner could get Bogotá to pay for his losses during a civil war. A Calvo Doctrine resolution came up at the First International Conference of American States in 1890 and only the United States voted against it. In 1902, another Argentine, foreign minister Luís Drago, advanced his own Drago Doctrine: that foreign armed intervention to enforce the payments of public debts was illegal.

A second trend was that, among U.S. citizens, knowledge about Latin America spread after World War I. The spectacle of Europeans massacring each other by the millions made Latin Americans seem peaceful and sophisticated in comparison. Travel and interest in Mexico especially grew. While in 1910 only 5000 U.S. high schoolers studied Spanish, by 1920 that number skyrocketed to 260,000. Books and magazine articles about Latin America flourished. By the late 1920s, radio and telegraph communication with Latin America increased, direct steamship lines to South America left San Francisco and New York, and New Yorkers could fly directly to Buenos Aires.

As U.S. journalists reported more Latin American news, some began to doubt the marine version of interventions. Before Nicaragua's Augusto Sandino even came on the scene, Will Rogers, the era's most popular news commentator, contrasted U.S. backing of a Conservative puppet with Latin America's perspective. "We say that [Adolfo] Díaz is the properly elected president of Nicaragua, but Brazil, Argentina, Peru, Chile, Mexico, Ecuador, Costa Rica, Cuba, Guatemala, Colombia, Uruguay, Paraguay – all those say that the other fellow is the properly elected president. It's funny how we are the only ones that get everything right."[2]

Scholars and labor leaders were increasingly critical of U.S. interventions, as was *The Nation* magazine. "For what are the marines in Nicaragua to die?" it asked.[3] In 1928, *The Nation* published journalist Carleton Beals's exclusive interview with Sandino, proving to the world not only that the Nicaraguan was alive but also that he had well-defined political ideas.

While those on the political left tended to focus on the unseen economic causes of marine landings, the right emphasized consequences – how interventions dragged Washington into the dark world of Caribbean politics, and pacifists and religious leaders were morally repulsed by the atrocities committed by marines. When the Haitian occupation did not end after Senate investigations in 1921–1922, Emily Balch, an opponent of the war in Europe, led a group of black and white U.S. citizens to Haiti in 1926, a mission that produced an important book, *Occupied Haiti*. They presented their findings to President Calvin Coolidge and later influenced President Herbert Hoover's take on Haiti.

The Latin American press, too, awakened to the occupations of the Caribbean and Central America, especially when Sandino became a global sensation. One Buenos Aires reporter repeated Sandino's warning "that the Yankee menace is a danger to all of our America." In the tradition of the Calvo and Drago doctrines, the press affirmed "the rights of weak States and the necessity that they be respected and that right must be defended against force."[4]

European diplomats and newspapermen, meanwhile, pointed to U.S. hypocrisy. Why criticize the British in India or the French in Algeria when Washington had similar colonies in the Caribbean? Most opposed to interventions were Europeans with a Latin-based language such as the French, Spaniards, and Italians. Many had citizens in cities such as Buenos Aires, who funded and raised hell in the press. In 1927 *Foreign Affairs* described Spaniards as "our bitterest and most relentless foe in Latin America."[5]

Latin American diplomats also increasingly confronted their U.S. counterparts directly. Either while stationed in Washington or at inter-American conferences, they protested, distributed pamphlets, and denounced occupations to the Latin American press. The Sixth International Conference of American States held in Havana, Cuba, in early 1928 was almost dominated by denunciations of the U.S. intervention against Sandino. Thirteen Latin American states, including Haiti and the Dominican Republic, voted for a Salvadoran resolution ordering, "No state has a right to intervene in the internal affairs of another."[6]

Joining the fray was an important minority of the U.S. Congress, a mishmash of pacifists, isolationists, and xenophobes united against anything smacking of U.S. imperialism. Some argued that none of these small wars were legal since the Congress had not authorized them. After reading the Beals articles, Minnesota senator Henrik Shipstead sharply questioned General John Lejeune's assumption that Sandino was a "bandit."[7]

The most important senator was William Borah of Idaho, who opposed every intervention in the Americas because he suspected loans to be tools of imperialism and felt that the Monroe Doctrine did not give Washington the right to overthrow governments. He judged

U.S. behavior in the hemisphere as no better than how Japan treated Korea or how Russia dominated Siberia.

Most important, Borah and his ilk introduced – and sometimes passed – resolutions in Congress that either forced the executive branch to hand over documents about interventions, set up investigative commissions, or cut off funds to occupiers.

Despite its desire for independence from Congress, the State Department was also changing. In the 1920s, a new generation of Spanish-speaking, professional diplomats staffed the Latin American Division at the State Department. They were still somewhat paternalistic toward the region, but men such as Francis White, Leo Rowe, and Sumner Welles believed in the self-governing abilities of Latin Americans and thought occupations were an outdated form of international relations.

They did not see economic exploitation as a cause or a consequence of interventions, but many diplomats abroad reported on boycotts or lost trade because of Latin American resentment at intervention. And, since U.S. investments in Latin America more than tripled and exports almost tripled from 1914 to 1929, there was much to lose by incurring the region's wrath. In 1927, U.S. trade with Latin America was greater than trade with Great Britain, Germany, and France combined.

And so, according to one of these new Latin Americanists, Dana Munro, "from 1923 on there was a definite trend toward a policy of less interference in the internal affairs of the Central American and West Indian [Caribbean] republics." The trend included a 1930 re-examination of the Monroe Doctrine. In what is now called the Clark Memorandum, the State Department agreed with Latin Americans that the Doctrine did not justify the taking of Latin American republics, only the checking of European invasions. The following year, Secretary of State Henry Stimson reiterated that the Monroe Doctrine was "a declaration of the United States vs. Europe, not of the United States vs. Latin America."[8]

Yet the practice of intervention could not really end until the president was on board. Three Republican presidents – Warren Harding, Coolidge, and Hoover – set the stage for the formal abandonment of sending marines.

U.S. leaders had talked of being a "good neighbor" to Latin America since 1815. Secretary of State Elihu Root, the architect of many interventions, had said it in 1907. But not until 1920 did a president at least avoid starting new interventions. Because World War I was over, isolationists wanted troops to come home from Europe and Latin America, and Germans no longer threatened the Panama Canal. Republican presidential candidate Harding criticized Woodrow Wilson's occupations of Haiti and the Dominican Republic, and when he won office, he and his Secretary of State, Charles Evans Hughes, had a clear policy of avoiding new interventions by marines. Under Coolidge, sending Stimson to design the Tipitapa accords was an attempt to shorten the marine intervention in Nicaragua's 1926–1927 civil war. Yet Coolidge did send the marines into Honduras in 1924 and in Nicaragua in 1926, and they stayed to hunt down Sandino.

Hoover took a giant leap over these baby steps. He had the Clark Memorandum published when Coolidge would not, and he reduced the political appointees – who tended to know little about the area, compared to career diplomats – sent to Latin America from 15 to one. A Quaker, Hoover was an anti-militarist and wanted no U.S. troops abroad except for self-defense. He opposed the Haitian and Dominican occupations as early as 1922, and thought it wrong to have marines collect loans. As secretary of commerce, he saw how interventions harmed trade in the hemisphere.

After he won the 1928 presidential election, Hoover did something unequaled before or since. He took a seven-week tour of 10 Latin American countries from November 1928 to early January 1929. He said the words "good neighbor" on his first stop, in Honduras, and several times thereafter. In Argentina, he promised that "no intervention policy predominates or will prevail in my country."[9] The month after he walked into the Oval Office, he rejected intervention to protect U.S. investors in Mexico, and in 1929–1930 he declined to meddle in a Cuban revolution. He avoided intervening in Panama, Peru, Honduras, and El Salvador in response to events that in the past would have drawn the marines. Hoover, finally, inaugurated the first ever Pan-American Day, an opportunity to declare friendship and shared values throughout the Americas.

Franklin Delano Roosevelt, however, did the most to formalize and publicize the Good Neighbor Policy and to expand it beyond a promise of nonintervention. He had previously backed occupations, boasting that he had written Haiti's 1918 constitution and calling its inhabitants "little more than primitive savages."[10] But by the early 1930s, he was following prevailing political winds. Roosevelt announced the Good Neighbor Policy during his first inaugural address. A few months later, at the Pan-American Union on April 12, 1933, he tied it to Latin America: "the essential qualities of a true Pan Americanism must be the same as those which constitute a good neighbor, namely, mutual understanding, and, through such understanding, a sympathetic appreciation of the other's point of view." That same year, at the Seventh Inter-American Conference in Montevideo, Uruguay, Secretary of State Cordell Hull declared that "no government need fear any intervention on the part of the United States under the Roosevelt administration." In December 1936, Hull and FDR both went to a Buenos Aires conference to sign on to a statement that condemned "intervention by one state in the internal or external affairs of another State" and declared illegal the "forcible collection of pecuniary debts."[11] Few noticed the loophole: "by one state" meant that several states could intervene, and every overt U.S. intervention since then has been in some way multilateral.

In contrast to his Republican predecessors, FDR also encouraged cultural exchanges with Latin America, signed trade agreements that lowered tariffs on imports to and from the region, and provided credits to finance U.S. goods through the Export-Import Bank. A new era had begun, one marked by fewer military interventions but deepening U.S.–Latin American relations.

Nicaragua, 1928–1933

When Washington recalled U.S. Minister Dana Munro from Managua to head the Latin American Division in the late 1920s, he noted a new atmosphere in Washington: "There had been much criticism of intervention in anti-imperialist circles and in Congress, and the Sandino affair in Nicaragua had shown how unpleasantly action in one Latin American country could affect our relations with the others."[12] Sandino, by 1928, had amassed not only a lot of sympathizers abroad but also a transnational network that helped him materially and diplomatically. He famously said of himself, "Sandino is Indo-Hispanic and he has no frontiers in Latin America." Just among his officers, that was true: there were 11 Hondurans, six Salvadorans, three Guatemalans, three Mexicans, two Venezuelans, two Colombians, two Costa Ricans, one Peruvian, and one Dominican. In Tegucigalpa, Honduras, magazine editor Froylán Turcios was Sandino's loudspeaker, publishing the Nicaraguan's inspirational letters and funneling him mail and money. Some funds came from Mexico City, New York, and other centers of communism and anti-imperialism. U.S. workers sent him medical supplies.

World pressure to withdraw from Nicaragua mounted, but marines on the ground pushed back. They wanted to leave a more or less representative government that would not fight yet another civil war that might drag them back in. In November 1928, led by Brigadier General Frank McCoy, they oversaw elections that were the fairest in Nicaragua's history and brought the Liberal Party to power. It grew more difficult now for Sandino to claim that the marines made his country less democratic.

In mid-1929, Sandino left for Mexico to reinvigorate his supporters abroad, but there the Mexicans, in a deal with Washington, kept him in near-poverty in the remote state of Yucatán. He was losing allies among foreign governments and rich Central Americans, so he returned to Nicaragua in mid-1930 and expanded his war beyond the mountainous Segovias of the north. He now identified only with the "noble and generous" workers and peasants and called his army the "chosen ones" who would bring "Divine Justice" to Nicaragua. His fighting force peaked at 2000 with another 1800 in reserves, and he claimed that it controlled eight departments.[13]

Meanwhile, the Departments of State and Navy were rethinking Nicaragua. The October 1929 Wall Street crash made impossible a new canal in Nicaragua, a policy announced in mid-1932. Partly to save money, half the U.S. force left after the 1928 elections, leaving only 2500. After eight marines were killed and two wounded in an ambush on New Year's Eve 1930, Stimson announced full withdrawal weeks later, reducing the force from 1300 to 500 by June.

In spring 1931, Stimson made another momentous policy choice: to stop protecting any U.S. property endangered by war. U.S. farm and plantation owners kept asking the State Department for marines to guard their property. Stimson countered that it was too expensive, and that besides, marines only attracted more violence. This sounded the death knell of Dollar Diplomacy – and debunked the thesis of many anti-imperialists that the protection of private property was the main cause of most U.S. interventions.

In 1932, the Latin American Division declared that the remaining marines would leave after another marine-supervised election that year "since public opinion in this country would not understand them remaining any longer, and their presence there was a fruitful cause of misunderstanding and criticism in Latin America."[14] The statement demonstrated the power of U.S. *and* Latin American public opinion in ending occupations.

U.S. military officials in Managua, meanwhile, contested ending the occupation because they were distraught that State seemed to be abandoning its reform of Nicaraguan politics. They had been trying to teach Nicaraguans *more* nationalism, for instance by banning partisan talk in the constabulary and teaching its guards to march with the Nicaraguan flag and chant the national anthem.

But politics in Nicaragua just got more partisan. After the 1932 elections, the occupation made the monumental decision to place Anastasio Somoza in charge of the constabulary. U.S. Minister Matthew Hanna was certain that Somoza would "maintain the non-partisan character of the Guardia [the constabulary]," and in a sense he was right: Somoza followed no political leader – but himself.[15] He mastered the instruments of national repression – the constabulary, the roads, the telegraph, and the disarmament of all potential opponents – and began to challenge President Juan Sacasa.

On February 2, 1933, Sandino responded to the election of Sacasa and the withdrawal of the marines by laying down his own weapons. Somoza responded to that by perceiving Sandino as the last threat to his personal power. On February 21, 1934, Sandino came to Managua to discuss disarmament with Sacasa. Somoza's men took Sandino and two of his generals to an airfield, forced them to their knees, shot them dead, and buried them. On the same day, Somoza's constabulary massacred the 300 men, women, and children among Sandino's followers who had formed a farming co-operative in northern Nicaragua.

Haiti, 1930–1934

In Haiti, meanwhile, much of the discontent at the presidency of Louis Borno since 1922 was building up a head of steam, but with no outlet.

Then came an apparently minor student strike. On October 31, 1929, elite students walked out of a U.S.-run agricultural training school because it wanted to give some of its scholarships to poorer students. Other schools joined the elite students in a sympathy strike, then other towns joined. This first student strike in Haitian history resented an occupation that told Haitians how to develop without giving them enough tools and by disrespecting their culture. Schools administrator George Freeman, an Alabaman, treated Haitians as if they were second-class citizens, not realizing that Haitians hated being compared to African Americans (elite Haitians, especially, saw African Americans as uncultured and subordinated to whites).

Backing the strike were radical young men such as writer Jacques Roumain, who were inspired by either socialism or *noirisme*, a burgeoning movement of pride in Haiti's African heritage. When the U.S. High Commissioner invited Roumain to an invitation, the writer placed his response in the newspaper: "The black Jacques Roumain does not dine with the white racist [John] Russell."[16] Older Haitians, raised with French *politesse*, never would have been so openly controversial about race. Roumain founded the underground Haitian Communist Party in 1932.

Opposition politicians also backed the student strike, mostly because they could use it to chase Borno out of office. Peasants, meanwhile, blamed Borno for the fall in the price of their coffee exports. Context continued to matter as the Great Depression cut Haiti–U.S. trade by about half.

The now-general strike reached a climax on December 6, 1929, in the city of Aux Cayes, where 20 marines felt cornered by 1500 Haitians and fired into the crowd, killing 12 and wounding 23.

The Aux Cayes "massacre," as Haitian immediately called it, got the attention of the U.S. media and groups lobbying for Haiti. The National Association for the Advancement of Colored People and the American Civil Liberties Union called for ending the occupation. The Communist Party held rallies in New York and Washington.

President Hoover had already decided to hasten the end of the occupation. Three days before Aux Cayes, he publicly vowed "to arrive at some more definite policy than at present."[17] On December 7, he asked Congress for a commission, a group of five men – all of whom spoke French and two of whom were Catholics – who arrived in Haiti on February 28, 1930.

The Haitian opposition was ready for these investigators, in contrast to their amateurish reception of the Senate investigation in 1921–1922. Conservative and radical Haitian opponents of Borno set aside their conflicts and, almost to a man, testified before the Forbes Commission, as the five men were called, that if Borno did not resign and a new assembly was not elected, poor Haitians would revolt and blood would run in the streets. The performance was admirably "on message."

It worked. Though the marines and High Commissioner Russell explained that their hard work in transforming Haiti into a stable, middle class country was nowhere close to being finished, the Forbes Commission called for elections in October 1930 and a phase-out of the occupation by the expiration of the 20-year convention in 1936. The most anti-occupation party won the National Assembly and chose Sténio Vincent as Haiti's new president.

The end of the occupation was approaching, but the phase-out was plagued with conflict. "We are trying to give way to the Haitians gradually," wrote Secretary Stimson in a typically racist (though private) comment for 1931, "but of course that is not the way to deal with Negroes."[18] As in the Dominican Republic, a portion of Haitians wanted immediate withdrawal of the marines, *pure et simple*. As they prepared to leave, occupiers witnessed the same political behaviors that had brought them in 1915: corruption among political parties, assassinations, and deep division and distrust along lines of color and class.

Still, President Roosevelt had rejected Wilson's constitutionalism: no longer would the United States intervene in Latin America unless threatened. In the first ever visit to Haiti by a foreign head of state, in July 1934 FDR sailed to Cap-Haïtien to celebrate Haiti's independence, express hope for mutual friendship, and remind Haitians that the U.S. intervention "tried to help the people of

Figure 6.1   President Franklin Delano Roosevelt and Haitian President Sténio Vincent in Haiti, 1934. United States Marine Corps.

Haiti."[19] U.S. occupiers enumerated the ways: 1000 miles of roads, 210 bridges, nine airfields, 1250 miles of telephone lines, 82 miles of irrigation, 11 hospitals, and 147 rural clinics. The last U.S. troops left Haiti on August 15, 1934, two years ahead of schedule.

Cuba, 1933–1934

FDR had barely outlined his Good Neighbor Policy in spring 1933 when a Cuban crisis tested it. Sumner Welles, one of the new men at the Latin American Division of the State Department, largely shaped the president's Cuban diplomacy of 1933–1934. By then, Welles had served in Buenos Aires, learned Spanish, monitored elections in Cuba, visited Haiti, designed the withdrawal from the Dominican Republic, and even published a two-volume history of the Dominican Republic.

In Cuba, the political and economic system that had evolved under the U.S.-imposed Platt Amendment was breaking apart. U.S. citizens had $1 billion invested in the island, but the rise in sugarcane production in the 1910s and 1920s, mostly led by U.S. sugar barons who enjoyed stratospheric prices, collapsed in the early 1930s. President Gerardo Machado, an authoritarian nicknamed "the Butcher," tried to crush a violent revolution from students, professionals, and workers and peasants made poorer by plunging sugar prices.

In April 1933, FDR named Welles as special presidential ambassador to Cuba to offer "friendly mediation," assisted by the not so friendly cruiser *Richmond*, the battleship *Mississippi*, and more than 20 other warships.[20] By August, backed with this firepower, Welles negotiated the resignation of Machado and the interim government of his friend, Carlos Manuel de Céspedes. But, on September 5, an alliance of student radicals and noncommissioned officers led by Sergeant Fulgencio Batista, a man Welles called "extraordinarily brilliant and able," overthrew the De Céspedes government in what was called the "Sergeants' Revolt."[21]

Here was a defining moment for the Good Neighbor Policy. Welles was disturbed by the Sergeants' Revolt. He wanted to adhere to Wilson's constitutionalism and restore De Céspedes through a U.S. military intervention. But FDR and his Secretary of State, Cordell Hull, decided instead to showcase their new policy of nonintervention, which in theory left alone all regimes, whether dictatorships or democracies. They rejected Welles's request.

On September 10, the student junta nominated Dr Ramón Grau San Martín as president, the first since 1898 to take power without official U.S. sanction. With the slogan "Cuba for Cubans," Grau's coalition called for eight-hour days, protection for rural workers, votes for women, and the end of the Platt Amendment.[22] Disliking those reforms, Welles warned that communists were taking over and, given the new constraints of the Good Neighbor Policy, he responded with an ingenious new strategy: intervention through nonintervention.

Welles withheld Washington's recognition of Grau. In those days of U.S. hegemony in the Caribbean basin, such a withholding signaled a green light for a president's enemies. In January 1934, Batista, now the army chief of staff, led another coup – this time against Grau. Batista backed a U.S.-friendly government behind Carlos Mendieta. This time, U.S. recognition came within five days.

On June 9, 1934, FDR proclaimed a Treaty of Relations with Cuba that rescinded the Platt Amendment but added that "stipulations with regard to the naval station at Guantánamo shall continue in effect."[23]

Panama, 1936–1939

Finally, in Panama, the Roosevelt administration formalized the Good Neighbor Policy with the signing of the Hull–Alfaro Treaty in 1936.

After nationalist President Harmodio Arias in 1933 made a surprise visit to Washington, FDR said the Panamanian initiative "does illustrate the practical way of taking up problems that occur between different countries."[24] In the spirit of the Good Neighbor,

Roosevelt agreed to changes, for instance banning Canal Zone sales to noncanal employees and thus forcing Panamanians to spend their dollars in Panama itself.

Arias remained dissatisfied, however, and negotiators revised the Treaty of 1903 that they found so humiliating. When U.S. envoy Sumner Welles complained that his counterpart Ricardo Alfaro was reversing the Biblical saying to read, "It is more blessed to receive than to give," Alfaro contested, "We gave all we could in 1903."[25] Hull–Alfaro increased the U.S. annual payment to Panama from the canal to $430,000, ended the U.S. right to acquire land in Panama, allowed Panamanians to operate radio stations, and promised equal treatment of Panamanian and U.S. employees of the canal. Washington also renounced its right to intervene unilaterally in Panama, and so the "protectorate" status of the republic ended. However, the treaty kept the Canal Zone and its bases in U.S. hands, thus allowing its soldiers to be sent potentially to other parts of the Caribbean. And practically none of Hull–Alfaro's provisions were enforced. Such small concessions were still too much for many in the U.S. Senate, which took until 1939 to ratify the treaty.

Tragically, the end of direct military intervention in the 1930s did not mean less violence for Central America and the Caribbean, and in some ways it caused more bloodshed and terror. In Nicaragua, Somoza, a product of the U.S. occupation, ruled with an iron fist, deposing the president and beginning a half-century of dictatorship carried on through his sons. Dominicans, meanwhile, suffered the dictatorship of Rafael Trujillo. Like Somoza, Trujillo rose through the ranks of the U.S.-designed constabulary during the occupation of his country. Once that occupation was over, he proved far more brutal than the occupation had been, especially for the 10,000–18,000 Haitians whom he had massacred in 1937. And in Cuba, the nonintervention of 1933–1934 resulted in the ascent of Batista, another ruthless autocrat.

The marines had not necessarily planned to bring these strongmen to power, but military interventions had primed the pump. Occupiers had aimed to stop revolutions, and to do that, they disarmed the general population, stripped small armies from regional politicians, and gave the constabularies the monopoly of force by building roads by which they could take down any challenger. The pledge of nonintervention of the Good Neighbor Policy, moreover, made it more difficult for U.S. foreign policymakers to order marines back to the region to overthrow these dictators. In any case, nobody called for such interventions because dictators achieved political stability – the overall goal of the U.S. government. They also protected U.S. private property and partook in the growing influence of U.S. culture. Some in the State Department hated the dictators, but many in the military were only too happy to have them keep the Caribbean free of external influence – another important goal of the Good Neighbor Policy. Among the many consequences of the Good Neighbor Policy, the dirty work of U.S. interventions had now been outsourced to Latin America and the Caribbean.

Notes

1   Interviewed by *La Nación*, reproduced in "The Hoover Idea on Argentina," *The Review of the River Plate* (Buenos Aires), December 21, 1928, 13–19.
2   Cited in Richard White, *Will Rogers: A Political Life* (Texas Tech University Press, 2011), 101.
3   "Can We Get Out of Nicaragua?" *The Nation* 126: 3268, February 22, 1928, 201.
4   Manuel Antonio Valle, "Viva Sandino," *The Living Age*, translated from *Nosotros* (Buenos Aires), 243 (November 1932), 248; cited in "Disputes Moncada on Our Occupation," *New York Times*, December 19, 1929, 8.
5   Clarence H. Haring, "The Two Americas," *Foreign Affairs* (April 1927), 376; Bailey W. Diffie, "The Ideology of Hispanidad," *Hispanic American Historical Review* 23: 3 (August 1943), 457–8.
6   Greg Grandin, *Empire's Workshop: Latin America, the United States, and the Rise of the New Imperialism* (Metropolitan Books, 2006), 32.
7   "Testimony of the Major General Commandant before the Senate Committee of Foreign Relations," February 18, 1928, folder Nicaragua – U.S. Senate Inquiry, box 30, Operations and Training Division,

Intelligence Section, 1915–1934, Record Group 127, National Archives and Records Administration, Washington, D.C., 64–5.

8   Dana G. Munro, *The United States and the Caribbean Republics 1921–1933* (Princeton University Press, 1974), 15; cited in Lejeune Cummins, *Quijote on a Burro: Sandino and the Marines, A Study in the Formulation of Foreign Policy* (La Impresora Azteca, 1958), 41.

9   "The Hoover Idea," 13–19.

10 Cited in Grandin, *Empire's Workshop*, 28.

11 Cited in Mark Gilderhus, *The Second Century: U.S.–Latin American Relations since 1989* (Scholarly Resources, 2000), 78.

12 Dana G. Munro, "The American Withdrawal from Haiti, 1929–1934," *Hispanic American Historical Review* 49: 1 (February 1969), 5.

13 Sandino to Turcios, El Chipotón, June 10, 1928, in Robert Edgar Conrad, ed. and trans., *Sandino: The Testimony of a Nicaraguan Patriot, 1921–1934* (Princeton University Press: 1990), 202, 203; my translation. Sandino, manifesto, El Chipotón, February 15, 1931, E-001, C-005, 000234, Collección ACS (Augusto César Sandino), Centro de Historia Militar, Managua, Nicaragua.

14 Wilson, Washington, February 3, 1932, 817.00/7323, Central Decimal Files Relating to Internal Affairs of Nicaragua, 1930–1944, Record Group 59, National Archives and Records Administration, College Park, Maryland.

15 Cited in Karl Bermann, *Under the Big Stick: Nicaragua and the United States since 1848* (South End Press, 1986), 216.

16 Magdaline W. Shannon, *Jean Price-Mars, the Haitian Elite and the American Occupation, 1915–1935* (St Martin's Press, 1996), 81.

17 Cited in British Library of Information, "U.S.A. Press to December 10th, 1929," 13 December 1929, file A8860, reference 13485, Foreign Office 371, Public Record Office, Kew, UK.

18 Stimson, 22 April 1931, reel 3, vol. 16; and September 30, 1931, reel 3, vol. 18, both in Stimson Diary, Franklin Delano Roosevelt Library.

19 Roosevelt, "Address of the President," Cap-Haïtien, July 5, 1934, box 18, Speeches, President's Personal File, Franklin Delano Roosevelt Library.

20 Cited in Gilderhus, *Second Century*, 77.

21 Welles cited in Robert Holden and Eric Zolov, eds., *Latin America and the United States: A Documentary History* (Oxford University Press, 2000), 145.

22   Cited in Gilderhus, *Second Century*, 77.

23   Cited in Stephen Irving Max Schwab, *Guantánamo, U.S.A: The Untold History of America's Cuban Outpost* (University Press of Kansas, 2009), 4.

24   Cited in Michael L. Conniff, *Panama and the United States: The Forced Alliance* (University of Georgia Press, 1992), 90.

25   Cited in Lester Langley, *The United States and the Caribbean in the Twentieth Century*, rev. ed. (University of Georgia Press, 1985), 156.

7

Warding Off Global Ideologies, 1935–1954

They would have overthrown us even if we had grown no
bananas.

José Fortuny, Guatemalan labor leader[1]

The 20 years or so following the withdrawal of U.S. troops from
the Caribbean and Central America were not as free of military
intervention as the term "good neighbor" implied. The overwhelming
and urgent *context* of World War II brought to Latin America the
greatest U.S. occupation force ever, concentrated in British islands of
the Caribbean and in Panama. The postwar period then saw one of
the first, and the most *consequential*, indirect military interventions
when the Central Intelligence Agency organized a coup in Guatemala.
Both of these interventions had a common *cause*: the desire to keep
political ideologies out of the hemisphere – first fascism during the
war, then communism in the Cold War. U.S. leaders considered these
systems of thought to be "foreign" to the Western Hemisphere.

The means by which the United States excluded fascism and
communism, however, were more controversial. To be sure, Latin
Americans by and large *collaborated* with World War II-era interventions, and several leaders helped militarily or diplomatically with the

A Short History of U.S. Interventions in Latin America and the Caribbean,
First Edition. Alan McPherson.
© 2016 John Wiley & Sons, Inc. Published 2016 by John Wiley & Sons, Inc.

coup in Guatemala, because they shared the fear of totalitarian systems that fascism and communism often brought. But many Latin Americans *contested* interventions when they saw too many foreign troops landing too quickly, or when those troops behaved badly, or when they seemed more interested in protecting U.S. corporations than in promoting democracy.

A New Continental Security

As President Franklin Delano Roosevelt's Good Neighbor Policy evolved into a tolerance for dictators in the Caribbean and Central America, the president was also concerned about casting a wide security net around the entire hemisphere, from northern Canada to the Strait of Magellan at the southern tip of South America. Inter-American conferences in Lima (1938), Panama (1939), and Havana (1940) no longer focused on keeping U.S. troops out but instead on creating a military alliance with Washington against the Axis powers of Germany, Japan, and Italy. The republics of the Americas, for instance, declared that an attack against any of them would be considered an attack on all.

Before World War II, Germany was mostly active on the hemisphere's economic front. Over one million ethnic Germans lived in Latin America, many of them merchants. German gunboats also landed on Latin America's shores, usually to demand debt payments. Adolf Hitler's Nazi Party aimed to create exclusive trade zones by using an inconvertible currency, and Berlin successfully kept the United States out of Brazilian trade. In 1940, however, the U.S. government bought massive amounts of raw materials from Latin America to deny them to Hitler.

After France fell to the Nazis in June 1940, Roosevelt ordered the development of Operation Pot of Gold, a plan to hurry 100,000 U.S. troops to Brazil whether Brazilians wanted them or not. Brazilian President Getúlio Vargas did agree to build airfields in northeast Brazil to help supply the Allies in Africa and in the China-Burma-India battlefields. Brazil also deployed forces under U.S. commanders in Italy.

Right after the Japanese attack on the U.S. base at Pearl Harbor, Hawai'i, on December 7, 1941, the Nazi gloves in the hemisphere came off. In 1942, German submarines sank a total of 336 ships, especially oil tankers from Mexico and Venezuela, around Trinidad, the Panama Canal, the Yucatán Channel, and the Windward Passage between Cuba and Haiti. The Axis Powers, however, only attacked Caribbean territory once during the war, in Aruba in February 1942. Most worrisome was the Panama Canal. The Federal Bureau of Investigation and military spies found out that the Japanese and Germans knew the technical weaknesses of the canal. Near the end of the war, the Japanese even built huge submarines meant to destroy the locks of the canal.

Fearing Nazis everywhere, U.S. diplomats pressured Latin Americans to blacklist, deport, or jail thousands of Axis nationals only because they could be spies or propagandists. In January 1942, the Pan-American Foreign Ministers' meeting in Rio de Janeiro produced Resolution 20, which called for the removal of Japanese individuals into internment camps. Cuba, Nicaragua, Costa Rica, Colombia, Ecuador, Mexico, and Venezuela housed some prisoners. By the end of the war, too, some 4058 Germans, 2264 Japanese, and 288 Italians from 15 Latin American countries ended up in large camps in the United States. While many countries handed over suspects willingly, the United States threatened to boycott Costa Rican and Guatemalan coffee and sugar unless officials complied.

World War II Interventions

U.S. armed interventions came about as part of Roosevelt's efforts to get around his own government's neutrality laws and arm the British and other allies. In 1941, the Lend-Lease Act – which was "neutral" because it did not technically sell anything – allowed him to credit $50.1 billion in war materiel not only to Europeans and the Soviet Union but also to Brazil.

A year earlier, the bases-for-destroyers deal – again, a trade rather than a sale and therefore "neutral" – transferred 50 U.S. Navy destroyers to Great Britain. In exchange, British Prime Minister Winston Churchill, desperate for those ships, gave away 99-year rent-free leases for airfields or naval bases in Newfoundland, Bermuda, and the Bahamas in the Atlantic, in British Guiana, and in Jamaica, St Lucia, Antigua, and Trinidad in the Caribbean. All were possessions to which the British had hung on from their imperial heyday.

In early 1941, the first U.S. intervention in Latin America during World War II began as hundreds of troops landed to build and occupy installations mostly in north Trinidad, in the nation of Trinidad and Tobago. Two years later, over 20,000 U.S. service members would be stationed there – arguably the largest mobilization for Latin American service since the Mexican War.

The Trinidadian response to the occupation was ambivalent. On one hand, budding nationalists hoping to be soon free of British colonialism contested the U.S. presence. On the other, new military installations brought well-paid jobs, taken up by tens of thousands of Trinidadians and other British West Indians.

U.S. troops also took to being in Trinidad. U.S. men and Caribbean women had intimate relationships, and jazzy Yankee fashions such as untucked jitterbug shirts and zoot suits influenced men especially. Calypso songs of the war, for instance the Andrews Sisters' cover of "Rum and Coca-Cola" – the cocktail itself denoting the mixing of Caribbean and U.S. elements – spoke of these pleasures:

> If a Yankee comes to Trinidad
> They got the young girls all goin' mad
> Young girls say they treat 'em nice
> Make Trinidad like paradise.[2]

Most of the U.S. wartime bases closed in 1949.

Panama was the site of the second U.S. military intervention to support the greater war. Washington first negotiated with the government of Arnulfo Arias. "Fufo" was as strong a nationalist as his brother

Harmodio, who negotiated the 1936 treaty between Panama and the United States. Initial positions were eons from each other – the U.S. War Department wanted 999-year leases while Arias demanded a rent of $4000 per hectare. After Arias was overthrown, however, the two countries penned a deal on May 18, 1942, to build and/or occupy military installations on Panamanian soil – that meant not just the Canal Zone, where U.S. troops were allowed by treaty to stay – for less rent but also shorter leases. By the end of the war, the U.S. military occupied 134 facilities outside the Zone. These included bases, runways, and radar and sonar stations. Thousands of U.S. troops had already guarded the canal since its opening but, in wartime, numbers grew from 11,000 to 67,000.

The infusion of money and 22,000 workers from Central America and the West Indies was a boon for Panamanian businesses. Sales of milk, sugar, electricity, and cattle almost doubled. In his novel *Luna verde*, Panamanian author Joaquín Beleño complained how this get-rich-quick frenzy left Panamanians envious and frustrated, especially when the war ended and jobs vanished.

The wartime agreement with Panama, known as Filós–Hines, specified that U.S. occupation of sites outside the Canal Zone would end one year after the war did. In 1947, the U.S. military's attempt to extend Filós–Hines caused major rioting in Panama, signaling the dawn of the Panamanian student movement.

Still, wartime expansion resulted in the 1946 creation of the U.S. Army Caribbean School at Fort Amador in the Zone, whose job it was to train Latin American military and police forces against leftist subversion. In 1949 it moved to Fort Gulick, and in 1963 it changed its name to the School of the Americas.

To counter the negative connotations of military interventions and to foster a sense of shared civilization in the Americas, the Roosevelt administration also developed cultural programs. FDR created the Office of the Co-ordinator for Inter-American Affairs (OCIAA), headed by Nelson Rockefeller, which promoted student exchanges, binational centers, libraries, and traveling movie projectors through-out Latin America. To counter Nazi propaganda, the OCIAA created a blacklist of newspapers and radio stations owned or influenced by the enemy. Its Motion Picture Division got U.S. film distributors to pull their reels from all theaters that also showed Axis movies, and it collaborated with Walt Disney Studios to produce the cartoon feature films *Saludos Amigos* and *The Three Caballeros*. This last film had Donald Duck befriending a Brazilian parrot, José Carioca, who taught Donald all about Latin America.

The Cold War Inter-American System

In some respects, anti-fascism continued to define U.S. policy in Latin America after the war ended in 1945. In Argentina in 1946, for instance, U.S. diplomat Spruille Braden set out to punish the Argentine government for breaking relations with the Axis only in 1944 and declaring war only the following year, when it was too late. Braden confronted Juan Domingo Perón, a militarist candidate for the presidency, by publishing the Blue Book, so called for the color of its cover. The book's documents detailed Argentina's ties with Nazi Germany, and Braden hoped it would promote U.S.-style democracy. But the Blue Book boomeranged: Perón confronted Argentines with the choice of an Argentina commanded by "Perón or Braden." Playing on traditional Latin American nationalism and fear of external intervention, voters chose Perón.

Toward most of Latin America, however, U.S. concerns were shifting from anti-fascism to anti-communism – what some simplistically called "red fascism," just another kind of totalitarianism. In March 1947, President Harry Truman declared that the United States would "support free peoples who are resisting attempted subjugation by armed minorities or by outside pressures." He meant it to apply mostly to European countries, notably Greece and Turkey, fighting violent insurrections by communists supported or not by Moscow. But the so-called Truman Doctrine reverberated around the world, including in Latin America. There, dictators and would-be dictators, who were concerned by recent democratic victories in the hemisphere, labeled their political opponents communists and thus enjoyed U.S. military

aid against them. Conveniently, the Roosevelt and Truman administrations also claimed that, because of the Good Neighbor Policy, they
were unable to intervene against noncommunist dictators.

The Inter-American System, or the network of institutions through
which diplomacy flowed, also adapted to the Cold War. The year of
the Truman Doctrine, delegates from the United States and 18 other
American republics met in Rio de Janeiro to sign the Inter-American
Treaty of Reciprocal Assistance. The Rio Pact, as it was known, promised that "an armed attack by any State against an American State shall
be considered as an attack against all the American States" and that all
member states would "assist in meeting the attack." For Latin
Americans, the agreement seemed to guarantee that the United States
would never again intervene in Latin America. For U.S. policymakers,
however, the American republics had just agreed to repel any intervention by the Soviet Union. The door was thus open to newfangled
U.S. interventions – if, that is, they could be spun as multilateral
responses to international communism.

In 1948, the year after the Rio Pact signing, 21 American republics
met to found the Organization of American States (OAS), a diplomatic
counterpart to the Rio Pact's military commitment. Again, intentions
diverged. Latin American leaders – being almost unanimously anti-
communist in 1948 – saw the logic in having a regional version of the
United Nations where they could discuss common projects and air
grievances in a forum in which the Soviets could not meddle. For
Washington, the OAS served that purpose too, but also provided
them with a place where they could impose Cold War priorities and
win votes by economic pressure and diplomatic arm-twisting,
especially if U.S. officials wished to launch an intervention.

Guatemala, 1954

The small Central American country of Guatemala is where the logic
of the Cold War Inter-American System allowed for the next U.S.
military intervention. Unlike previous ones, this U.S. intervention

was largely indirect: the Central Intelligence Agency (CIA) funded and trained an invasion force, but that force was made up of Latin Americans led by Guatemalans.

Guatemala was in the middle of a democratic spring. In 1944, a coalition of democrats forced dictator Jorge Úbico out of power and ushered in the reformist Juan José Arévalo. Arévalo gave the vote to all adults, ended forced labor, introduced a minimum wage and collective bargaining for workers, established a social security agency, and increased literacy. In 1951 came a second democratically elected president, Jacobo Arbenz, a military man who had helped overthrow Úbico.

More than Arévalo, Arbenz undertook reforms that U.S. officials perceived as threatening to U.S. interests. On June 17, 1952, he passed a land reform law that aimed to take 1.5 million uncultivated acres from large farms and distribute them to 100,000 peasant families, many of them indigenous peoples long marginalized in politics and landowning. Decree 900, as it was called, was meant to redress the injustice of 2 percent of the people owning 72 percent of the land.

The richest landowner in Guatemala was the Boston-based United Fruit Company (UFCO), which mostly exported bananas. Arbenz planned to expropriate – meaning to forcibly take but pay for – 234,000 uncultivated UFCO acres. But Arbenz refused to compensate the company what it declared it was now worth – $19,355,000 – but instead pay it only the $1,185,000 it had claimed on its returns to minimize its tax payments.

Some U.S. aid workers originally thought Decree 900 "constructive and democratic in its aims," similar to U.S. land redistribution in Asia after World War II.[3]

The Truman administration was concerned about this move against private U.S. property. "If the Guatemalans want to handle a Guatemalan company roughly that is none of our business," said one U.S. diplomat, "but if they handle an American company roughly it is our business."[4] In 1948, the Office of Policy Co-ordination was created to handle covert paramilitary actions, and by 1951 it fused with the CIA and showed growing concern over Guatemala. In 1952, the CIA approved a plan to give weapons to the Arbenz-hating Guatemalan Colonel Carlos Castillo Armas and have Nicaragua and Honduras provide air cover for an operation codenamed PBFORTUNE. But the plot was uncovered and abandoned a month later.

The new president in 1953, Dwight Eisenhower, was less interested in Good Neighbor niceties, taking down from White House walls the portraits of Latin American independence leaders. His Secretary of State was John Foster Dulles and his CIA director was Allen Dulles. The two brothers were also both former lawyers who had worked for UFCO. The family of John Moors Cabot, the Assistant Secretary of State for Inter-American Affairs, owned stock in UFCO.

More important, the Dulles brothers believed that the United States had a duty to overthrow even democratic governments if those governments threatened the independence of corporations, which were not only motors of economic growth but promoters of political freedom. If the Dulles brothers did not overthrow Arbenz, they reasoned, communism would flourish in the Americas. John Foster Dulles explained that, if the Arbenz government "gave a gold piece for every banana [it expropriated], the problem would still be Communist infiltration."[5]

In Guatemala, Arbenz *was* friendly with communists. Jacobo's wife, María, had communist sympathies, and some of his closest allies were communists from the workers' and peasants' unions. Arbenz may even have believed that communism would eventually triumph in his country. He had legalized the Guatemalan Communist Party, which changed its name in 1952 to the Guatemalan Workers' Party (PGT in its Spanish acronym).

Yet communists themselves advised the president only to modernize Guatemala from a semi-feudal economy into a modern, capitalist one, for instance by giving expropriated land to small farmers and not the state. Arbenz also followed the advice of the International Bank for Reconstruction and Development and built more highways, ports, and houses. The president was not a member of the Communist Party, which had only 4000 in a country of nearly 3 million and held only four of the 61 seats in the Congress. The communists also had next to no influence in the military.

Details mattered little to U.S. policymakers. Evidence of a PGT relationship to the Soviet Union was "largely circumstantial," admitted the State Department, but U.S. officials believed that "such a tie must exist."[6] One U.S. ambassador to Guatemala applied the "duck test" to Arbenz: if it walks like a duck, swims like a duck, and quacks like a duck, then it doesn't need to be called a duck for everyone to know it's a duck. Ambassador to Guatemala John Peurifoy made the test plain for a House committee: "I spent six hours with [Arbenz] one evening, and he talked like a Communist, he thought like a Communist, he acted like a Communist, and if he is not one, Mr Chairman, he will do until one comes along."[7] Peurifoy also believed that "Communism is directed by the kremlin [*sic*] all over the world, and anyone who thinks differently doesn't know what he is talking about."[8] His deputy added that the communists "were very honest, very committed. That was the tragedy: the only people who were committed to hard work were those who were, by definition, our worst enemies."[9]

Guatemala experts at the CIA feared that land reform would weaken the political power of conservative landowners while binding the majority of peasants to Arbenz and the PGT. So the problem was political more than economic.

The U.S. government found many enemies of its enemy in Central America: Castillo Armas had studied at the U.S. Army school in Fort Leavenworth, Kansas, and his troops trained in the Panama Canal Zone. Nicaraguan dictator Anastasio Somoza, who told U.S. officials "Just give me the arms, and I'll clean up Guatemala for you in no time," allowed planes to fly out from his country.[10] And more than a few conservative Guatemalans were horrified by Arbenz's reforms, which tended to help not only the poor but also indigenous Guatemalans. Anti-reform violence began in the countryside before any U.S.-led invasion.

In August 1953, Eisenhower approved the covert overthrow, whose chances of success Allen Dulles estimated at "better than 40 percent but less than even."[11] In December, the CIA authorized an initial $3 million for the plotters, on the way to $4.5 million – more than it had ever spent on a covert operation.

As the invasion force trained in neighboring countries, Secretary Dulles tilled the diplomatic soil to justify the intervention. At the Tenth Inter-American Conference held in Caracas, Venezuela, in March 1954, he strong-armed fellow foreign ministers into passing a resolution declaring that international communism represented "alien despotism" in all the Americas for "its antidemocratic nature and its interventionist tendency."[12] Dulles did not note the irony in intervening against interventionism.

Guatemala's Foreign Minister, Guillermo Toriello Garrido, responded that there was "nothing novel or alien" in Guatemala's democratic reforms. Aiming his fire at Washington, he bemoaned that "those who boast of encouraging other people to travel the road to economic and political liberty decide to bring them to a halt," and he denounced the "active intervention against the Guatemalan Government" that would follow from the Caracas resolution. If the Soviets are planning an attack, "say so," concluded Toriello. But to police "man's thought" ran against the Pan-American principle of nonintervention.[13]

The State Department also boycotted arms sales to Guatemala. Cornered because he knew an invasion was coming, Arbenz secretly ordered 2000 tons of Czech weapons to be brought on a Swedish ship, the *Alfhem*. The CIA followed the ship's movements and in May publicly denounced the arms shipment, which made it look like Arbenz was indeed a tool of Moscow. CIA Director Dulles suggested that Arbenz might use these weapons to attack the Panama Canal, and *Life* magazine added that, with these weapons, "the Kremlin will gain a de facto foothold in the Western Hemisphere."[14] Buying the *Alfhem*'s weapons proved a fatal mistake by Arbenz, especially since the arms turned out to be rusted and unusable.

On June 17, 1954, Operation PBSUCCESS, as the coup was code-named at the CIA, began. Castillo Armas's 480 soldiers, many wearing sandals, invaded Guatemala's south from Honduras and El Salvador. They met defeat at Gualán and Puerto Barrios, giving Arbenz hope that the army would do its job and crush Armas. But the CIA came to the rescue. It bombarded Guatemalan roads, bridges, military installations, and pro-Arbenz property owners. From Florida, it fed

Figure 7.1 Guatemalan President Jacobo Arbenz talking to a crowd on June 18, 1954, a day into the U.S.-led invasion of his country. Courtesy of Associated Press.

lies to Guatemalans through radio that Arbenz was about to ban the revered Catholic Holy Week, exile the archbishop, and force children into re-education centers.

At the United Nations, meanwhile, Minister Toriello sounded the alarm that Guatemala "had been invaded by expeditionary forces forming part of an unlawful international aggression." The United States disingenuously responded that "the situation does not involve aggression but is a revolt of Guatemalans against Guatemalans."[15]

By June 23, Castillo Armas had grown his army to 1500, but the Guatemalan army had 5000 and the defeat of the intervention seemed assured. But Arbenz made a second fatal error by assuming that the military would defend him. "I never imagined that in a case of foreign aggression in which the liberty of our country, its honor and independence were at stake, the army could betray us," he later recalled.[16] Many officers, strong anti-communists, disliked the president and his quarrel with Washington. They refused to follow his orders to resist or to give arms to the communist party or popular organizations. Instead, they told Arbenz to step down. He did so on June 27 and went into exile.

Arbenz turned over the presidency to Colonel Carlos Enrique Díaz, who he believed would protect his reforms. But Ambassador Peurifoy got Díaz to step down, and soon after a new junta elected Castillo Armas as president.

The occupation of the Caribbean during World War II was one of the most successful U.S. interventions ever. Its massive manpower and geographic scope helped prevent an Axis attack on the region – its major purpose. It also brought wealth to certain areas, although that wealth was fleeting and brought about resentment. The broader U.S. effort to seal off the hemisphere during World War II also demonstrated that, despite the Good Neighbor Policy, Washington was ready to cajole dictators and to spy and bully supposed allies to get what it wanted.

The Guatemalan intervention had more ambivalent results, to say the least. In the short run, it seemed a smashing success. Demonstrating that he could not only contain Soviet advances but also roll them back, Eisenhower himself celebrated his prevention of a "Soviet beachhead" in the Americas, and the U.S. press echoed him, avoiding the word "invasion" to describe the invasion of Guatemala. United Fruit got its land back. However, the Justice Department sued UFCO for anti-trust violations, competition increased, and the company's profit margin and share prices collapsed. In 1972, UFCO sold its Guatemalan land to Del Monte. It changed its name to United Brands, and in 1975, after being caught bribing the government of Honduras, its president, Eli Black, jumped to his death from his corner office of the Pan Am Building in New York. UFCO still sells bananas today as Chiquita.

Inside Guatemala, the Communist Party was banned, and Castillo Armas suppressed unions and political parties that had worked with Arbenz. The new regime also took land back from the 500,000 Guatemalans who benefited from Decree 900 and gave it to rich land-owners and opened the country to foreigners owning large tracts of land. As a reward, the United States showered Guatemala with millions in aid. Consequently, poor and indigenous Guatemalans never again trusted the government. Some organized into violent guerrillas, and a civil war raged for four decades, killing 200,000 by the 1990s. U.S.-supported right-wing regimes murdered the overwhelming majority of those Guatemalans. At the height of the killing in 1980, one U.S. official sighed, "What we'd give to have an Arbenz now."[17]

The U.S. government did not admit to its role in the 1954 coup until decades later.

Such U.S. arrogance, and blindness to arrogance, was part and parcel of the ideological causes that distinguished the World War II and Guatemalan interventions from those that came before. In both instances, economic motives were not absent. But those who ordered interventions subsumed economics under a larger defense of their very way of life – first against Nazi fascism, then against Soviet communism. Economic disputes were simply code for political ones. If someone threatened a U.S. corporation, for instance, they were therefore communists and thus controlled by Moscow. The tragic irony was that Latin Americans often shared the "American dream" and passed reforms so that they could get closer to it.

Notes

1   Cited in Piero Gleijeses, *Shattered Hope: The Guatemalan Revolution and the United States, 1944–1954* (Princeton University Press, 1991), 4.

2   "Rum and Coca-Cola" cited in Robert Holden and Eric Zolov, eds., *Latin America and the United States: A Documentary History* (Oxford University Press, 2000), 171.

3 Cited in Nick Cullather, *Secret History: The CIA's Classified Account of Its Operations in Guatemala 1952–1954* (Stanford University Press, 1999), 22.

4 Cited in Cullather, *Secret History*, 16.

5 Cited in George Black, *The Good Neighbor: How the United States Wrote the History of Central America and the Caribbean* (Pantheon, 1988), 101.

6 Cited in Michael Grow, *U.S. Presidents and Latin American Interventions: Pursuing Regime Change in the Cold War* (University Press of Kansas, 2008), 17.

7 Cited in Richard H. Immerman, *The CIA in Guatemala: The Foreign Policy of Intervention* (University of Texas Press, 1982), 181.

8 Cited in Cullather, *Secret History*, 16.

9 Cited in Gleijeses, *Shattered Hope*, 7.

10 Cited in Gleijeses, *Shattered Hope*, 229.

11 Cited in Martha L. Cottam, *Images & Intervention: U.S. Policies in Latin America* (University of Pittsburgh Press, 1994), 43.

12 Caracas Declaration of Solidarity: March 28, 1954, available at http://avalon.law.yale.edu/20th_century/intam10.asp

13 "Address by His Excellency Guillermo Toriello Garrido," Third Plenary Session, March 5, 1954. Central Intelligence Agency Documents, Freedom of Information Act, www.foia.cia.gov.

14 Cited in Black, *Good Neighbor*, 99.

15 Cited in Cole Blasier, *The Hovering Giant: U.S. Responses to Revolutionary Change in Latin America 1910–1985* (University of Pittsburgh Press, 1985), 169–70.

16 Cited in Blasier, *Hovering Giant*, 173.

17 Cited in Walter LaFeber, *Inevitable Revolutions: The United States in Central America*, 2nd ed. (W. W. Norton, 1993), 9.

8

Containing Revolution, 1959–1990

If you are going to pronounce a new law that "wherever there is communism imposed against the will of the people then the U.S. shall enter," then we are going to have really terrible wars in the world.

> British Prime Minister Margaret Thatcher, referring to the U.S. intervention in Grenada[1]

U.S. military interventions from 1959 to the end of the Cold War, by and large, were *caused* by the desire to prevent the success and spread of the Cuban Revolution. The revolution intensified the Cold War in Latin America and the Caribbean by upping the ante in Washington's imagined two-player poker game with the Soviets in the region, a match in which every win by the opponent was a loss for the United States. Two large, direct landings by U.S. troops, in the Dominican Republic and Grenada, were meant to avoid "another Cuba." Two indirect interventions that involved only small numbers of CIA assets, in Cuba and Nicaragua, intended to sabotage socialist governments.

As in the Guatemala intervention of 1954, the extra-hemispheric *context* was the Cold War, which intensified also in Europe, Africa,

A Short History of U.S. Interventions in Latin America and the Caribbean,
First Edition. Alan McPherson.
© 2016 John Wiley & Sons, Inc. Published 2016 by John Wiley & Sons, Inc.

the Middle East, and especially Asia from the 1950s to the 1980s. U.S. policymakers increasingly saw Latin American socialists and communists not only as puppets of the Soviets but also as enmeshed in a global network of terrorist subversion. In the Americas, Havana stood at the center of this network.

Latin Americans were sharply divided between supporting and fearing socialist revolutions. Some governments were only too happy to *collaborate* with the anti-communist crusade in Washington, and with the help of U.S. weapons, training, and spying, some became the worst abusers of human rights. Most Latin Americans, however, whether socialists or not, tended to *contest* U.S. interventions in their hemisphere if only for the fact that Washington seemed to be creating new justifications for old-fashioned interventions – new *botellas* for old *vino*.

Most interventions were on the whole successful in containing revolution to Cuba, and sometimes even in promoting elections. But other *consequences* included bringing brutally repressive dictators to power and crushing the dreams for development of moderate reformers.

Cuba, 1961

The first U.S. intervention of this period, the failed invasion at Cuba's Bay of Pigs in April 1961, followed the rapid radicalization of the Cuban Revolution. On January 1, 1959, rebel leader Fidel Castro and his bearded comrades overthrew U.S.-backed dictator Fulgencio Batista. Castro's 26th of July Movement declared itself democratic yet began to undermine the sources of U.S. power on the island. The *castristas* and their allies slashed rents and utility rates, desegregated beaches and closed down casinos, and passed an agrarian reform law more radical than that of Jacobo Arbenz in Guatemala. Fidel, his brother Raúl, and Argentine physician Ernesto "Ché" Guevara had learned from Guatemala in 1954 that the CIA took advantage of open societies to spread propaganda and influence military officers and opposition politicians. So they "closed" Cuba by curtailing press freedoms, dismissing elections, sandbagging liberal democrats, and executing, jailing, or exiling disloyal officers and even *castristas* who disagreed with the revolution's hardening.

By late 1959, when the State Department resolved that Castro should be "checked or replaced," the Cuban had already become too powerful and most of his opponents had left for Florida.[2] In February 1960, Castro also signed a major trade deal with the Soviet Union, moving into its Cold War orbit. Doors were closing quickly. In June, Castro ordered U.S. refineries in Cuba to process Soviet crude oil; Washington forbade them, so Castro took the refineries. In July, President Dwight Eisenhower suspended 900,000 tons of Cuban sugar sales to the United States, so Castro nationalized the sugar industry. In January 1961, Castro told all but 11 of the 300 U.S. employees of the embassy to go home, so Eisenhower broke diplomatic relations.

Months earlier, in March 1960, Eisenhower had approved the CIA's "Program for Covert Action Against the Castro Regime," which included plans for a paramilitary force "to be introduced into Cuba to organize, train and lead resistance groups."[3] Shortly after, the agency revised its plan into an invasion plot. In May, training by CIA operatives began in Guatemala – a side-benefit of the 1954 intervention. Others trained in Florida, while pilots prepared to take off from Nicaragua. Participants were almost all Cuban exiles, almost 200,000 of whom left Cuba between 1960 and 1962. Meanwhile, the CIA increasingly sidelined Cubans such as Manuel Ray, who argued for an internal uprising co-ordinated with an outside attack; because Ray wanted "Castroism without Castro," the CIA called him a communist.[4] By fall 1960, the plan mostly coalesced around a full-blown invasion, including U.S. air support, and Castro's suspicious delegate at the United Nations contested any such plots.

John Kennedy was elected president in November 1960, and he soon after learned of the secret plans. His tough talk against Cuba during the campaign compelled him to support some kind of invasion. He also had incompatible goals – military success with plausible deniability, or the ability to claim no responsibility and be believable. The invasion he wanted could only succeed with U.S. military help, but he fatally downsized the force by ordering that no U.S. citizen be involved in the actual landing.

Plotters presented flawed plans to the president. The first called for a landing near Trinidad, on Cuba's southern coast, from which Brigade 2506, as the invaders now called themselves, could escape into the Escambray Mountains. But Kennedy feared it would attract too much attention. So on April 4, 1961, he approved a new plan, Operation Zapata, at the more remote Bay of Pigs, but from which any surviving invaders would have to wade through a massive swamp to get to the mountains where they could regroup.

Kennedy's first CIA director, Allen Dulles, was a holdover from the Eisenhower administration. He and Deputy Director for Plans Richard Bissell, along with the Joint Chiefs, convinced Kennedy and others in the White House that Operation Zapata would work. When Kennedy asked about the plan's chances, he was told they were "fair." He was not told that "fair" meant one in four.[5] The Bay of Pigs invasion was a go.

On April 15, 1961, B-26 bombers attacked four Cuban airfields, but failed to destroy Castro's air force. Two days later, the real invasion began. The 1300-man-strong Brigade 2506 set off from Puerto Cabezas, Nicaragua, headed for the Bay of Pigs. At 2 am, frogmen went ashore at a beach called Playa Girón to set up lights, then two battalions followed while another landed at Playa Larga. They unloaded 900 tons of supplies and 4000 weapons.

The Cuban response was swift and effective. Castro's air force sank the invaders' command-and-control ship. Two other ships filled with supplies and weapons foundered offshore. Cuban T-33 jets shot down 10 of the 12 invading bombers. On the beaches, those who landed faced a Cuban force of 35,000 out of a total army of 200,000. Kennedy had already decided against providing overt U.S. air support to help the invasion.

Pounded by artillery and tanks, within three days the invaders were pushed back to their landing area at Playa Girón and soon surrendered. The final tally was 114 exiles killed, 1189 captured. In December 1962, Castro would release 1113 in return for $53 million in food and medicine.

The exiles had expected local populations to rise up spontaneously upon seeing them land. That did not happen. On April 20, Kennedy admitted that the U.S. government was behind the operation. One writer called the Bay of Pigs "one of those rare politico-military events: a perfect failure."[6] Kennedy called it "the worst defeat of his career," admitting he had, in his words, "fucked up."[7] He forced Dulles and Bissell to resign and elevated his brother Bobby, the Attorney General, to police Cuban affairs. Bobby Kennedy intensified Operation Mongoose, the name given to the many plots to assassinate Castro and sabotage his régime.

Latin Americans largely contested the invasion attempt as a slap in the face of the doctrine of nonintervention that had been the bedrock of inter-American relations since the Good Neighbor Policy. Riots occurred outside almost every U.S. embassy in the hemisphere.

The most serious consequences were in Moscow and Havana. Castro declared himself, and the Revolution, to be officially Marxist-Leninist and therefore to follow the model of the Soviet Union, which called for the government to own all property, for religion to be abolished, and for elections to be unnecessary since working people enjoyed a "dictatorship" over themselves. Rejecting this vision, many Latin Americans broke with the Cuban Revolution, which up to that point had seemed merely nationalist, anti-dictatorial, and anti-imperialist.

Back in Cuba, the entire country remained on high alert, fearing the next invasion. That gave Castro an excuse to jail opponents and force socialist unity behind his defense against Yankee imperialists. Ché Guevara sarcastically told U.S. officials he wanted "to thank us very much for the invasion – that it had been a great political victory for them."[8]

Before the Bay of Pigs, the Soviets had few soldiers in Cuba and little fear of it being attacked. After, Soviet Premier Nikita Khrushchev began a massive military buildup of conventional forces. In April 1962, he hit upon the idea of secretly shipping nuclear-tipped missiles to the island so as to protect Cuba from any further invasion. This gambit sparked the Cuban Missile Crisis in October of that year.

Dominican Republic, 1965–1966

Barely a month after the Bay of Pigs, in May 1961, assassins ambushed and killed Dominican dictator Rafael Trujillo as he was driven down a country road on his way to see a mistress. These Dominicans had had enough of Trujillo's 31-year iron-fisted rule. Washington, in the past an ally of the strong anti-communist, also abandoned him, and the CIA even provided a few rifles, some of which made it into the hands of the shooters.

After Trujillo, however, *le déluge*. The Kennedy administration briefly supported the democratically elected Juan Bosch, showering him with Alliance for Progress funds, meant to keep Latin American poverty from leading to "other Cubas." But the Kennedy men soon suspected Bosch of being too weak to resist communists. In September 1963, after just nine months, an authoritarian cabal allied with large landowners and with the Catholic Church overthrew Bosch.

In Washington, the new president, Lyndon B. Johnson, recognized the Dominican régime in December 1963. Johnson and his Assistant Secretary of State for Latin American Affairs, Thomas Mann, spoke of supporting progressive democrats, but insisted more on anti-communism and tolerated military cold warriors. They shoveled $100 million to the "Triumvirate" or three-man government in Santo Domingo.

On April 24, 1965, junior officers overthrew the government of Donald Reid Cabral. They called themselves Constitutionalists and demanded the return of Bosch and his constitution. Socialist militants following the Cuban, Soviet, or Chinese line joined them. Armed Constitutionalist civilians quickly took control of the military revolt and of colonial Santo Domingo, prompting many in the police to take off their uniforms and flee.

Facing these revolutionaries were the Loyalists, who argued that Bosch backers were *all* communists. Their leader was General Elías Wessin y Wessin of the Armed Forces Training Center (CEFA), who had helped overthrow Bosch. On April 27, CEFA planes strafed the city and its tanks faced off with Constitutionalists on the Ozama bridge separating CEFA's base from Santo Domingo. The Constitutionalists prevailed, shocking everyone. Their new leader was Colonel Francisco Caamaño.

During these chaotic days, Johnson received exaggerated intelligence. CIA and other agents viewed the civil conflict between Dominicans as a Cold War crisis ripe for outside intervention. Some said that heads of loyalists were being paraded on spikes in Santo Domingo, that all Americans were in danger. Most alarming to Johnson, reports came in that Constitutionalists had trained in Cuba.

It was true that Castro had made of Cuba a training site for would-be guerrillas from throughout Latin America. Since Castro himself had spread the myth that he had begun the revolution with only a dozen fighters, many believed that a small group of dedicated communists could take over a Caribbean country.

But Johnson stretched the evidence to suggest that Castro was *directing* the Dominican rebels. When advisers said that no Cubans were involved, the president pointed to the danger of not invading: "I sure don't want to wake up a few hours later and say, 'Well, we were awaiting developments,' and find out Castro's in charge."[9] Domestically, the president feared that, if he did not pre-empt Cuban involvement, however imaginary, Republicans would trounce his party at the next election.

So he ordered Operation Power Pack. On April 27, a few US troops began evacuating U.S. citizens. The next day, Washington asked embattled Loyalist General Antonio Imbert to request a U.S. military intervention. While these troops continued to evacuate, their mission was now also to keep the "communists" from winning. By mid-May, U.S. soldiers and airmen on Dominican soil peaked at just under 24,000. The intervention did end the fighting and probably saved lives. But while the public mission was to separate the Constitutionalists and Loyalists, U.S. troops were in fact to "step in and squeeze the rebels [Constitutionalists] down," as Secretary of Defense Robert McNamara explained. "The Loyalists would have more power than the rebels and would come out on top."[10] The U.S. military gave Wessin logistical support, jammed Constitutionalist radio stations, and manned a cordon between them and the Loyalists.

Figure 8.1   President Lyndon Johnson, leaning at center, in a meeting with advisers about the Dominican intervention on its first day, April 28, 1965. By Yoichi Okamoto, White House Photo Office. Lyndon Baines Johnson Library.

After the military intervention came the diplomacy. Johnson, realizing he had ridden roughshod over decades of inter-American efforts at nonintervention, worked with the Organization of American States to transform the unilateral U.S. move into a pan-American one. Some Latin American statesmen were aghast.

However, Brazil supported Washington. There, a generation of officers trained by the U.S.-run School of the Americas in the most modern military techniques, but also indoctrinated by anti-communism, launched a coup against leftist president João Goulart in 1964. The Johnson government, identifying these Brazilians as responsible military leaders and not tin-pot dictators who would embarrass the United States as Trujillo and others had, supported the coup with what one historian called "the quiet intervention."[11] The CIA funded opposition campaigns. Johnson increasingly withheld aid. And finally, Operation

Brother Sam set up a military task force to help the plotters. It was not an intervention, but it might have turned into one had the Brazilians failed. They succeeded, and Brazil lived under a military government until 1985.

Back in the Dominican Republic, on May 6, the OAS approved the creation of the Inter-American Peace Force. Six countries, most importantly Brazil, contributed 2000 troops to add to the 9100 from the United States. Five of these countries were dictatorships, paying back Washington for its support.

With this "peace" established, the White House failed to mediate between Caamaño and Imbert and handed the task to the OAS and to experienced U.S. diplomat Ellsworth Bunker. By late summer, the Constitutionalists accepted a provisional government headed by Héctor García Godoy.

García Godoy spent his short time in office preparing the next election, in which the choice came down to two familiar faces – Bosch against Joaquín Balaguer, Trujillo's former right-hand man who now promised democratic rule and a return to peace with firm anti-communism. On June 1, 1966, with covert U.S. support for his campaign, Balaguer won handily, and U.S. troops left that summer. In all, 26 U.S. troops had died versus 2850 Dominicans.

The consequences for Dominicans were tremendous. The Balaguer era meant a dozen years of an authoritarian government in cahoots with a strongly anti-communist military. It repressed students, labor leaders, and women's groups and easily crushed guerrilla uprisings. Coincidentally, the United States loosened its immigration law in 1965, and gave thousands of visas to supporters of Bosch so as to avoid another civil war.

While LBJ and his team – not to mention three-quarters of the U.S. public – saw the Dominican intervention as successful, Senator William Fulbright, the chair of the Foreign Relations Committee, chided the White House for always equating revolution with communism, violating "inter-American law," weakening the OAS, and alienating "reformers and young people throughout Latin America."[12]

Support for Military Régimes

The U.S. backing of right-wing revolutions in Brazil in 1964 and in the Dominican Republic in 1965–1966 fit a pattern begun in earnest in the Johnson administration (1963–1969) and intensified in the Richard Nixon (1969–1974) and Gerald Ford (1974–1977) administrations. These presidents moved away from the Eisenhower–Kennedy approach of monopolizing weapons sales in the Western Hemisphere away from Europeans and entrusting those arms to dictators such as Trujillo and Batista. The Cuban Revolution and the assassination of Trujillo had shown that, when almost all the power and all the money rested within one man, his family, and a few cronies, that man could grow isolated and lose his supporters and eventually his military.

New military régimes that arose in the 1960s were no less ruthless but far more sophisticated. They were often not controlled just by one man, but by a *junta* or a handful of men. Unlike the old dictators, if one junta member were killed, another would replace him. Juntas were also more competent to run the economy, avoiding communism like a plague, of course, but also preventing the concentration of too much land or industry in the hands of one family or one corporation. Captains of industry came to trust juntas. These new "bureaucratic-authoritarian" régimes, finally, were far more efficient at spying, jailing, torturing, and killing political opponents. All fiercely anti-communist, deeply Catholic, and often fascist in their ideology, they believed in a "national security doctrine," or the idea that all critics of their rule, not just armed communists, were to be treated as enemies of the state, stripped of their rights, and hunted down.

From 1961 to 1966, nine Latin American countries suffered military coups and became such régimes. In 1962–1963 alone, democracies fell to coups in Argentina, Peru, Guatemala, Ecuador, Honduras, and the Dominican Republic. By the mid-1970s, the most powerful military régimes had emerged in Chile, Argentina, Brazil, Paraguay, and Uruguay. These machines of repression not only hunted "subversives" inside their borders but also formed Operation Condor to kill 50,000, "disappear" 30,000, and arrest and imprison 400,000 abroad.

The United States considered all these governments to be allies because of their anti-communism, and, apart from the Jimmy Carter administration (1977–1981), it rarely compelled them to respect human rights.

Washington was most directly involved in the rise and maintenance of the Augusto Pinochet dictatorship in Chile, which lasted from 1973 to 1990. For decades before that, Chile had been a stable and relatively prosperous democracy, a shining exception among its South American neighbors. But a charismatic doctor named Salvador Allende, a Marxist and leader of a coalition of leftists, won the presidential election of 1970 when his opponents split the conservative vote. He promised to nationalize the companies that extracted copper, Chile's main export.

The Nixon government panicked. Including copper companies, U.S. investors owned $1 billion of Chile, and some, such as PepsiCo and International Telegraph and Telephone, approached Nixon to help pay to prevent Allende from taking office after he had won the election. In the White House and the State Department, the greater fear was that Allende would show the peaceful, democratic road to socialism – *la vía chilena* or the Chilean way, as Chileans called it. Before Allende could be confirmed president by the legislature, Nixon ordered the CIA to "make the economy scream" and to "save Chile!"[13]

"The President asked the Agency to prevent Allende from coming to power or to unseat him," concluded CIA Director Richard Helms from the president's instructions. Nixon had indeed said he wanted to "smash" the Chilean.[14] The CIA thus provided Chilean coup plotters with submachine guns, gas grenades, and masks, and encouraged kidnapping René Schneider, the Chilean army commander-in-chief who was to oversee Allende's confirmation. The plot failed, but days later an overlapping group did capture and then kill Schneider.

This was the most direct U.S. intervention against Allende. But it failed. Chilean lawmakers, horrified by this interruption of their constitution, confirmed the president-elect. Then came the U.S.-assisted screams from the economy. Over the next three years, the CIA spent $8 million to fund opponents of Allende, pay for radio stations and newspapers, and support a major strike uniting truckers, merchants, and professionals. Nixon scrapped new Export-Import Bank guarantees to Chile, stopped all new aid programs except for food, delayed existing programs, and pressured foreign investors to pull out of Chile.

Allende called these moves "the invisible blockade," but it was not an intervention as defined in this book.[15] It had no U.S. boots on the ground. Pinochet was no puppet, and his military was not a "proxy" as the Bay of Pigs brigade had been. However – and this was a big "however" – Pinochet may never have come to power or remained in power if the United States had defended the principle of democracy in Chile. Pinochet grabbed the presidency along with his junta in a bloody attack on the presidential palace on September 11, 1973, that soon killed over 3000. Nixon and Kissinger welcomed him with open arms.

Nicaragua, 1979–1990

Despite the shift toward U.S.-friendly right-wing military governments in the 1960s and 1970s, in the 1980s, Washington grew frustrated, unable to overthrow a second socialist régime in the Americas. In Nicaragua as in Cuba, Washington stood helplessly while a years-long guerrilla war unseated a U.S.-supported dictator – in this case, Anastasio "Tachito" Somoza Debayle, the son of the National Guard leader of the same name who had Augusto Sandino assassinated in 1934. In response, the CIA, as in the Bay of Pigs, formed a proxy army to overthrow a régime it disliked. This indirect Nicaraguan U.S. intervention, conceived as "low-intensity warfare," was much longer lasting than the Bay of Pigs. In the short term, it also failed. But after a decade, it contributed to convincing Nicaraguan voters to abandon their socialist leaders.

The Sandinista revolution that triumphed against Somoza on July 19, 1979, was not friendly to the United States. With backing from Washington, Somoza had not only enriched his own family but also promoted exports and concentrated land in the hands of few, leaving many landless. After a devastating Managua earthquake in 1972, his National Guard *sold* foreign aid to desperate Nicaraguans. One observer noted how Guardsmen sold "anything from a small electric generator to a water purifier, electric torches, pickaxes and spades, [and] complete factory-sealed blood transfusion equipment."[16] In 1978, gunmen pulled up to opposition journalist Pedro Joaquín Chamorro's car and riddled him with bullets. Such brazen despotism sickened Nicaraguans, who turned to the Sandinista National Liberation Front (FSLN in its Spanish acronym). The Carter administration cut off aid to Tachito and approached the FSLN not as puppets of Moscow or Havana but as homegrown revolutionaries. Yet Carter's diplomats were never able to find a viable, middle-class, democratic alternative to Somoza and the FSLN.

The FSLN, led by Daniel Ortega, began radical social programs in health, farming, and literacy to undo what they saw as the damage caused by decades of a U.S.-friendly thieving dictatorship. By 1980, 2000 Cubans and 200 Soviets worked in Nicaragua.

All of this was legal and legitimate for a sovereign state. What was unacceptable to Washington was the FSLN's sale of weapons to a neighboring rebellion in El Salvador by the Farabundo Martí National Liberation Front (FMLN in Spanish), also fighting a U.S.-supported right-wing régime. This attempt to spread revolution to another country prompted Carter to send $19.5 million to nonmilitary opponents of the FSLN and to end $75 million in promised aid to Nicaragua.

Ronald Reagan took the White House from Carter in 1980 partly by arguing that the FSLN victory exposed a weak Democratic president. Reagan warned that Nicaragua not only helped spread communism in Latin America but also threatened Mexican oil fields, the Panama Canal – which Carter had agreed to hand over to Panamanians – and Caribbean sea lanes. "The national security of all the Americas is at stake in Central America. If we cannot defend ourselves there, we cannot expect to prevail elsewhere. Our credibility would collapse, our alliances would crumble, and the safety of the homeland would be put in jeopardy."[17] Hollywood hopped on the paranoid bandwagon, releasing 1984's *Red Dawn*, a survivalist fantasy in which Nicaraguans, allied with Cubans and Soviets, somehow took over the United States, only to meet resistance from Colorado teens organized into a guerrilla force.

In reality, the Reagan administration was not united in *how* to undermine the Nicaraguan government. Since the United States had lost the Vietnam War in 1975, a consensus of sorts existed that U.S. troops, to be sent abroad, had to defend a vital national interest, fully commit resources, express clear objectives, reassess goals and resources, gain U.S. public and Congressional support, and be used as a last resort.

"I *never* considered sending U.S. troops to fight in Latin America," Reagan wrote in his memoirs.[18] And Congress did not believe that the small, poor revolution in Nicaragua threatened U.S. security. Reagan did attempt negotiations, but there was too much distrust between him and the FSLN. To pressure them, on November 23, 1981, the president ordered the CIA to begin covert operations through a fighting force of collaborators called the Contras, short for *contrarevolucionarios* or counter-revolutionaries. Most were former Somoza soldiers, others were former guerrillas disenchanted with the hardening revolution, while still others were peasants frustrated by the new socialist régime's atheism, rationing, and low prices for their crops and live-stock. The military junta in Argentina, in power since 1975, had already financed and trained these Contras for months in El Salvador, Guatemala, and Honduras. When Reagan began funding the Contras, they numbered 500. By November 1983, they were 12,000 strong.

Funding the Contras fit into a greater context, a global "Reagan Doctrine": supporting guerrillas against Soviet-backed governments not only in Central America but also in Afghanistan, Cambodia, and Angola.

On paper, the Contras were only supposed to stop the flow of weapons to El Salvador. But their true war aim, and that of the White House, was to overthrow the Nicaraguan government. When evidence surfaced that the FSLN had curtailed gun running in 1981 and that there was no export of weapons in 1986, the Reagan administration stuck to its story. Reagan also described the Contras as "the moral equivalent of our Founding Fathers and the brave men and women of the French Resistance," yet one of his operatives told the Contras, "The only way to defeat Communism is by using the same means, the same tactics. Kidnap, kill, torture, rob. Democratic means are not effective."[19] The Contras also trafficked drugs on CIA planes and laundered money.

Angered, Congress passed two amendments in 1982 and 1984, both sponsored by Edward Boland, chair of the House Intelligence Committee. The first prohibited spending any money in Nicaragua "for the purpose of overthrowing the government of Nicaragua or provoking a military exchange between Nicaragua and Honduras." Reagan was incensed: "The Sandinistas have openly proclaimed Communism in their country and their support of Marxist revolutions throughout Central America. They're killing and torturing people! Now, what the hell does Congress expect me to do about that?"[20] What he did was to use funds to prohibit guns going from Nicaragua to El Salvador. So Congress passed Boland II, which was more explicit:

> No funds available to the Central Intelligence Agency, the Department of Defense, or any other agency or entity of the United States involved in intelligence activities may be obligated or expended for the purpose or which would have the effect of supporting, directly or indirectly, military or paramilitary operations in Nicaragua by any action, group, organization, movement or individual.

"There are no exceptions to the prohibition," added the amendment's author.[21]

The Contra intervention was not all indirect. To intimidate the FSLN, the U.S. military itself conducted massive exercises off the coast of Nicaragua and in the Caribbean. Washington also increased military aid to Nicaragua's hostile neighbors – El Salvador, Guatemala, and Honduras. Most directly, in 1983–1984 the CIA sent its own U.S. employees into Nicaragua. They and the Unilaterally Controlled Latino Assets, who were scuba divers and other operatives, dove off CIA ships and dropped mines into the water of Nicaraguan ports – all approved by Reagan but hidden from Congress. The CIA told the

Contras to take credit for the mining, whose purpose was to make shipping insurance more expensive and thus discourage trade with Nicaragua.

Mining the harbor of another country was an act of war, not to mention that ships from third countries such as the Soviet Union and the Netherlands struck the mines. When it found out about the mining, the U.S. Senate condemned it 84 to 12. Nicaragua sued the United States at the International Court of Justice (ICJ). In 1986's *Nicaragua v. The United States of America* case, the ICJ judged U.S. Contra support "a clear breach of the principle of nonintervention."[22] The United States argued that the ICJ lacked jurisdiction, then refused to participate. It also stopped the United Nations Security Council from enforcing the judgment.

The Boland amendments were a clear warning to stop funding the Contras. So in summer 1984, the National Security Planning Group met in the White House to think about how to get around the air-tight prohibition. What if private sources funded the Contras? Secretary of State George Shultz and others warned that such a route might be "an impeachable offense." Reagan was more worried about keeping the plan secret. "If such a story gets out," he said to close the meeting, "we'll all be hanging by our thumbs in front of the White House until we found out who did it."[23]

In defiance of Boland, in summer 1984, a White House group including National Security Adviser John Poindexter, CIA Director William Casey, and Lieutenant Colonel Oliver North raised funds secretly from private individuals, private organizations such as Pat Robertson's Christian television program *The 700 Club*, and allied governments from Taiwan to Israel to keep the Contras active. Enterprise members joked about donations as "Contra-butions."[24] Saudi Arabia gave the biggest Contra-bution – $32 million. Reagan knew about all this. He allegedly was kept isolated, however, from a plan to divert profits from overpriced weapon sales to Iran – already against policy – into the coffers of the Contras.

When this last scheme was exposed, it became the Iran–Contra scandal. Three investigations exposed what many considered illegal and immoral actions by Reagan's close advisers. Proponents countered that North and others had done nothing illegal and had defended the U.S. Constitution because they fought communism. Ironically, right before the Iran–Contra scandal erupted, Congress reversed course and sent $100 million to the Contras. Between 1981 and 1990, the U.S. government would give them $322 million.

No matter how much they received, however, the Contras – who a Reagan insider admitted were "men of unproven abilities and sometimes unclear motives" – remained unable to win over towns or other territory from the FSLN.[25] One high-level Contra explained how their brigades would "arrive at an undefended village, assemble all the residents in the town square and then proceed to kill – in full view of the others – all persons suspected of working" with the government.[26] They also mutilated, tortured, and raped. The Contras eventually turned to sabotaging the revolution's economy and morale, hitting schools and health centers, co-operatives, power stations, and oil depots, inflicting hundreds of millions of dollars in damage. In 1988, Nicaraguan inflation peaked at 36,000 percent. Tens of thousands became refugees.

This war against civilians took a psychological toll. In 1990, the Ortega government agreed to a second election. It had handily won the election in 1985 when its opponents withdrew. Now, anti-FSLN groups united behind the candidacy of Violeta Chamorro, Pedro Joaquín's widow and a grandmotherly symbol who promised peace after a decade of war – something Ortega could not deliver. The George H.W. Bush administration provided $30 million in covert funding, and Chamorro won. The people of Nicaragua, a majority of whom had backed the FSLN throughout the decade, voted to end their seemingly endless national nightmare.

By 1990, the changing global context had lowered the stakes in Nicaragua. The Soviet Union was slowly collapsing and had for years been in negotiations with the United States to diminish the nuclear threat. Eastern Europe had revolted against Soviet-communist control, and the Berlin Wall had come down. And, devastating for Fidel Castro and the FSLN, the Soviet government had ceased to fund them.

The consequences of the Contra intervention for Nicaragua included a devastating loss of 30,000 lives – not counting the 10,000 who perished in the war against Somoza in 1978–1979. An equivalent war in the United States would have killed over 3 million. Daniel Ortega lost the 1990 election but remained at the helm of the FSLN, which became only one political party among others. In 2007, it carried Ortega back to the presidency, from which he continued to contest U.S. policies in Latin America. In 2011 he suggested resurrecting the claim of $17 billion that he had advanced after the ICJ judgment in 1986 and that "Violeta" had dropped in 1991.

Grenada, 1983

In the middle of its proxy war in Nicaragua, the Reagan administration also flexed its muscles against the tiny, English-speaking Caribbean island of Grenada, but this time in a direct, massive mobilization of U.S. troops. The cause was similar to that of the Nicaraguan Contras – to fight the spread of Cuban-Soviet influence in the hemisphere.

U.S.–Grenadian relations began to sour in March 1979, when Maurice Bishop led his New Jewel Movement to a bloodless coup. Similar to Ortega of Nicaragua, Bishop was a Marxist and had close relations with the Cubans and Soviets. In response to the U.S. Ambassador to Barbados and the Eastern Caribbean's warning to Bishop not to seek aid from Cuba, the Grenadian went on the radio to proclaim, "Nobody has the right to tell us what to do or how to run our country or who to be friendly with … We are not in anybody's backyard and we are not for sale."[27] Economically, Grenada was insignificant – a former British colony of 110,000 souls, the size of Martha's Vineyard, that exported cocoa, nutmeg, and bananas. Under Bishop, most land and businesses remained in private hands.

Still, Reagan called for an overthrow, if not yet a U.S. invasion. On October 4, 1983, he signed National Security Decision Directive 105, which ordered plans for destabilizing the economy of Grenada, for routing its government, and for ridding the island of Cuban and Soviet influence. Then Reagan got the best gift he could have asked for when the island fell under a far more radical régime. Because they considered Bishop too moderate, Bernard Coard, his wife Phyllis, and the armed forces overthrew him on October 13, and on October 19 soldiers executed Bishop along with Cabinet members. The Revolutionary Military Council (RMC) headed by General Hudson Austin eventually took over and announced a curfew: "No one is to leave their house. Anyone violating this curfew will be shot on sight."[28]

Reagan's national security adviser for Latin America saw in this crisis "an excellent chance to restore democracy in Grenada while assuring the safety of our citizens."[29] The Reagan administration set its sights on Cuban construction crews helping build a 10,000-foot airstrip, saying it would serve as a Soviet base. From the Oval Office, Reagan showed blurry satellite photos of the airfield: "Grenada does not even have an air force. Who is it intended for?"[30]

Tourists, said the Grenadians. Contractors, including U.S. and European companies, also denied military capabilities. The project had been planned since 1955.

But, as in Nicaragua, Reagan thought primarily of the global context and saw outside communist penetration in the Americas. U.S. officials hoped an invasion would "send some shivers up Castro's spine about whether or not they might be next."[31]

As the immediate cause of the intervention, Reagan argued that some 600 U.S. medical students, the bulk of about 1000 U.S. citizens in Grenada, would be taken hostage. He, like many others, feared a repeat of the 444 days from 1979 to 1981 when Iranians kept dozens of U.S. diplomats hostage and made the United States look impotent. With Iran and Vietnam on their minds, therefore, military planners called for an overwhelming force to protect U.S. lives and overthrow the RMC. Naval forces on their way to the Mediterranean turned around and headed to Grenada. Still, said a Navy spokesperson on October 21, "there are not going to be any landings or anything like that."[32]

On October 23, a suicide bomber drove a truck filled with explosives and gases into the marines' barracks in far-off Lebanon, killing 241. Immediately, the chairman of the Joint Chiefs of Staff suggested that one war was enough for the moment and that diplomats could probably get the students out of Grenada. Still, on the evening of the Lebanon bombing, Reagan signed the invasion plan. Next to his name he wrote one word: "Go."[33]

Democrats and Republicans in Congress objected that no U.S. citizens had been threatened and that the Constitution said nothing about the president ordering régime changes. But Reagan insisted on his powers and on a military solution without a declaration of war. "You are informing us," Speaker of the House Tip O'Neill chided Reagan, "not asking us."[34] And, to help make up for Lebanon, the role of the Marine Corps in Grenada expanded.

In the early hours of October 25, 1983, 12 days after the coup against Bishop, Operation Urgent Fury began. A battle group was shaped around the aircraft carrier *Independence* and the 22nd Marine Amphibious Unit, supported by the amphibious assault ship *Guam*. Two Ranger battalions, a brigade of the 82nd Airborne Division, and special operations forces joined them from the mainland. The marines commanded in the north, the Army in the south.

The invasion did not go as smoothly as it should have, considering that Grenada only had a 2000-man army and no navy. Planning teams sometimes worked with maps dating from 1895, and those on the ground had nothing but tourist maps of "Grenada: The Isle of Spice." The SEAL Team Six intending to parachute near the island even failed to account for a one-hour daylight saving time change. "It was pitch black outside. We couldn't see a thing," recalled the jumpmaster. Sixteen men jumped too low to the water, with high winds keeping their chutes inflated in the surging waves. Four men were never found.[35] Once on the island, communications were spotty. A marine team erroneously called in an airstrike on an army command post, wounding seven U.S. soldiers and killing one. Seventeen of the 19 U.S. dead were from friendly fire or accidents. Navy pilots mistakenly blew up a psychiatric hospital, killing 18 patients.

Incompetence resulted partly from secrecy. Planners failed to share with the National Security Agency, which in turn could have provided intelligence on phone calls and radio traffic. Reagan also kept the mission from the British, even though Grenada was a member of the British Commonwealth, a free association of former colonies. And, in a break with tradition, reporters were kept in as much darkness as the SEAL team. When asked directly about military action in Grenada, National Security Adviser John Poindexter – who would also be caught lying in the Iran–Contra affair – responded, "Preposterous!"[36]

The Reagan administration also had no diplomats on the island, and the U.S. Ambassador to the Barbados had forbidden his team from visiting Grenada or contacting its leaders. They simply assumed that all law and order had broken down and that the U.S. medical students at St George's University School of Medicine were essentially hostages.

Once landed, the marines encountered little resistance and moved south. Rangers parachuted into Point Salinas airport and overwhelmed the Cubans and Grenadians firing at them. Without contacting anyone at St George's, without finding out that the students were perfectly safe, the Rangers "rescued" the students. Or at least some of them: more than two-thirds were at another campus a few miles away. The students had been in their dorms for 36 hours after the first troops landed, with no Grenadians or Cubans threatening them. When their dean asked if they wanted to leave Grenada, 90 percent said no.

Most combat was over two days later on October 27. Eight thousand U.S. forces had participated, at a cost of $135 million. The casualties were light. The U.S. military suffered 19 deaths and 116 injuries; Cubans, 25 deaths and 59 injuries; Grenadians, 45 deaths and 358 injuries. Seventy-one percent of U.S. citizens approved. The U.S. military considered it a success, and Reagan's approval rating jumped from the thirties to the sixties.

The rest of the world was not in such a celebratory mood. Prime Minister Margaret Thatcher, usually a Reagan fan, was furious. The United Nations Security Council voted 11–1 "deeply deploring" the invasion as a "flagrant violation of international law," but the United States vetoed the resolution.[37] When told that a hundred more nations agreed with the resolution, Reagan quipped, "It didn't upset my breakfast at all."[38]

On the plus side for Washington, Barbados, Jamaica, and small states in the Eastern Caribbean supported the invasion. Many of their conservative leaders had warned of dangers to U.S. citizens, and the seven-member Organization of Eastern Caribbean States had formally requested U.S. intervention on October 23. Perhaps most heartening, 91 percent of Grenadians were "glad the United States troops [had come] to Grenada."[39]

The U.S. military quickly gave way to a civilian government backed by a multinational force and referred to Article 8 of its treaty to justify the "pre-emptive defensive strike."[40] The invasion uncovered several buildings full of arms and secret military agreements with the Soviet Union, Cuba, and North Korea. They called for training Grenadians. But there were no plans for a Soviet or Cuban military base.

U.S. military interventions in Latin America and the Caribbean from 1961 to the 1980s reflected two sets of causes. On one hand, they mirrored other U.S. overt and covert military adventures to help locals fight communist aggression. They reflected the paranoia that communists were everywhere and able to manipulate every situation to their advantage. On the other hand, they also reflected U.S. thinking about Latin Americans – that they were unable to govern themselves and that communists would easily fool them. The national security apparatus in Washington thus demanded control over any anti-communist crusade. One common consequence was the neglect not only of Latin American democracy but also, often, of the U.S. Congress and Constitution.

Notes

1 Cited in Robert J. Beck, *The Grenada Invasion: Politics, Law, and Foreign Policy Decisionmaking* (Westview Press, 1993), 2–3.
2 Cited in Michael Grow, *U.S. Presidents and Latin American Interventions: Pursuing Regime Change in the Cold War* (University Press of Kansas, 2008), 37.

3   Grow, *U.S. Presidents*, 38.
4   Cited in Lester Langley, *The United States and the Caribbean in the Twentieth Century*, rev. ed. (University of Georgia Press, 1985), 220.
5   Lester Langley, *America and the Americas: The United States in the Western Hemisphere*, 2nd ed. (University of Georgia Press, 2010), 201.
6   Theodore Draper cited in George Black, *The Good Neighbor: How the United States Wrote the History of Central America and the Caribbean* (Pantheon, 1988), 106.
7   Theodore Sorensen and Kennedy cited in Grow, *U.S. Presidents*, 28.
8   Cited in Hal Brands, *Latin America's Cold War* (Harvard University Press, 2010), 35.
9   Recording of telephone conversation between Johnson and National Security Advisor McGeorge Bundy, 29 April 1965, 9.48 am, WH6504.06, Lyndon Baines Johnson Library.
10 Recording of telephone conversation between Johnson and McNamara, 19 May 1965, 12.37 pm, WH6506.26, Lyndon Baines Johnson Library.
11 Phyllis R. Parker, *Brazil and the Quiet Intervention, 1964* (Kent State University Press, 1990).
12 Cited in Robert Holden and Eric Zolov, eds., *Latin America and the United States: A Documentary History* (Oxford University Press, 2000), 248.
13 CIA, Richard Helms handwritten notes, "Meeting with the President on Chile at 1525," 15 September 1970, reproduced in Kornbluh, *The Pinochet File*, Chapter 1, Document 1.
14 CIA memorandum, 16 September 1970, reproduced in *ibid.*, Chapter 1, Document 2.
15 Paul Sigmund, *The United States and Democracy in Chile* (Johns Hopkins University Press, 1993), 57.
16 Cited in Black, *Good Neighbor*, 129.
17 Rachel Maddow, *Drift: The Unmooring of American Military Power* (Crown Publishers, 2012), 78.
18 Ronald Reagan, *An American Life: The Autobiography* (Simon & Schuster, 1990), 475.
19 Cited in Christopher Dickey, *With the Contras: A Reporter in the Wilds of Nicaragua* (Simon & Schuster, 2008), epigraph; cited in Brands, *Latin America's Cold War*, 212–13.
20 Reagan, *An American Life*, 479.
21 Cited in U.S. House and Senate, *Report of the Congressional Committees Investigating the Iran-Contra Affair*, 100th Cong., 1st Sess. (Washington, D.C.: USGPO, 1987), 398.

22 International Court of Justice judgment, "Nicaragua v. United States of America," 27 June 1986, available at www.icj-cij.org/docket/?sum=367&p1=3&p2=3&case=70&p3=5

23 Cited in Maddow, *Drift*, 109.

24 Maddow, *Drift*, 107.

25 Robert Kagan, *A Twilight Struggle: American Power in Nicaragua, 1977–1990* (Free Press, 1996), 221.

26 Cited in Greg Grandin, *Empire's Workshop: Latin America, the United States, and the Rise of the New Imperialism* (Metropolitan, 2006), 115.

27 Bishop cited in Cole Blasier, *The Hovering Giant: U.S. Responses to Revolutionary Change in Latin America 1910–1985* (University of Pittsburgh Press, 1985), 282.

28 Maddow, *Drift*, 75.

29 Maddow, *Drift*, 79.

30 Cited in Grow, *U.S. Presidents*, 145.

31 Cited in Grow, *U.S. Presidents*, 155.

32 Cited in Stephen Kinzer, *Overthrow: America's Century of Regime Change from Hawaii to Iraq* (Henry Holt, 2006), 219.

33 Kinzer, *Overthrow*, 232.

34 Maddow, *Drift*, 83.

35 Maddow, *Drift*, 72, 71.

36 Cited in Beck, *The Grenada Invasion*, 162.

37 Cited in Reynold A. Burrowes, *Revolution and Rescue in Grenada: An Account of the U.S.-Caribbean Invasion* (Greenwood Press, 1988), 94.

38 Cited in Beck, *The Grenada Invasion*, 66.

39 Cited in Beck, *The Grenada Invasion*, 2.

40 Cited in William C. Gilmore, *The Grenada Invasion: Analysis and Documentation* (Facts on File, 1984), 43.

9

Identifying Post-Cold War Political Threats, 1986–2016

It isn't important whether [Manuel Noriega] was a communist.

Col. Samuel Dickens (Ret.)[1]

U.S. interventions in post-Cold War Latin America and the Caribbean were contradictory. On one hand, they did not elicit as much criticism as before, for two reasons. First, post-Cold War interventions shifted even further toward multilateralism, and this time not the superficial multilateralism seen during the Guatemalan, Dominican, and Grenadian episodes of the Cold War. This time, *collaboration* by other nations of the hemisphere was offered earlier, more willingly, and almost exclusively by democratic governments. In Panama – and technically still within the era of the Cold War, which ended in 1991 – the United States acted in a traditional manner: by itself and seeking diplomatic cover later. Yet two Haiti interventions showed an evolution toward multilateralism prior to intervention.

Second, new U.S. military interventions had more pragmatic and less ideological overtones. Especially since 1989, interventions reflected, as they always had, larger *contextual* changes in international politics. Simply put, the Soviet Union no longer existed and thus no longer helped Cuba, and Cuba itself plunged into an economic crisis

A Short History of U.S. Interventions in Latin America and the Caribbean,
First Edition. Alan McPherson.
© 2016 John Wiley & Sons, Inc. Published 2016 by John Wiley & Sons, Inc.

that made it difficult for the island to train or subsidize leftists elsewhere. In response, U.S. interventions no longer reflected concerns about communism in the hemisphere. Instead, the new *causes* were post-Cold War U.S. worries about Latin American politics: fragile democracies, drug trafficking and narcorégimes, and desperate refugees flooding U.S. shores. For that reason, U.S. policymakers were no longer willing to ally with any anti-communist, no matter their record on human rights. Also for that reason, Latin Americans' responses were less ideologically charged, and they became more likely to tolerate U.S. troops on their soil.

On the other hand, many U.S. citizens and Latin Americans did continue to *contest* U.S. interventions. Sometimes it was merely on the principle that American republics should respect nonintervention. At other times, critics pointed to specific negative consequences stemming from interventions, such as the death of innocents or the ousting of democratic leaders. And finally, others warned that a growing U.S. military presence in the hemisphere was, in itself, evidence of the continuing desire by Washington to control its southern neighbors. Such fears demonstrated the weight of memory and history in the consciousness of the hemisphere.

Panama, 1989

Operation Just Cause, the code name of the U.S. invasion of Panama on December 19, 1989, stemmed from several causes that developed over the preceding years.

One cause – the most public, but maybe not the most important – was the U.S. turn toward "democracy promotion" against the ruthless rule of General Manuel Noriega. Noriega had never been a democrat, but, as chief of military intelligence in the 1970s, was subordinated to President Omar Torrijos. In 1981, Torrijos died in a mysterious plane crash, and many suspected the hidden hand of Noriega, now the commander of the Panama Defense Force (PDF), whose job became more political than military. Many so-called presidents of Panama in the 1980s were puppets of Noriega, a borderline psychopath who murdered political opponents such as Hugo Spadafora, who was found decapitated and mutilated in 1985.

In June 1987, Noriega announced that the second most powerful man in Panama, Colonel Roberto Díaz Herrera, was "retiring." Díaz in turn accused the strongman – nicknamed "pineapple face" for his severe acne – of murder, drug trafficking, corruption, electoral fraud, and orchestrating Torrijos's plane crash. The opposition organized the National Civic Crusade (NCC), which hit the streets calling for Noriega's departure.

The U.S. Congress and State Department sided with the NCC, and the Central Intelligence Agency (CIA) secretly gave it $10 million. Noriega responded by sending a mob of Panamanians to stone the U.S. embassy. In December, the government of Ronald Reagan cut off military and economic aid to Noriega because tensions with the Soviets were easing and Panama posed no communist threat. In the minds of conservatives such as Assistant Secretary of State for Inter-American Affairs Elliott Abrams, democracy promotion went hand in hand with the Contra war in Nicaragua, since both aimed to end dictatorships and usher in fair elections and other elements of democracy. One model used in Panama was the People Power Revolution in the Philippines, which had recently taken down strongman Ferdinand Marcos.

A second cause of the invasion – and its legal justification – was Noriega's long history of drug trafficking. From the late 1950s to the early 1980s, Noriega had been "in bed" with the CIA, giving it intelligence in exchange for being left alone to run drugs and guns and launder money. By itself, allowing Colombians to clean up their drug profits in Panamanian banks brought Noriega $4 million per *month*. Pineapple Face was on the payroll of at least 10 intelligence agencies, including in Colombia, El Salvador, Syria, and Palestine. Noriega even sold intelligence to the Cubans, and Washington knew it. "Sure, Noriega worked for the Cubans," explained one intelligence officer. "But we calculated he belonged twenty percent to them and eighty percent to us."[2] This included in 1976, when Noriega met with George H.W. Bush, the Director of the CIA who, as president in 1989, would order the invasion.

Against the wishes of the CIA and the Drug Enforcement Administration, in February 1988, two U.S. grand juries brought indictments against Noriega for drug trafficking. The State Department and U.S. Southern Command (SOUTHCOM) were even caught by surprise, and SOUTHCOM prepared contingency plans for a buildup of U.S. forces in the Panama Canal Zone, the evacuation of U.S. military and civilians, combat against the PDF, and postconflict reconstruction.

After those indictments, events in Panama sped up. On March 16, part of the PDF, along with the Christian Democratic Party, failed to overthrow Noriega, who cracked down on his opposition. The following month, Reagan banned any transactions with the Panamanian government. While SOUTHCOM built up its forces, Noriega switched from buying U.S. to Soviet weapons.

U.S. government agencies were split. Diplomats largely wanted Noriega out, while the military, spies, and anti-drug officials considered Noriega too valuable. Admiral William Crowe of the Joint Chiefs of Staff argued that other countries hosting U.S. bases might fear they were next: "How do you expect those governments would react to the specter of the U.S. using its bases to overthrow a country's leadership?"[3] Others weighed domestic politics: it was safer to wait until after the November 1988 elections in which Vice President Bush was the Republican candidate. Noriega agreed to hold his own elections on May 7, 1989, so Washington watched and waited.

Campaigning for the Panamanian election appeared free. But after the vote, Noriega stopped the count before the final tally. The candidates who were supposed to have won took to the streets and were savagely beaten by the Dignity Battalions ("Dingbats" for short), Noriega's paramilitary thugs. Presidential candidate Guillermo Endara was sent to the hospital, while Guillermo "Billy" Ford, his second vice presidential candidate, appeared bloodied by the Dingbats on magazine covers and television screens around the world. In response, a brigade of the 7th Infantry Division arrived in the Canal Zone, U.S. families left off-base housing, and the embassy sent nonessential personnel stateside. On October 3, a failed coup by Major Moses Giroldi, leaked to the U.S. military days before, only increased tensions. On December 15, Noriega declared himself head of government and said "a state of war" existed in Panama.[4] It was not a declaration of war but rather an accusation against Washington. A third cause was that Noriega, given his involvement in drugs, assassinations, and double-dealing, knew too much. He had met with Oliver North of the Iran–Contra affair to discuss financing the Contras and bombing Nicaragua. Vice President Bush, Noriega revealed, wanted his help so much that he looked the other way on money laundering and dictatorship in Panama. Bush's 1988 Republican challenger, Bob Dole, accused Bush of "playing footsie with this guy" even though Noriega "was up to his eyeballs in dirty drugs and anti-American politics."[5] Explaining the invasion, former CIA Director Stansfield Turner declared of Noriega, "I don't think we can afford to let him tell everything he knows about the U.S. intelligence organizations."[6]

Fourth, Bush wanted to nullify the "wimp" factor. As vice president and as president, he was accused of timidity against the Soviet bloc and China. But the Panama invasion began to redeem Bush. "Showing his steel [in Panama]," wrote the *New York Times*, "has shown him [to be] a man capable of bold action."[7]

The fifth and most immediate cause of the invasion was the harassment of U.S. personnel living in Panama, who numbered roughly 20,000. Armed intruders in the Canal Zone began clashing with U.S. forces, sometimes on U.S. defense sites. Beginning in 1988, the PDF stopped and searched U.S. individuals and vehicles, even detaining nine school buses of U.S. children.

Meanwhile, U.S. economic sanctions against Noriega were having an impact. The Panamanian economy lost $500 million, its gross domestic product contracted by 27 percent, and unemployment shot up to 30 percent. Elites saw their trade with the United States prohibited and their assets in U.S. banks frozen. In October 1989, the PDF missed a payroll. Noriega was losing allies.

On December 16, 1989, the day after Noriega's "state of war" pronouncement, four off-duty marines in Panama took a wrong turn into a PDF checkpoint. All of a sudden, black T-shirted

Machos del Monte, members of Noriega's elite force, ordered them out of the car with Kalashnikov rifles.

"Shit, it's the fucking Machos!" said one marine. "They just locked and loaded!" the driver shouted. "Let's get the hell out of here!"[8] The driver tried to escape, and the PDF shot his back seat passenger, First Lieutenant Robert Paz. Two witnesses, a U.S. Navy lieutenant and his wife, were arrested. The PDF allegedly beat the lieutenant and fondled his wife and threatened her with rape before releasing them.

Summing up all these causes, Chairman of the Joint Chiefs of Staff Colin Powell explained that Washington needed to reaffirm that the "superpower lives here."[9] Panama was once again about to suffer the consequences of having the Canal Zone on its territory.

U.S. personnel in Panama canceled their Christmas parties and prepared for war. On December 17, President Bush renamed the invasion plan Just Cause and fixed D-day for December 20.

At 12.45 am on that day, almost 26,000 U.S. forces moved into the Republic of Panama, hitting the first of 27 targets in the largest U.S. combat operation since Vietnam. Some parachuted in, others invaded by land, water, and chopper. Abrams tanks, Apache attack helicopters, and Stealth fighter-bombers were tested in battle, sometimes "just for show," as Powell admitted. Against the invasion stood a mere 16,000 PDF and local police, and within that, only 3000 combat-ready Panamanian soldiers. Within two days, the United States controlled all major PDF sites in the canal area. In the provinces, the U.S. military called PDF officers to inform them of the imminent fall of Noriega, and they all surrendered. Some PDF remnants and Dingbats resisted, but it was over in four days.

As in Grenada in 1983, the invasion proved popular with the U.S. and Panamanian publics, 80 and 90 percent respectively approving. And, as with the Dominican intervention of 1965, U.S. diplomacy within the hemisphere took place after the military victory. On December 22, the Organization of American States (OAS) voted 20 to 1 "to deeply regret" the intervention and call for the removal of U.S. troops, but rejected a resolution by Nicaragua to condemn the intervention. One U.S. diplomat called the OAS resolution "a mixed bag …

Figure 9.1   A US Army M113 armored personnel carrier during the 1989 invasion of Panama. By PH1 (SW) J. Elliott. Department of Defense.

We're a little disappointed. It certainly wasn't an extreme resolution, but it's a little detached from what is really happening in Panama."[10] A week later, the United Nations (UN) General Assembly voted 75 to 20 to label the invasion a violation of international law.

Noriega himself temporarily evaded the invasion. With a $1 million bounty on his head, on Christmas Eve he took refuge at the papal nunciature – the Vatican's embassy in Panama. The nuncio did not want him, but he had a tradition of harboring any refugee. After nine days of SEAL Team Four blasting loud music toward him – a psychological war called Operation Nifty Package that included, appropriately enough, "I Fought the Law" by The Clash and "Panama" by Van Halen – Noriega surrendered.

Operation Just Cause officially ended on January 31, 1990. Its consequences were quite favorable to the United States, though observers differed on its consequences for Panama.

First, controversy erupted over casualties. The U.S. government reported 26 dead GIs, plus 516 Panamanians. The Catholic Church calculated around 300 Panamanian deaths, while human rights organizations in Panama countered with at least 2000 deaths, adding that thousands more were arrested, including union leaders and university professors, simply for opposing the invasion. The Chorrillo slum, next to PDF headquarters in Panama City, burned down during the invasion, and Panamanians and U.S. citizens accused one another of setting the fires. The U.S. military provided for Chorrillo refugees after the invasion.

Second, Noriega was tried on eight counts of drug trafficking, racketeering, and money laundering in 1992. His U.S. prison sentence ended in September 2007, but Panama and France wanted him for murder and money laundering. In April 2010 he was moved to Paris, where he was sentenced to seven years in prison. The following year, however, he was extradited to Panama to serve 20 years.

Third, though its banks continued to clean dirty money, Panama reverted to a democracy. Right before the invasion, the U.S. military facilitated the swearing in of Endara and the other denied candidates of the May 1988 election at Fort Clayton in the Canal Zone. A month after Just Cause, Bush announced a $1 billion aid package to the new government. Endara served until 1994 and then passed on power peacefully.

Haiti, 1994

A few years after Panama, the United States sent an intervention force into the poorest nation in the hemisphere. Haiti was the size of Massachusetts, but with 2 million more souls and living off 2 percent of its wealth. The causes of this intervention were the twin desires of restoring democracy while also keeping a wave of migrants from reaching U.S. shores. The UN, not the United States, directed this intervention, and it involved not only U.S. soldiers but also Caribbean Community (CARICOM) armed forces.

In September 1991, an illegal junta headed by Commander-in-Chief of the Army Raoul Cédras overthrew the democratically elected Haitian president Jean-Bertrand Aristide, in office only seven months. Cédras hated Aristide's nationalization of industries, land reform, and distribution of wealth. Aristide fled to Venezuela. The Department of Defense considered sending a force to evacuate U.S. citizens and other nationals, but threats against them soon dissipated.

In the following months, pressures mounted on the international community to unseat Cédras. Hundreds of Haitians fled by boat after Cédras unleashed his forces on Aristide supporters, and the U.S. Coast Guard, after intercepting them, brought them first to Guantánamo Bay, Cuba, and later directly back to Haiti. Members of the Black Congressional Caucus such as New York's Charles Rangel called President Bush's policy "racist and discriminatory" since Cubans, by contrast, could stay in the United States.[11] Bush also rejected Haitian political refugees. The junta denied access to Haiti to human rights observers from the United States and UN. In October, the OAS instituted an embargo on Haiti and a freeze on its assets.[12]

President Bill Clinton had never wanted intervention. He signed Presidential Decision Directives 25 and 56 to tighten requirements and planning before any peacekeeping or military intervention. The Congress, the press, and Latin Americans also argued against intervention in Haiti. No Europeans threatened Haiti, and Aristide was a fair-weather friend at best, an anti-American at worst.

While running for president, Clinton had called Bush's repatriation of Haitians a "cruel policy." But days after his own inauguration, he did the same after learning that a raft construction project might bring 100,000 Haitians to U.S. shores. In hearings, U.S. officials admitted the link between restoring democracy and keeping would-be emigrants in Haiti:

> Senator Carl Levin (D-MI): The only way to stem [immigration] is if somehow or other there is a democratic government in Haiti …
>
> Undersecretary of Defense Walter B. Slocombe: That is absolutely our most direct and concrete interest.[13]

In March 1993, Clinton vowed to restore Aristide and rebuild Haiti's economy. Cédras first agreed to resign, then changed his mind. Pushed by members of Congress and by nongovernmental organizations such as TransAfrica, in June Clinton froze all the U.S. assets of those doing business with the junta. That same month, the UN Security Council banned petroleum sales to Haiti and froze financial assets. This brought Cédras to Governor's Island, New York, where he and mediators reached agreement on July 4 whereby Cédras would resign and Aristide would nominate a prime minister and grant amnesty to Cédras and others who plotted the coup against him.

To implement the Governor's Island agreement, a first intervention came peacefully. In the wee hours of October 11, lightly armed U.S. Special Forces and marines wearing UN insignia steamed toward Port-au-Prince aboard the USS *Harlan County*. Contrary to what he was told, the ship's captain, Marvin E. Butcher, discovered a harbor filled with ships and a pier busy with the junta's police. Gunshots were ringing out to warn the *Harlan County* away. Hours later, a drunken mob, also organized by the junta, showed up to attack a U.S. diplomat's car and intimidate Butcher. "Somalia! Somalia!" some shouted, a reference to the 18 U.S. soldiers killed a week earlier in Africa. To avoid violence, Butcher and his force stayed on their ship. When Haitian armored vehicles rolled up on the docks and gunboats circled his ship, Butcher left for Guantánamo.

The intimidation of the *Harlan County* crew humiliated the Clinton administration. "If we cannot support duly elected democratic governments 800 miles from our shores," rhetorically asked Senator Tom Harkin, who worried about U.S. credibility, "what kind of message will we send to potential coup leaders?"

"I'm never going to wimp out like I did in Haiti again," was Clinton's own vow.[14]

The Department of Defense began planning to remove Cédras by force. By January 1994, those plans included the U.S. Army 18th Airborne Corps from Fort Bragg, North Carolina, along with others. According to Operation Plan (OPLAN) 2370, these units would form Joint Task Force 180, remove the junta, neutralize the Haitian army and police, restore order and public services, and protect U.S. citizens and their property, other foreigners, and some Haitians. In July, CARICOM forces from eight Caribbean countries joined the plot. Twenty-five nations would eventually join under a UN mandate.

In summer 1994, Clinton felt increasing heat again when 20,000 more Haitians fled political violence by boat, headed for U.S. shores. The UN Security Council, meanwhile, passed Resolution 940, to "use all means necessary to restore Aristide."[15] This was a first: a green light from the UN to intervene in Latin America. Washington still hoped Cédras would step down and make an intervention unnecessary, so OPLAN 2380 was developed for such a case. OPLAN 2375 combined the first two if the junta dissolved in the first two days of an invasion.

On September 14, Clinton publicly gave Cédras an ultimatum: "Your time is up. Leave now or we will force you from power."[16] The next day, he ordered an invasion for September 19.

Cédras heard of troop movements and turned for help to former president Jimmy Carter. On September 17, Carter gathered a negotiation team that included General Powell and headed for Haiti. Powell later recalled that, once he was in Cédras's military headquarters,

> I leaned across the table. "Let me make sure you understand what you're facing," I said. I began ticking off my fingers: two aircraft carriers, two and a half infantry divisions, twenty thousand troops, helicopter gunships, tanks, artillery. I kept it up, watching the Haitians' spirits sink under the weight of the power I was describing.[17]

The next day, paratroopers from North Carolina were in the skies. Army Rangers from Georgia were almost in the air. Sailors and marines were ready to pounce from their off-shore ships.

Cédras's junta then agreed to leave Haiti in return for calling off the invasion. U.S. officials agreed, but still deployed 10th Mountain Division soldiers to Port-au-Prince. Lieutenant General Hugh Shelton met with Cédras at the Haitian National Palace, stripped him of his power, and arranged to exile the rest of the junta and to bring back Aristide.

The rest of the intervention, officially called Operation Uphold Democracy, went relatively smoothly. U.S. and CARICOM soldiers patrolled the cities, while Special Forces fanned out in the countryside. In Cap-Haïtien, Haitian soldiers engaged in a firefight with U.S. marines and 10 of the Haitians died. The U.S. occupation that followed lasted six months, and the mission as a whole cost more than $2 billion. On March 31, 1995, the UN Mission in Haiti (UNMIH) officially took over. A year after that, only 400 U.S. combat troops remained and the UN began a mainly humanitarian mission.

Haiti, 2004

On February 29, 2004, almost a decade later, the United States headed another UN intervention into Haiti. Again, the causes were the long-term failure of democracy and the short-term fear of massive migration.

Although the UN was officially in charge after 1995, the United States remained involved, not only helping to fund and staff the UNMIH but also investing millions to create, train, and equip the Haitian National Police. Washington also aimed to teach Haitians good governance through reforming its courts and supporting elections.

U.S. influence in Haiti also grew. From 1980 to 2004, Haiti's debt to foreign banks and governments grew from $302 million to $1.134 billion, much of it owed to the United States. U.S. intelligence agencies also bankrolled Emmanuel "Toto" Constant, the founder of the Revolutionary Front for Haitian Advancement and Progress (FRAPH in its French acronym), a paramilitary death squad.

Aristide's influence was disintegrating. Despite the 1994 intervention, U.S. troops worked with pro-coup business elites. Also, instead of disarming FRAPH, they protected it. Aristide dissolved the army, which he saw as the elite's tool. "Before the foreigners leave, they have to destroy the army," his supporters pleaded to reporters. "Every night, they break into our houses and rape our daughters and wives. Don't leave any of them."[18]

During elections in 1995 and 2000, Aristide's handpicked successor, his party, Lavalas Family, and he himself won overwhelmingly, but only 15–25 percent of Haitians voted. Opponents banded together as the Democratic Convergence (DC) and were headed by U.S.-born André Apaid, who owned garment factories supplying Disney, among others. Apaid hated Aristide for trying to raise the minimum wage, frozen since 1983, above $1.60 per day. It eventually doubled to about $3.00 but did not even catch up with inflation. The International Monetary Fund assessed that the raise "should not affect the good prospects for the export sector," and one labor watchdog organization added that "more than half of the approximately 50 assembly plants producing in Haiti for the U.S. market pay less than the legal minimum wage."[19]

The DC disputed only eight parliamentary seats out of 7500 filled in the 2000 elections, nevertheless convincing many in the United States that, despite being overwhelmingly popular, Aristide and his party were anti-democratic, even dictatorial.

Several international lenders began cutting off Haiti while pressuring Aristide to privatize state-owned industries. Under President George W. Bush, the State Department slowed down help for Haiti's currency. The U.S. ambassador, Brian Dean Curran, also accused the International Republican Institute, a self-styled democracy promoter, of telling the opposition to "cripple" Aristide.[20] Washington also pressured Europeans to suspend hundreds of millions in credit and aid. The Inter-American Development Bank held back $400 million. The International Monetary Fund, the World Bank, and the European Union denied credit.

On December 17, 2001, thugs almost overthrew the president in his own palace. U.S. Special Forces were training a 600-man force in the neighboring Dominican Republic to destabilize Aristide, with $1.2 million from the U.S. Agency for International Development. In addition, about $68 million in yearly U.S. aid went to the opposition from 2000 to 2003. Canada, France, and the European Union helped not just with UN peacekeeping and the financial boycott but also with funding the opposition.

Aristide grew scared and desperate. He offered concessions, but the opposition wanted him gone, and he refused. Many said he grew corrupt and turned to gangs to protect him. Haitian politics were at an impasse.

In 2003, former members of the Haitian military raided Haiti from bases in the neighboring Dominican Republic. They burned police stations, killed Lavalas activists, and captured towns. By early 2004, they controlled Haiti's north, where revolutions usually began, and then moved south into Port-au-Prince. In mid-February, Guy Philippe, a former police chief trained at a U.S. facility in Ecuador and accused of drug smuggling by the U.S. embassy, emerged as the commander of the rebel army. He had declared the previous year that he "would support a coup: we have to get rid of the dictator." He also revealed that the DC "helped us with money and weapons."[21]

Aristide asked for foreign help to contest a "coup d'état in motion," but Colin Powell, now Secretary of State, initially responded that Washington had "no enthusiasm" for a military solution – if it were to save Aristide.[22] On February 9, Secretary of Defense Donald Rumsfeld explained that "everyone's hopeful that the situation, which tends to ebb and flow down there, will stay below a certain threshold and … we have no plans to do anything."[23]

That threshold, as in the 1990s, was the refugees. Throughout February, the White House assured journalists that "we have a plan in place to stop any boats … That's been our policy and that remains our policy." But there was still no "surge" in refugees.[24] On February 24, after rebels rejected a power-sharing offer, Aristide warned, "The wave of violence sweeping through here is going to provoke the flight of many Haitians." *El Caribe* of Santo Domingo condemned "Aristide's veiled threat that the 'fire of violence will spark the departure of many Haitians.'" The next day, Bush said he would *consider* an international security force. Republican Mark Foley of Florida presented a grimmer ultimatum: "[Aristide is] either going out in a Learjet or he's going out in a body bag."[25]

On that infamous leap day, February 29, 2004, Philippe and his men were closing in on the capital. The U.S. military told Aristide that, if he did not escape with them, he would be overthrown, maybe killed. Aristide claimed that the U.S. soldiers pretended that they were bringing him to a press conference but then turned toward the airport where an unmarked plane waited. "It was a kidnapping and under the cover of a *coup d'état*," he told a journalist. "He left of his own free will," countered Vice President Dick Cheney. "He signed a resignation letter on his way out."[26] After a 20-hour flight, Aristide ended up in the Central African Republic, which U.S. officials said Aristide chose as his destination while Aristide alleged that he was kept in the dark until he landed.

Aristide's departure elevated an interim president in an unelected government. But power on the ground lay with Philippe, who declared, "I am the chief, the military chief. The country is in my hands."[27] Following his orders, police and paramilitaries killed and imprisoned thousands of Lavalas members. They even threatened the interim president, who requested UN assistance.

This cry for help resulted in the UN Security Council passing Resolution 1529 to authorize Operation Secure Tomorrow. It created a Multinational Interim Force (MIF) of about 3700, with 2000 from the United States, 900 from France, 330 from Chile, and 530 from Canada. This was far less than the 20,000 who occupied Haiti a decade previous.

Abandoning the Roosevelt Corollary of a century earlier, the Pentagon declared that it refused to act like "cops on the beat."[28] The United States also contributed only one-eighth of the budget to the first 14 months. Still, as the largest contributor, it prepared the mission. SOUTHCOM in Miami co-ordinated the arrival of soldiers, humanitarian aid, and communications, among other things. The force commander was a U.S. citizen; his deputy, French.

Also unlike past interventions, this one would not encourage a takeover by a brutal dictator but instead insist on a democratic government. Guy Philippe was allowed to head it, but the UN warned him to keep things peaceful – or else. There remained some rebels who fought back, and also some *chimères*, or Aristide supporters named after a mythical monster that was part snake, part goat, and part lion. Within a week of the MIH's arrival, however, the violence died down. Two months later, a prime minister was selected. Where UN troops were stationed – in most big cities – Haitian life returned more or less to normal. Ports and airports reopened. Humanitarian aid arrived. The massive wave of migrants that Washington dreaded never materialized.

Elsewhere, the national police fell apart, many police abandoning their stations. Gangs stepped into the vacuum and violence continued. MIH units confiscated illegal weapons and looked for weapons caches.

In 2005 was completed the transfer from SOUTHCOM's MIH to the UN Stabilization Mission in Haiti, better known for its French acronym, MINUSTAH. Brazil headed it, and troops from Brazil, Argentina, Chile, and elsewhere trickled in. MINUSTAH remained in Haiti for at least another decade, but the U.S. role in the Haitian intervention was over.

The Drug Wars, 1972–2016

The U.S.-led drug wars in Latin America do not fit this book's definition of an intervention. U.S. forces were on the ground, but they trained rather than fought, and they only deployed when invited by Latin American governments and usually in collaboration with Latin American soldiers or police. Yet the trillion dollars spent by Washington since the 1970s on the drug war in Latin America have often produced consequences similar to an intervention. U.S. approaches to countering drugs also drew a similar contestation, especially from those who suspected darker motives.

President Richard Nixon's 1972 White House meeting with aging rock star Elvis Presley was not an auspicious start to the "war on drugs." First was the matter that Elvis insisted on being "deputized" even though he was himself a drug abuser who died of an overdose five years later. Second was the word "war," which suggested a military solution to what many saw as a public health or a law enforcement problem.

Nineteen-eighty-six was a landmark year for further defining the U.S. approach to drugs. That year, Washington began to "certify" Latin American governments that were "co-operating fully" with U.S. authorities in the war. If a country lost certification – as did Bolivia in 1995 and Colombia in 1996 and 1997 – it also lost the U.S. Congress's anti-drug funds.

Also in 1986, Reagan called drug trafficking a national security threat and began to use the U.S. military to interdict shipments from Latin America. In Bolivia, for instance, U.S. troops, with six Blackhawk helicopters and 160 support personnel, undertook Operation Blast Furnace, to back the Bolivian National Police's find-and-destroy operations against coca processors. Since these facilities were in villages, many Bolivian peasants felt targeted. Some 6000 in a town called Santa Ana de Yacuma expelled 150 U.S. soldiers and Bolivian police officers.

As Operation Blast Furnace made clear, the U.S. government pointed to Latin American supply rather than U.S. demand as the problem, and it became a lucrative problem for weapons manufacturers. In the decades that followed, almost $9 out of every $10 law enforcement and military aid sent to Latin America went to counter-narcotics. Defense contracts for guns, satellites, radar equipment, tear gas, Kevlar helmets, and airport runways skyrocketed from $119 million in 2001 to $629 million a decade later. The U.S. government itself spent over $20 billion over the first decade of the twentieth century on U.S. Army troops, Air Force pilots, and Navy ships with Coast Guard anti-drug teams chasing down drug smugglers. By the 2010s, at any given time, about 4000 U.S. troops were taking part in counter-narcotics in Latin America, along with as many as four U.S. Navy ships. Many of those troops trained Latin American law enforcement and military personnel.

"Plan Colombia" was the most prominent and expensive U.S. program. President Andrés Pastrana of Colombia proposed it, and 80 percent of its funds went to his military and police. Between 2000 and 2008, U.S. funding for Plan Colombia averaged $540 million per year. (The Colombians chipped in $812 million per year, 1.2 percent of their GDP.) Initially, Washington spent its money strictly on counter-narcotics and not on fighting the Revolutionary Armed Forces of Colombia (FARC in Spanish), a decades-old allegedly Marxist guerrilla organization that protected many of the cocaine growers. But after the terrorist attacks of September 11, 2001, the U.S. government slid down the slippery slope of intervention by redefining the enemy as "narcoterrorists." By 2004, there were 800 U.S. military personnel in Colombia, mostly to protect oil pipelines.

That number was too small, according to President Álvaro Uribe. He argued that drugs were a greater threat than Iraq, where the United States had sent about 200 times more troops the year before, so "why don't they consider an equal, similar deployment, to put an end to this problem?"[29] Critics of Plan Colombia, however, pointed to the 15,000 lives it cost and the almost 6 million people displaced inside the country.

But did Plan Colombia achieve its goal of reducing drug trafficking? On one hand, it devastated the FARC, most of whose members had either surrendered or were in negotiations to do so by 2015. It also halved coca production in Colombia between 2000 and 2013. On the other hand, coca yields increased in neighboring Peru and Bolivia, and Andean cocaine exports stayed at the same level while its price increased. Finally, cocaine became increasingly a drug of choice in Latin America, for instance Brazil.

In response to the idea of U.S. intervention, resistance to U.S. counter-narcotics operations grew outside Colombia, part of a larger protest against U.S.-led neoliberalism or the promotion of global market forces rather than social inclusion. Bolivian President Evo Morales, who as a former coca farmer remembered Operation Blast Furnace, expelled all U.S. Drug Enforcement Administration agents from his country after a revolt in 2008 killed 30. The following year, Ecuador's Rafael Correa refused to renew a rent-free U.S. base near the Pacific coast town of Manta from which the Pentagon ran anti-drug operations. Observing the asymmetry of such bases, Correa joked, "We'll renew the lease if the U.S. lets us set up a base in Miami."[30]

Accusations of intervention also followed Washington's 2009 signing of an agreement to use seven bases in Colombia. U.S. troops claimed they were there only to fight narcotraffickers and guerrillas in Colombia. But the U.S. Air Force added that the deal offered a "unique opportunity" for "conducting full spectrum operations" against several threats, including "anti-U.S. governments."[31] Hugo Chávez, president of neighboring Venezuela, called the agreement a threat to his country. Even the Colombian constitutional court ruled it unconstitutional. The U.S. personnel level in Colombia stayed at 1400, allowed by previous agreements.

Perhaps because of Mexico's own bitter history of U.S. interventions, U.S. military personnel have been largely absent from that country's war against drug cartels. Still, up to early 2015, the United States had provided $2 billion in military and police assistance and $4 billion in weapons to Mexico City. It also trained more than 16,000 Mexican security personnel. In 2014, U.S. Marshals disguised themselves as Mexican marines in order to arrest drug kingpins and extradite them to the United States to face justice.

As the drug war in Mexico infiltrated its southern neighbors with crime and corruption, Central America became vital to debates over U.S. intervention. In 2015, 200 marines arrived in Honduras to help prepare the country for the hurricane season, build schools, and repair roads. Some suspected that this "humanitarian mission" was instead going to "destroy democracy." The root of the suspicion was the already 600-strong U.S. force working in Honduras on anti-narcotics operations. "Two hundred today, two thousand tomorrow," one critic predicted, adding that Washington used the drug war to "create a military basis for intervention in Latin America."[32]

Increasingly, many Latin Americans, including former heads of state, called for demilitarizing the fight against drugs. Bolivia legalized the growing of coca leaves. In 2013, Uruguay legalized and regulated marijuana. In 2015, Colombia abandoned the aerial spraying of herbicide glyphosate on coca fields.

Observers of post-Cold War U.S. interventions in Latin America and the Caribbean were divided on whether they signaled a departure. Some noted that democracy promotion was something new, that true multilateralism had been achieved, and that teaching good government, while less paternalistic than in the days of Woodrow Wilson, was a consistent goal. Others pointed out that, no matter the specific circumstances, all interventions stemmed from the desire to remind the hemisphere of U.S. hegemony, and that U.S. military and economic interests were always present. Contestation and collaboration continued.

Notes

1 Cited in Christina Jacqueline Johns and P. Ward Johnson, *State Crime, the Media, and the Invasion of Panama* (Praeger, 1994), 91.

2 Cited in Michael Grow, *U.S. Presidents and Latin American Interventions: Pursuing Regime Change in the Cold War* (University Press of Kansas, 2008), 163.

3 Cited in Martha L. Cottam, *Images & Intervention: U.S. Policies in Latin America* (University of Pittsburgh Press, 1994), 153.

4 Cited in Michael L. Conniff, *Panama and the United States: The Forced Alliance* (University of Georgia Press, 1992), 163.

5 Cited in Grow, *U.S. Presidents*, 170.

6 Cited in Johns and Johnson, *State Crime*, 39.

7 Cited in Grow, *U.S. Presidents*, 183.

8 Cited in Stephen Kinzer, *Overthrow: America's Century of Regime Change from Hawaii to Iraq* (Henry Holt, 2006), 253.

9 Cited in Hal Brands, *Latin America's Cold War* (Harvard University Press, 2010), 245.

10 Cited in "OAS Voices 'Regret' on Panama Invasion: Latin America: Resolution also Urges Immediate End to Fighting but Does not Condemn the U.S. Action," *Los Angeles Times*, December 22, 1989, available at http://articles.latimes.com/1989-12-22/news/mn-942_1_latin-american

11 Cited in Russell Crandall, *The United States and Latin America after the Cold War* (Cambridge University Press, 2008), 194.

12 Cited in Crandall, *The United States*, 193.

13 Cited in Philippe R. Girard, *Clinton in Haiti: The 1994 U.S. Invasion of Haiti* (Palgrave Macmillan, 2004), 56.
14 Both cited in Girard, *Clinton in Haiti*, 43, 44.
15 Cited in Crandall, *The United States*, 200.
16 Clinton cited in Carl M. Cannon, "Clinton Gives Ultimatum 'Your Time Is Up,' President Tells Haiti's Leaders," *Baltimore Sun*, September 16, 1994, available at http://articles.baltimoresun.com/1994-09-16/news/1994259012_1_haiti-clinton-cedras
17 Cited in Girard, *Clinton in Haiti*, 5.
18 Cited in Stephen Hallward, *Damming the Flood: Haiti, Aristide, and the Politics of Containment* (Verso, 2007), 54.
19 Both cited in Hallward, *Damming the Flood*, 61.
20 Cited in Crandall, *The United States*, 208.
21 Cited in Hallward, *Damming the Flood*, 122, 128.
22 "Powell Rejects U.S. Military Aid for Haiti," *Fox News*, February 17, 2004, available at www.foxnews.com/story/2004/02/17/powell-rejects-us-military-aid-for-haiti/
23 Cited in Howard LaFranchi, "As Rebels Gain, How to Help Haiti?" *Christian Science Monitor*, February 24, 2004, available at www.csmonitor.com/2004/0224/p01s01-usfp.html
24 "Press Briefing by Scott McClellan," February 24, 2004, *The American Presidency Project*, available at www.presidency.ucsb.edu/ws/?pid=73956
25 Cited in Alan McPherson, *Intimate Ties, Bitter Struggles: The United States and Latin America* (Potomac Books, 2006), 128.
26 Aristide and Cheney cited in Noam Chomsky, Paul Farmer, and Amy Goodman, *Getting Haiti Right This Time: The U.S. and the Coup* (Common Courage Press, 2004), 108, 115.
27 Cited in Chomsky, Farmer, and Goodman, *Getting Haiti Right This Time*, 30.
28 Cited in Crandall, *The United States*, 207.
29 Cited in Robin Kirk, *More Terrible than Death: Drugs, Violence, and America's War in Colombia* (Public Affairs, 2004), 291.
30 Cited in Greg Grandin, "Muscling Latin America," *The Nation*, 21 January 2010, available at www.thenation.com/article/muscling-latin-america

31 Cited in Benjamin Dangl, "U.S. Bases in Colombia Rattle the Region," *The Progressive*, undated, available at http://progressive.org/danglmarch10.html

32 James Petras, cited in Abraham Zamorano, "Qué busca EE. UU. con su mayor despliegue military en Centroamérica," *BBC Mundo*, 14 May 2015, available at www.bbc.com/mundo/noticias/2015/05/150513_marines_honduras_centroamerica_eeuu_az

Conclusion
Multitudes of Interventions

Do I contradict myself?
Very well then I contradict myself,
(I am large, I contain multitudes.)

Walt Whitman, "Song of Myself"

This book has explored the Five C's as themes of U.S. interventions in Latin America and the Caribbean – causes, consequences, contestation, collaboration, and context. Of those five, the causes are the most important. Without them, the next three would not have occurred, and the fifth would be irrelevant.

And of those causes for intervention, this book has argued that political causes were the most important. The key word here, however, is "mostly." Seen as a group, the thousands of small interventions and dozens of large ones in the region almost all stemmed from more than one motivation. Diversity was also evident in the many forms that interventions took. U.S. adventures in the region displayed a dizzying variety not only in intent but also in size, cost, duration, historical context, resistance, allies, reception, and legality. Like the great U.S. poet Walt Whitman, interventions contained multitudes, and students of

A Short History of U.S. Interventions in Latin America and the Caribbean,
First Edition. Alan McPherson.
© 2016 John Wiley & Sons, Inc. Published 2016 by John Wiley & Sons, Inc.

them should appreciate their contradictions as a representation of the complexity of U.S. power in the world.

Still, patterns emerged. To simplify them, this conclusion will suggest binaries that were most common and consequential in the causes and forms of U.S. interventions in Latin America and the Caribbean.

Humanitarianism v. Revenge

U.S. citizens liked to imagine themselves as exceptional or morally superior to other nations, and thus tended to frame interventions as humanitarian. Many hearts broke when gazing upon depictions of Cuban *reconcentrados* victimized by Spaniards before 1898. Images of emaciated children made their way into U.S. newspapers, and tales of harassed (white) Cuban women set up a narrative of gallantry for Uncle Sam. It was no coincidence that President William McKinley called for a war "in the name of humanity." In the Cold War, too, U.S. officials saw themselves "saving" Guatemala, the Dominican Republic, Nicaragua, and Grenada from communism.

However, the desire to exact vengeance from Latin Americans should not be underestimated as a cause for interventions. While the impulse to rescue Cubans existed for years before 1898, it was the explosion aboard the *Maine* in February of that year that truly whipped up war fever. A half-century earlier, U.S. citizens sang of their desire to punish Mexicans who shed *gringo* blood supposedly on U.S. soil. The 1854 bombing of tiny San Juan del Norte in Nicaragua and the taking of Veracruz in 1914 were also instances of disproportionate retaliation. And of course, the Punitive Expedition against Pancho Villa in 1916 might as well have been called the Revenge Excursion. Except for Villa's attack in New Mexico, an undisputed fact, all other revenge narratives were based on *perceived* wrongs done to the United States. U.S. proponents of intervention either ignored the lack of evidence or else exaggerated slights into full-blown international incidents.

Both humanitarianism and revenge were mighty motivators because they called forth powerful emotions – pathos and narcissism in the former, fear and wrath in the latter. Once evoked, these emotions proved difficult to resist and thus unifying for the nation. The precursors to U.S. reactions to Pearl Harbor in 1941 and the Al Qaeda attacks of 2001 are to be found in U.S. interventions in the hemisphere.

Economics v. Politics

Just as humanitarianism and vengeance reinforce one another, economic and political goals were not incompatible. In fact, they not only often supported each other but were also both necessary. To argue for one at the exclusion of the other is to engage in a false dichotomy – a contradiction that isn't.

Economic goals were present in almost all interventions, but sometimes in abstract, indirect ways. In the Mexican War and filibustering expeditions, land acquisition was a central motif, and large U.S. landowners and slaveholders were cheerleaders for war. But most U.S. citizens were more concerned with national greatness and racial hierarchies. The "liberation" of Cuba in 1898 was even less economic, since sugar producers were divided and would only later recognize the advantages of acquiring Cuban lands. Cold War interventions, meanwhile, were economic only in that they aimed to protect capitalism – but, with the exception of United Fruit in Guatemala and copper companies in Chile, not specific capitalists. The apex of U.S. economic motives came with the rash of small interventions and large occupations in the first third of the twentieth century. To be sure, this speaks to the importance of economic motives such as land purchases, tariff revisions, acquisitions of markets abroad, and extensions of Wall Street loans. But even in that overtly imperialist era, interventions such as the Punitive Expedition had next to no economic rationale.

Political goals were always present, and in most cases were the primary definition of success for U.S. government officials, if not for corporations or the U.S. public. It was those officials, after all, who ordered interventions, managed occupations, and withdrew troops. Moreover, true economic or geostrategic transformation or stability could not be achieved without the collaboration of at least some Latin American and Caribbean politicians. U.S. officials, civil and military, aimed to change these politicians' attitudes and habits so that they would produce stable, nonviolent societies that would enable U.S. investment and trade, provide allies in war, and secure passageways to the Panama Canal. Politics were the lynchpin of all other causes. Ideologies such as liberalism, racism, xenophobia, and anti-communism only added to the political brew.

Direct v. Indirect

Just as there existed no single goal to interventions, there was also no single form to them. The greatest distinction in the kind of interventions in the hemisphere was that between those undertaken directly by U.S. troops and those in which the U.S. government trained, equipped, and funded proxy invasion forces or armies.

The great majority fell into the first category. The Mexican War, the War of 1898, the Cuban interventions, the Panama revolution of 1903 and other interventions in Central America, the Wilsonian interventions, the World War II occupations, the Dominican Republic in 1965, Grenada in 1983, Panama in 1989, and Haiti in 1994 and 2004 were all examples of the U.S. president ordering regular U.S. troops to fight, or at least to exercise coercion aboard gunboats or at checkpoints (as in Panama in 1903 and the Dominican Republic in 1965, respectively). The Mexican War also included thousands of U.S. volunteers who engaged in combat at the behest of the U.S. government.

The indirect interventions of the Cold War were an important late twentieth-century phenomenon. Ironically, they emerged from

U.S. agreements during the Good Neighbor years of the 1930s *not* to intervene. Governments in the Americas pledged to refrain from intervention into one another's affairs.

But there were two loopholes. One was the assumption that interventions were always done by a country's armed forces and did not include funding or training foreigners to overthrow their own government. Much of U.S. military strategy after the Good Neighbor, therefore, jumped through that loophole. Washington sent weapons to Latin American and Caribbean governments for strictly internal security and reserved the right to do the same with those governments' internal opponents if the political tide turned against the United States. As a consequence, during the Cold War, governments and rebels were armed to the teeth and trained to use those arms against one another.

The second loophole of Good Neighbor pledges of nonintervention was that American governments could band together for an intervention if its purpose was to repel a threat from beyond the hemisphere. During the Cold War, subversion by the Soviet Union was suspected everywhere. It took little imagination – and not much more diplomacy – for U.S. officials to get Latin American governments to join them in preventing or rolling back "communist" governments in Guatemala, the Dominican Republic, Nicaragua, and Grenada, among others.

Perhaps because U.S. armed forces were not doing the killing in proxy wars, Washington felt less responsibility to restrain the killers, and the consequences of these supposedly low-intensity wars could be even greater. Nicaragua in the 1970s and 1980s is the best example.

Unilateral v. Multilateral

The trend of increasingly multilateral interventions has largely overlapped with that of indirect ones, but not entirely. Its origins also date from the agreement among American states that only collective interventions can be allowed against extra-hemispheric threats. Thus, since the 1965 Dominican intervention, almost all direct U.S. landings have been done in concert with other nations of the hemisphere or the world. The Dominican intervention gained the support of an inter-American peace force. The Organization of Eastern Caribbean States requested the Grenada invasion. United Nations (UN) resolutions, meanwhile, provided cover for Haiti interventions in 1994 and 2004. The sole exception was the Panama intervention of 1989, which the international community condemned. And still, Washington tried to smooth over the resentment among the hemisphere's governments.

Legal v. Illegal

A closely related – and complex – binary is whether interventions were legal or illegal. If one allows a broad definition of "legal," then almost all of them were. To simplify, U.S. interventions in Latin America or the Caribbean could be legal in one of four ways.

First, they could be considered wars under the U.S. Constitution if the Congress passed a declaration of war. Article I of the Constitution states that only the Congress – not the president – has the power to do so, and that Congress must also raise and maintain military forces. World War II partially qualified because its declaration resulted in troops in the hemisphere, but it was not a war declared against any of the hemisphere's nations. Otherwise, the only two declared U.S. wars in Latin American history were the Mexican War and the War of 1898 – and even this latter one was against Spain, not Cuba.

Second, the U.S. Congress can give the president the authority to use force without declaring a formal war. That authority derives from Article II of the U.S. Constitution, which establishes the president as the commander in chief of the U.S. military with the authority to conduct war. Congressional resolutions, meanwhile, define the scope of a military campaign. A good example is the 1914 occupation of Veracruz, Mexico, justified by Joint Resolution 251, which gave

President Woodrow Wilson the authorization to use force. There was also the little-known Paraguay expedition of 1858, when U.S. Navy ships steamed toward Asunción to demand an apology for the shelling of the USS *Water Witch*. The Congress authorized the ships, Paraguay apologized, and the Navy never entered Paraguayan territory.

Third, treaties or other legal documents negotiated with foreign governments have helped to justify U.S. interventions. The Platt Amendment toward Cuba and the Treaty of 1903 with Panama both explicitly allowed the United States a right of intervention. The Wilson administration strong-armed the Haitian government in 1915 into a Haitian–American Convention that allowed U.S. security and economic oversight – after the troops had already landed. Closely related to these instances were those where Latin American governments invited U.S. landings on their own territory. This occurred in Cuba in 1906, Nicaragua in 1912 and 1926, Panama in 1925, and the Dominican Republic in 1965.

Fourth, the international community, through resolutions passed in international bodies such as the Organization of American States or the UN, legalized U.S. military actions, even after the fact. As mentioned above, the Haiti actions of 1994 and 2004 were such examples.

Interestingly, the Congress also has the authority to interdict funding to a war or an intervention, but rarely has it done so. The Boland Amendments against arming the Nicaraguan Contras in the 1980s were an exception, but even then U.S. officials maneuvered around them and later claimed to have done so legally.

In 1973, in response to the perceived constitutional excesses of presidents during the Vietnam War, Congress passed the War Powers Resolution, which stated that the president needed to notify Congress within 48 hours and obtain congressional authority within 60 days – possibly extending to 90 days – of sending troops into a warlike situation. The intent was to restrain the president, but in reality the president thereafter had a 60- or 90-day window to use force for virtually any reason. In the invasions of Grenada and Panama, congressional critics argued that the president did not fully comply with the War Powers Resolution.

In many interventions, U.S. presidents claimed authority despite none of the conditions above applying. Some military actions were intended to defend U.S. persons, property, or national interests. These justified, for instance, the initial landings in Haiti in 1915 or in the Dominican Republic in 1965. The original "self-defense" rationale was the 1811 No Transfer Resolution, which justified the very first intervention in Latin America by the United States' "due regard to their own safety." Other actions fell short of traditional war, for instance a bombing or the dispatch of the *Harlan County* to Haiti in 1993.

A few U.S. interventions were plainly illegal, but rarely were there consequences for U.S. policymakers. President Theodore Roosevelt and his attorney general knew that the fomenting of a rebellion in Panama in 1903 was illegal, but they boasted of it. Wilson skirted the edge of the law often, but most U.S. citizens were uninterested. The bases-for-destroyers deal that sent the United States to Trinidad and Tobago and elsewhere arguably violated the Neutrality Acts, but President Franklin Roosevelt plowed forth anyway. The Iran–Contra scheme was the most notorious. It resulted in dozens of indictments, but either they were vacated or overturned on appeal and the perpetrators not retried, or else President George H.W. Bush, himself possibly involved, pardoned convicted officials.

The legality or illegality of U.S. interventions in Latin America and the Caribbean is, in the end, academic but also revealing. That the president was able to send troops to the region with sometimes the slightest legal authority reveals two cold realities of inter-American relations. First was the general consensus in U.S. society that interventions in the hemisphere were in the national interest. Second is that U.S. hegemony in that hemisphere was so great that no Latin American or global opposition could successfully challenge it, which reinforces the argument that the national interest was indeed to further that hegemony. The overall lesson to be drawn from U.S. military interventions in the region, therefore, is not about goals or forms, but about power: the United States did what it did because it could.

Bibliography

Abbot, Willis J. *The Naval History of the United States*. Peter Fenelon Collier, 1890.

Beck, Robert J. *The Grenada Invasion: Politics, Law, and Foreign Policy Decisionmaking*. Westview Press, 1993.

Bermann, Karl. *Under the Big Stick: Nicaragua and the United States since 1848*. South End Press, 1986.

Black, George. *The Good Neighbor: How the United States Wrote the History of Central America and the Caribbean*. Pantheon, 1988.

Blasier, Cole. *The Hovering Giant: U.S. Responses to Revolutionary Change in Latin America 1910–1985*. University of Pittsburgh Press, 1985.

Boot, Max. *The Savage Wars of Peace: Small Wars and the Rise of American Power*. Basic Books, 2002.

Bradley, Ed. "Fighting for Texas: Filibuster James Long, the Adams-Onís Treaty, and the Monroe Administration," *Southwestern Historical Quarterly* 102: 3 (January 1999), 322–41.

Brands, Hal. *Latin America's Cold War*. Harvard University Press, 2010.

Burrowes, Reynold A. *Revolution and Rescue in Grenada: An Account of the U.S.-Caribbean Invasion*. Greenwood Press, 1988.

Butler, Smedley. *Old Gimlet Eye: The Adventures of Smedley D. Butler as told to Lowell Thomas*. Farrar & Rinehart, 1933.

Calder, Bruce. *The Impact of Intervention: The Dominican Republic during the U.S. Occupation of 1916–1924*. University of Texas Press, 1984.

Calhoun, Fredrick S. *Power and Principle: Armed Intervention in Wilsonian Foreign Policy*. Kent State University Press, 1986.

A Short History of U.S. Interventions in Latin America and the Caribbean,
First Edition. Alan McPherson.
© 2016 John Wiley & Sons, Inc. Published 2016 by John Wiley & Sons, Inc.

Challener, Richard D. *Admirals, Generals, and American Foreign Policy, 1898-1914*. Princeton University Press, 1973.

Chávez, Ernesto. *The U.S. War with Mexico: A Brief History with Documents*. Bedford/St Martin's, 2008.

Chomsky, Noam, Paul Farmer, and Amy Goodman. *Getting Haiti Right This Time: The U.S. and the Coup*. Common Courage Press, 2004.

Collin, Richard. *Theodore Roosevelt's Caribbean: The Panama Canal, the Monroe Doctrine, and the Latin American Context*. Louisiana State University Press, 1990.

Collings, Harry T. "Misinterpreting the Monroe Doctrine," *Annals of the American Academy of Political and Social Science* 111 (January 1924), 37-9.

Conniff, Michael L. *Panama and the United States: The Forced Alliance*. University of Georgia Press, 1992.

Conrad, Robert Edgar, ed. and trans., *Sandino: The Testimony of a Nicaraguan Patriot, 1921-1934*. Princeton University Press: 1990.

Cooper, Donald B. "The Withdrawal of the United States from Haiti, 1928–1934," *Journal of Inter-American Studies* 5: 1 (January 1963), 83–101.

Cottam, Martha L. *Images & Intervention: U.S. Policies in Latin America*. University of Pittsburgh Press, 1994.

Crandall, Russell. *The United States and Latin America after the Cold War*. Cambridge University Press, 2008.

Cullather, Nick. *Secret History: The CIA's Classified Account of Its Operations in Guatemala 1952-1954*. Stanford University Press, 1999.

Cummins, Lejeune. *Quijote on a Burro: Sandino and the Marines, A Study in the Formulation of Foreign Policy*. La Impresora Azteca, 1958.

DeLay, Brian. *War of a Thousand Deserts: Indian Raids and the U.S.-Mexican War*. Yale University Press, 2008.

Dickey, Christopher. *With the Contras: A Reporter in the Wilds of Nicaragua*. Touchstone, 1987.

Diffie, Bailey W. "The Ideology of Hispanidad," *Hispanic American Historical Review* 23: 3 (August 1943), 457–82.

Eisenhower, John S.D. *Intervention! The United States and the Mexican Revolution, 1913-1917*. W. W. Norton, 1993.

Eisenhower, John S.D. *So Far from God: The U.S. War with Mexico: 1846-1848*. University of Oklahoma Press, 1989.

Ellsworth, Captain Harry Allanson. *One Hundred Eighty Landings of United States Marines, 1800-1934*. History and Museums Division, U.S. Marine Corps, reprint 1974.

Escobar, Francisco. *"I Took the Isthmus": Ex-President Roosevelt's Confession, Colombia's Protest, and Editorial Comment by American Newspapers on "How the United States Acquired the Right to Build the Panama Canal."* M. B. Brown, 1911.

Ferguson, Niall. *Colossus: The Rise and Fall of the American Empire.* Penguin Books, 2004.

Foos, Paul. *A Short, Offhand, Killing Affair: Soldiers and Social Conflict during the Mexican-American War.* University of North Carolina Press, 2002.

Francisco Borgen, José. *Una vida a la orilla de la historia.* Dilesa, 1979.

Friedman, Max Paul. *Nazis & Good Neighbors: The United States Campaign against the Germans of Latin America in World War II.* Cambridge University Press, 2003.

Fuller, Captain Stephen and Graham Cosmas. *Marines in the Dominican Republic 1916-1924.* History and Museums Division, U.S. Marine Corps, 1974.

Gaillard, Roger. *Les blancs débarquent,* vol. 3, *Premier écrasement du cacoïsme: 1915.* No pub., 1981.

Gaillard, Roger. *Les blancs débarquent,* vol. 6, *Charlemagne Péralte le caco, 1918-1919.* No pub., 1982.

Gilderhus, Mark. *The Second Century: U.S.-Latin American Relations since 1989.* Scholarly Resources, 2000.

Gilmore, William C. *The Grenada Invasion: Analysis and Documentation.* Facts on File, 1984.

Girard, Philippe R. *Clinton in Haiti: The 1994 U.S. Invasion of Haiti.* Palgrave Macmillan, 2004.

Gleijeses, Piero. "1898: The Opposition to the Spanish-American War," *Journal of Latin American Studies* 35: 4 (November 2003), 681-719.

Gleijeses, Piero. *Shattered Hope: The Guatemalan Revolution and the United States, 1944-1954.* Princeton University Press, 1991.

Gobat, Michel. *Confronting the American Dream: Nicaragua under U.S. Imperial Rule.* Duke University Press, 2005.

González Canalda, Maria Filomena. *Línea noroeste: testimonio del patriotismo olvidado.* Universidad Central del Este, 1985.

Graebner, Norman A. "War Aims," in *The Mexican War: Crisis for American Democracy,* ed. Archie P. McDonald. Heath, 1969, 23-5.

Grandin, Greg. *The Last Colonial Massacre: Latin America in the Cold War.* University of Chicago Press, 2004.

Grandin, Greg. *Empire's Workshop: Latin America, the United States, and the Rise of the New Imperialism.* Metropolitan Books, 2006.

Grieb, Kenneth J. *The Latin American Policy of Warren G. Harding*. Texas Christian University Press, 1976.

Grow, Michael. *U.S. Presidents and Latin American Interventions: Pursuing Regime Change in the Cold War*. University Press of Kansas, 2008.

Hallward, Stephen. *Damming the Flood: Haiti, Aristide, and the Politics of Containment*. Verso, 2007.

Hart, John Mason. *Empire and Revolution: The Americans in Mexico since the Civil War*. University of California Press, 2002.

Heinl, Robert Debs, and Nancy Gordon Heinl. *Written in Blood: The Story of the Haitian People 1492-1971*. Houghton Mifflin, 1978.

Henríquez García, Enriquillo. *Cartas del Presidente Francisco Henríquez y Carvajal*. Sánchez, 1970.

Holden, Robert and Eric Zolov, eds., *Latin America and the United States: A Documentary History*. Oxford University Press, 2000.

Immerman, Richard H. *The CIA in Guatemala: The Foreign Policy of Intervention*. University of Texas Press, 1982.

Johns, Christina Jacquline and P. Ward Johnson. *State Crime, the Media, and the Invasion of Panama*. Praeger, 1994.

Kagan, Robert. *A Twilight Struggle: American Power in Nicaragua, 1977-1990*. Free Press, 1996.

Kinzer, Stephen. *Overthrow: America's Century of Regime Change from Hawaii to Iraq*. Henry Holt, 2006.

Knetsch, Jon and Nick Wynne, *Florida in the Spanish-American War*. History Press, 2011.

LaFeber, Walter. *The New Empire: An Interpretation of American Expansion, 1860-1898*. Cornell University Press, 1963.

LaFeber, Walter. *The Panama Canal: The Crisis in Historical Perspective*. Oxford University Press, 1978.

LaFeber, Walter. *Inevitable Revolutions: The United States in Central America*, 2nd ed. W. W. Norton, 1993.

Langley, Lester. *America and the Americas: The United States in the Western Hemisphere*, 2nd ed. University of Georgia Press, 2010.

Langley, Lester. *The Banana Wars: United States Intervention in the Caribbean, 1898-1934*. Scholarly Resources, 2002.

Langley, Lester. *The United States and the Caribbean in the Twentieth Century*, rev. ed. University of Georgia Press, 1985.

Langley, Lester, and Thomas Schoonover. *The Banana Men: American Mercenaries & Entrepreneurs in Central America, 1880-1930*. University Press of Kentucky, 1995.

Linderman, Gerald F. *The Mirror of War: American Society and the Spanish-American War.* University of Michigan Press, 1974.

Lockmiller, David A. *Magoon in Cuba: A History of the Second Intervention, 1906–1909.* University of North Carolina Press, 1938.

Logan Jr., John A. *No Transfer: An American Security Principle.* Yale University Press, 1961.

Loveman, Brian. *No Higher Law: American Foreign Policy and the Hemisphere since 1776.* University of North Carolina Press, 2010.

Lugo, Américo. *El Plan de Validación Hughes-Peynado.* La Cuna de América, 1922.

Maddow, Rachel. *Drift: The Unmooring of American Military Power.* Crown Publishers, 2012.

Martin, John Bartlow. *Overtaken by Events: The Dominican Crisis – From the Fall of Trujillo to the Civil War.* Doubleday & Company, 1966.

May, Robert E. "Young American Males and Filibustering in an Age of Manifest Destiny: The United States Army as a Cultural Mirror," *Journal of American History* 78: 3 (December 1991), 857–86.

May, Robert E. *The Southern Dream of a Caribbean Empire, 1854–1861,* 2nd ed. University Press of Florida, 2002.

McCaffrey, James M. *Army of Manifest Destiny: The American Soldier in the Mexican War, 1846–1848.* New York University Press, 1992.

McCullough, David. *The Path Between the Seas: The Creation of the Panama Canal, 1870–1914.* Touchstone, 1977.

McPherson, Alan. *Yankee No! Anti-Americanism in U.S.-Latin American Relations.* Harvard University Press, 2003.

McPherson, Alan. *Intimate Ties, Bitter Struggles: The United States and Latin America.* Potomac Books, 2006.

McPherson, Alan, ed. *The Encyclopedia of U.S. Military Interventions in Latin America.* ABC-CLIO, 2013.

McPherson, Alan. *The Invaded: How Latin Americans and Their Allies Fought and Ended U.S. Occupations.* Oxford University Press, 2014.

Missall, John and Mary Lou Missall, *The Seminole Wars: America's Longest Indian Conflict.* University Press of Florida, 2004.

Munro, Dana G. "The American Withdrawal from Haiti, 1929–1934," *Hispanic American Historical Review* 49: 1 (February 1969), 1–26.

Munro, Dana G. *The United States and the Caribbean Republics 1921–1933.* Princeton University Press, 1974.

Munro, Dana G. *The Five Republics of Central America: Their Political and Economic Development and their Relationship with the United States*. Russell & Russell, 1967.

Musicant, Ivan. *The Banana Wars: A History of United States Military Intervention in Latin AAmerican from the Spanish-American War to the Invasion of Panama*. Macmillan, 1990.

Musicant, Ivan. *Empire by Default: The Spanish-American War and the Dawn of the American Century*. Henry Holt, 1998.

Notter, Harley. *The Origins of the Foreign Policy of Woodrow Wilson*. Johns Hopkins University Press, 1937.

Pagano, Dom. *Bluejackets*. Meador, 1932.

Parker, Phyllis R. *Brazil and the Quiet Intervention, 1964*. Kent State University Press, 1990.

Pérez Jr., Louis A. *Intervention, Revolution, and Politics in Cuba, 1913-1921*. University of Pittsburgh Press, 1978.

Pérez Jr., Louis A. *Cuba between Empires, 1878-1902*. University of Pittsburgh Press, 1983.

Pérez Jr., Louis A. *The War of 1898: The United States and Cuba in History and Historiography*. University of North Carolina Press, 1998.

Pérez Jr., Louis A. *Cuba in the American Imagination: Metaphor and the Imperial Ethos*. University of North Carolina Press, 2008.

Porter, Kenneth Wiggins. "Negroes and the Seminole War, 1817-1818," *Journal of Negro History* 36: 3 (July 1951), 249-80.

Quirk, Robert E. *An Affair of Honor: Woodrow Wilson and the Occupation of Veracruz*. University of Kentucky Press, 1962.

Rabe, Stephen G. *U.S. Intervention in British Guiana: A Cold War Story*. University of North Carolina Press, 2005.

Rabe, Stephen G. *The Killing Zone: The United States Wages Cold War in Latin America*. Oxford University Press, 2012.

Reagan, Ronald. *An American Life: The Autobiography*. Simon & Schuster, 1990.

Renda, Mary. *Taking Haiti: Military Occupation & the Culture of U.S. Imperialism*. University of North Carolina Press, 2001.

Ruck, Rob. *The Tropic of Baseball: Baseball in the Dominican Republic*. University of Nebraska Press, 1998.

Schwab, Stephen Irving Max. *Guantánamo, U.S.A: The Untold History of America's Cuban Outpost*. University Press of Kansas, 2009.

Schmidt, Hans. *The United States Occupation of Haiti, 1915–1934.* Rutgers University Press, 1995.

Shannon, Magdaline W. *Jean Price-Mars, the Haitian Elite and the American Occupation, 1915–1935.* St Martin's Press, 1996.

Sonneborn, Liz. *The Acquisition of Florida: America's Twenty-Seventh State.* Chelsea House, 2009.

Stiles, T. J. *The First Tycoon: The Epic Life of Cornelius Vanderbilt.* Knopf, 2009.

Stout Jr., Joseph A. *Schemers and Dreamers: Filibustering in Mexico 1848–1921.* Texas Christian University Press, 2002.

Wexler, Alice. "Pain and Prejudice in the Santiago Campaign of 1898," *Journal of Interamerican Studies and World Affairs* 18: 1 (February 1976), 59–73.

White, Richard. *Will Rogers: A Political Life.* Texas Tech University Press, 2011.

Wienberg, Albert K. "The Mission of Regeneration," in *The Mexican War: Crisis for American Democracy,* ed. Archie P. McDonald. D. C. Heath and Company, 1969.

Wise, Frederic M. Col. USMC, *A Marine Tells it to You: As told to Meigs O. Frost.* J. H. Sears & Co., 1929.

Index

Note: Page numbers in italics indicate photographs.

A Short History of U.S. Interventions in Latin America and the Caribbean,
First Edition. Alan McPherson.
© 2016 John Wiley & Sons, Inc. Published 2016 by John Wiley & Sons, Inc.

218   *Index*

Made in the USA
Columbia, SC
18 March 2021

34690892R00134